616.891 Lambrou, Peter T.,
LAM   1947-

         Instant emotional
         healing.

DATE			

Instant
Emotional
Healing

Acupressure for the Emotions

Peter Lambrou, Ph.D., and
George Pratt, Ph.D.

BROADWAY BOOKS   NEW YORK

BROADWAY

Broadway Books titles may be purchased for business or promotional use or for special sales. For information, please write to: Special Markets Department, Random House, Inc., 1540 Broadway, New York, NY 10036.

BROADWAY BOOKS and its logo, a letter B bisected on the diagonal, are trademarks of Broadway Books, a division of Random House, Inc.

Visit our website at www.broadwaybooks.com

The techniques outlined in this book are designed to help you restore emotional balance at times of distress. The authors make no claims with regard to physical healing or to the cure of mental or psychiatric disorders. The methods in this book should not be used in place of proper medical or psychological treatment. If you are having serious physical or emotional problems, it is important that you seek proper professional assessment and treatment.

Library of Congress Cataloging-in-Publication Data

Lambrou, Peter T., 1947–
    Instant emotional healing: acupressure for the emotions / by
Peter Lambrou and George Pratt. — 1st ed.
        p.   cm.
    Includes bibliographical references and index.
        1. Mind and body therapies.   2. Mental health.   3. Acupressure.
    4. Self-management (Psychology)   5. Emotions.   I. Pratt, George J.
    II. Title.
    RC489.M53L36   2000
    616.89′1—dc21   99-36506
                                                                CIP

ISBN 0-7679-0392-7

FIRST EDITION

Designed by Mauna Eichner
Illustrated by Beatrice Benjamin

00   01   02   03   04   10   9   8   7   6   5   4   3   2   1

This book is dedicated to our wonderful families

In memory of Peter P. Lambrou

To Mary, Dottie, Brenden, and Larissa Lambrou

And to Sally, George Sr., Vonda, and Whitney Pratt

CONTENTS

ACKNOWLEDGMENTS

We want first to acknowledge the pioneers in the field of energy psychology, from its roots to its many branches. The foundational work of George Goodheart, John Diamond, and Roger Callahan has become the cornerstone of this field. They have paved the way for those who have carried on to explore, expand, and evolve the methods and theories they first laid down.

Margret McBride, our literary agent, has kept the faith and belief in this project, and has inspired and guided us through the labyrinthine hurdles along the publication pathway. She and her staff, Donna DeGutis, Kris Sauer, and others, have been wonderful in helping move this book through the various stages of publishing and beyond.

At Broadway/Random House we want to thank Bill Shinker, who believed in the project; Bob Asahina, who carried it forward; Lauren Marino, who shepherded it through the publication process; Rebecca Holland, for her attentive assistance with graphics and production; Ann Campbell and Cate Tynan, who took care of so many details; and Robert Allen, Kathy Spinelli, Adrianna della Porta, Eleanor Branch, Bob Walter, and many others whose efforts furthered the book on its journey.

Many of our family, friends, and colleagues have contributed feedback, encouragement, and ideas that furthered this project and helped us in a variety of ways. A heartfelt thank you to: Leigh and Tom Adkins; Brian Alman; Marcia and Greg Andrews; Sandra Bagley; Sheila and Paul Banko; Carol and Terry Bassett; Dick Bayer; Nancy and Chris Benbow; Beatrice Benjamin; Ken Blanchard; Cynthia Bolker, Sheldon Bowles; Scott Buchanan; Gregg Burnett; Stacy and Daniel Canfield; Gaetan Chevalier; Zang-Hee Cho; Becky, Dan, Jacob, Mathew, and Luke Cinadar; Melinda Clements; Steve Cobb; Linda Comer; Deane and Doris Dana; Steve and Maureen Dime; Steve Doyne; Brad Eli; Rich Elrod; Scott Finley; Sandy Flynn; Susan Frazar; Fred Gallo; Susan Gawlinski; Julie Gildred; Terry Gopadze; Rebecca and

David Grudermeyer; Nancy and David Haller; Sue Hannible; John Hinsey; Tom Horvath; Robert Howes; Kathy and Ron James; Kitty and Dirk Kingma; Margaret Knight; Kathy and Cliff Koerner; Errol Korn; Lacey Kinelowech; Ann and Mike Kriozere; Pat Kyle; Tammy and Milton Lambrou; Marilyn Lauer; Bruce Lipton; Judy Liu; Nancy Maher; Margie Dana-Mattingly; Gerald McCracken; Susana Mendez; Cheri and Todd Morgan; Mary Morgan; Mary Jo Mundahl; Mike Nagle; Pam Nathan; Erika Novak; Barbara and K. D. Nyegaard; John Osborne; Audrey Phillips; Karen, David, Grace, and Audrey Pike; Steve Pinterics; Pam Polcyn; Ophelia, Floyd, Sandra, Kenny, Kyle, and Whitney Prater; Pat, David, Chad, Ginger, and Jill Pratt; Patti Quint; Greg Rizzi; Shyla Roberts; Adrienne Rogers; Stu Schrieber; Liza Siegel; Stan Silbert; Cindy Simunec; Greg Smith; Benjamin Spock; Ken Squires; Kay Talley; Toni Thomas; and Marshall Williams.

Our wives, Dottie Lambrou and Vonda Pratt, deserve a special appreciation for their patience and encouragement and for the loving help they provided in taking on extra responsibilities as we focused so much of our energies on completing this book.

An important acknowledgment to Greg Nicosia, who so generously gave of his knowledge, experience, and innovative creativity to help us develop and refine our abilities and to expand our understanding and skills in energy psychotherapy. Greg is not only a psychologist, he is a true healer of the pain and suffering of others. His commitment and dedication to helping others is an inspiration to those who know him. We deeply appreciate Greg's open sharing of his ideas and his feedback on the manuscript.

A very special thanks to our collaborative editor, Laura Torbet, who reshaped our manuscript, reorganized it, fleshed out those areas that were badly in need of structure, smoothed and polished the words, and gave literary life to our case examples. As if that were not a tremendous contribution in itself, Laura also contributed her background in graphic arts to design and direct the graphic elements of this book that are so valuable in helping to explain the intricacies of our methods. We immensely appreciate her literary and visual creativity that blended to make this book so readable and understandable. Every bit as important as her skills were to the book's form, her good humor combined with professionalism made our work together a pleasure. Thank you, Laura, also affectionately known as Lulu.

Introduction

We are traditionally trained psychologists, originally from the Midwest, who today find ourselves at the leading edge of exciting and controversial new therapies that make extravagant promises.

It wasn't always this way. Early in our practices, we both relied strongly on the well-established cognitive and behavioral approaches to psychotherapy. However, throughout our professional careers we have been open to new ideas that could help our clients heal their emotional pain, particularly tools that foster self-reliance and speed up the therapeutic process. Both of us were drawn to hypnosis long before we met.

For a quarter century, George has been a clinical psychologist in private practice, specializing in psychotherapy and performance enhancement. Years before hypnosis became a common therapeutic tool, he was teaching it to physicians, dentists, and psychologists. Along with his gastroenterologist colleague Errol Korn, M.D., he authored hypnosis textbooks as well as videotapes for clinical training.

Peter, who began his career as a professional writer, became fascinated with self-hypnosis when he sought a way of dealing with his own stress. Work pressure had brought on the jaw-clicking and pain that can signal the onset of temporomandibular joint disorder (popularly known as TMJ). After enrolling in a course on self-hypnosis for stress management, a growing friendship with the instructor developed into a collaboration on a book. That writing project in the early 1980s, with hypnosis specialist Brian Alman, Ph.D. (who also had coauthored a book with George), turned Peter in the direction of clinical psychology.

Shortly after our mutual colleague Dr. Alman introduced us, we collaborated on a book that applied self-hypnosis and other skills to achieving business goals. Now, fifteen years later, our personal and professional lives have crossed in many ways. We are in private practice together and are on staff at Scripps Memorial Hospital in La Jolla, California. We also teach at the University of California at San Diego and other professional schools.

As conventionally schooled psychologists, we have cautiously examined therapies that are not well studied and validated by mainstream psychology. Certainly we accept the fundamental connection of mind and body and have approached mental and emotional healing from this perspective for most of our careers. Hypnosis is one potent tool for change. In the past ten years, we have achieved rapid results with EMDR (Eye Movement Desensitization and Reprocessing), a powerful and evolving therapy modality developed by psychologist Francine Shapiro, Ph.D.

However, nothing we have ever used as a treatment technique equals the rapid action and success rate of the approach we call Emotional Self-Management^{SM}, or ESM, which is presented in *Instant Emotional Healing*. ESM is one of several therapies that fall under the heading of Thought Field Therapy, which combines Western cognitive approaches with Eastern acupressure techniques. Thought Field Therapy is a synthesis of the work of a number of researchers, clinicians, and theorists, as we'll explain in Chapters 2 and 3.

Our work with this new method of releasing negative emotions has shown that a 95 percent success rate is practical and achievable in a clinical setting. In most cases we are talking not about temporary relief of symptoms but about ridding clients of their distress forever; for example, in cases involving past emotional trauma or phobias.

But the techniques in this book go beyond eliminating negative emotions that affect functioning. These methods can be used to manage the full spectrum of life's stressors, including some types of physiological problems, and to maximize individual performance and effectiveness. ESM can help people from all walks of life, and in all arenas of life, with issues from parenting to personal relationships and public speaking. *Instant Emotional Healing* is not just a self-help book; it is a foundation for a new way of optimizing your life and your performance in all areas.

From Skeptics to Believers

When we first started using these therapies, we were skeptical ourselves. We couldn't believe that anything so simple and quick could be so effective. With hypnosis and EMDR especially, we had seen what we believed to be rapid resolution of emotional pain. But nothing prepared us for the immediate and rewarding results we were getting with Thought Field Therapy.

We would begin by asking clients who came in for hypnosis if they were open to trying something new. Even though our description of the process might seem far out (even to clients already experienced with hypnosis or EMDR), they usually were open to consider "anything that might help." Ten minutes later they'd be saying "I don't believe it, my problem is gone!"

In those early days, we were as astounded as our clients, who were seeing results immediately, right there in our offices. We were pinching ourselves to be sure we weren't dreaming or making it up. In the world of psychotherapy, such relief is, unfortunately, rare. Many times, the best psychology can do is help people suffer more effectively. Never before in our careers had we seen so many grateful clients with such wonderful stories of success. You will be reading about many of these successes.

The response to these new techniques, from our office staff, graduate students, and colleagues on the psychology staff at Scripps Memorial Hospital, has been incredible. Not surprisingly, many of our physician and psychologist colleagues were highly doubtful and made no bones about it. We got used to their good-natured ribbing about our "miracle cures." Until they tried it. Often we'd have to cajole them: "C'mon," we'd say, "it only takes ten minutes, the time you'd spend talking to a friend." Or we'd back them into giving it a shot. "Here's your chance to prove us wrong. What have you got to lose?" One physician colleague, who was in a stew about an upcoming court appearance as an expert witness, grudgingly agreed to try it. He was astonished when his anxiety was completely gone five minutes later. "I'll be damned," he declared. "I didn't believe any of this energy crap." He's since been back to deal with other issues, and we've seen his wife and his two sons. We now treat, and train, many once-skeptical physicians and other clinicians.

As news of these dramatic successes spread within the therapeutic community, and as the speed and effectiveness of these procedures became more widely known, other therapists frequently sent us challenging patients and "treatment failures" (patients who have not responded to conventional treatments).

I GROANED INWARDLY WHEN Suzanne came to see me, referred by another therapist who was at wits' end about how to help her. There were hardly any problems that Suzanne *didn't* have. Where to begin? When I asked

Suzanne if there was anything that she would like to address using ESM, she mentioned her freeway driving phobia. "I'd like to be able to drive on the highway again," she said. Ten years earlier Suzanne had been in an accident in which she was forced off the highway by a big-rig truck. The broken leg and collar bone had healed, but since that day she hadn't been able to drive on the freeway without having a panic attack. Suzanne had pretty much avoided driving. When driving was unavoidable, she used side roads. It was a serious limitation in her life.

Without much hope that we would get results, given the depth and number of complicating issues, I administered the treatment protocol for trauma. As we went through the process, Suzanne evaluated her anxiety level at several steps along the way. With each step, the fear evaporated, and within fifteen minutes the anxiety was gone. She was astounded but still couldn't believe that the fear wouldn't come flooding back once she was on the road.

Next I worked with Suzanne to install a positive cognition about highway driving, using a variation of the procedure we'd used to eliminate her distress. The phrase she chose was "I enjoy driving on the freeway," which seemed preposterous to her. On the drive home Suzanne called on her cell phone to report that she felt great. "I had forgotten how wonderful it can feel to travel quickly and comfortably on the freeway. Thank you."

STORIES LIKE THESE and those of hundreds of other people who have called or written to report their surprise and thanks have inspired us to write this book.

ESM works wonders with common distress and the often deeply in-grained emotional patterns that do not reach the threshold for professional intervention yet can be unproductive and can interfere with the enjoyment of life. It is a powerful tool for dealing with habits and phobias and for helping children.

ESM also works to facilitate other treatment modalities such as hypnosis and cognitive therapy—eliminating the distress that allows the person to access information, emotions, thoughts, memories, and to overcome the avoidance that prevents cure. Able to think clearly, they can reverse deep-rooted traumas and unproductive behaviors.

However, these methods are not meant to be a replacement for seeking qualified professional help for serious problems such as physical ailments, habitual substance abuse, eating disorders, and serious pathologies including schizophrenia, major depression, and bipolar disorders. The psychological component of addictive urges *is* treatable with ESM techniques, although other treatment approaches and skills development may be necessary. While in these situations the procedures need to be reapplied periodically, the problem of compulsive urges seems to improve over time. The treatments last longer, and the urges subside; clear thinking is restored. In treating habits and addictive urges, the power to self-administer the treatments seems to be a crucial factor in successful outcomes.

A Little Background on Emotional Self-Management

Thought Field Therapy is the umbrella term for a number of hybrid technologies based on what Albert Einstein originally called the "subtle energy" systems of the body. These therapies are based on an understanding of the Eastern meridian systems of the body and the way that cognitive thought energy fields interact with the body—where energy, thought, and emotion overlap. Emotions, in this framework, are believed to result from the influence of electromagnetic energy created by our thoughts and the electrical and chemical changes that occur within the body.

As clinicians, we are involved in developing and using procedures and techniques that are safe, and which help people reduce or eliminate their stress. It is typical of professionals in the healing arts that we are inclined to apply what is safe and effective, and to look for the explanation later. Thought energy therapies are evolving even as we use them and continue to explore how they work.

Among mental health professionals, Thought Field Therapy is rapidly gaining advocates and practitioners. Attendance at workshops and public presentations—including those that we offer—is increasing rapidly. In our own practices, we have administered well over 18,000 treatments, with repeatable, reliable results. Emotional Self-Management principles fit within the new model of mind/body energy systems. In developing the techniques of ESM, we have added new elements to the basic Thought Field Therapy process that amplify its effects. We predict that in the next ten years, many therapies will incorporate the fundamentals of Thought Field Therapy, which itself is a branch of what is called Energy Psychology. Energy therapies will evolve to become a standard approach for health care professionals, for athletes, for business consultants, for coaches and teachers—anyone interested in optimum performance. They will be widely available for helping people remove blocks to enjoying happier, healthier, and more productive lives.

About Instant Emotional Healing

We've divided the book into four sections. Part I presents a broad picture of the many applications of Emotional Self-Management and of the learning process. Chapter 2 examines the paradigm, or frame of reference, on which ESM is based and discusses the paradigm blindness that keeps us from making sense, and use, of the information and discoveries at our disposal. Chapter 3 explores the fascinating discoveries and energy theories behind ESM and presents some ideas about how it works. You will learn the Balanced Breathing exercise, along with the basic techniques for "tapping" at the designated acupressure meridian sites used in most of the procedures. The exercise for correcting Polarity Reversals, which is the foundation step for addressing specific emotional issues, is presented in Chapter 4.

Effectively managing our emotions is at the heart of *Instant Emotional Healing.* Part II discusses the role that emotions play in our lives. It looks at the importance of emotional health, the ways in which emotions get stuck and out of balance, and how we can attain mastery over our emotions. There are guidelines for correctly identifying emotions, an important preliminary step to self-administering the ESM protocols. You will learn to accurately measure the level of your distress, using something called the Subjective Units of Distress scale. There is information on how to work with "layered" emotions as they arise. Each emotion is cross-referenced to the appropriate protocol in Chapter 9. And you'll find the quick-fix Rapid Relaxer, a potent stress reliever.

In Part III we come to the heart of the matter: the emotion-specific ESM protocols. Chapter 8 takes you on a step-by-step run-through of the basic procedure and tells you everything you need to know to administer these procedures yourself. You'll learn all the rest of the "tapping" sites here. Chapter 8 also explains how to diagnose difficulties and make corrections if you do not get immediate results, and tells you where to find the help you need. The twenty-eight emotion-specific protocols appear in Chapter 9, one to a page for quick reference. Chapter 10 details the Five-Step Breathing exercise, the remedy for polarity disorganization, which can hamper the success of any treatment.

Part IV opens with a chapter devoted to the performance and productivity applications for ESM. Follow-up and maintenance are the subjects of Chapter 12, which offers a suggested program for using ESM to maintain optimal emotional health and tips for developing fluency and confidence in the techniques. You'll find guidelines on how to teach, or administer, ESM techniques to others. Chapter 13 covers highly effective ways to work with children using ESM techniques. The book closes with a vision for the future of ESM and energy therapies.

As new discoveries illuminate the workings of the brain and body, novel applications are being found for energy therapies. The techniques of Thought Field Therapy are a natural for self-administration, yet so far no book has taught people to use these simple practices on their own. We wrote this book so people everywhere can gain access to these amazing tools.

Readers of this book will be at the leading edge of knowledge and information about subtle energy systems and Eastern ways of healing. We will not be surprised if this method and other energy therapies will do for people with emotional pain what aspirin did for physical pain earlier in this century.

NOTE: *Although we refer to ourselves as "we" in this book, the pronoun "I" is sometimes used in the anecdotes and case histories.*

PART I

All About Emotional Self-Management

Could This Be Magic?

A Vietnam vet, sole survivor and sole witness to the death of his entire squad during a fierce jungle battle, tormented by survivor's guilt.

A college senior, distraught over the breakup with his high school sweetheart, on the verge of flunking out.

A prominent NFL player wanting to improve his game performance.

A four-year-old girl, jealous and threatened by her new adopted brother.

A highly successful sixty-six-year-old executive who has lived his life under a cloud of depression and self-recrimination since accidentally shooting his best friend when he was sixteen.

A woman dangerously postponing an operation because she is too frightened to have the surgery.

A young lawyer whose boyfriend's slovenly habits are driving her up the wall.

A man with a history of panic attacks, dreading seeing his father at his upcoming wedding after many years of not speaking.

What do these seemingly diverse people have in common? All of them experienced immediate and lasting relief from their troubles, many after years of painful suffering, using the techniques of Emotional Self-Management℠.

True Tales of ESM

Does the idea that you can instantly get over your fears or your sadness, that you could feel more relaxed and balanced in your everyday life, sound too good to be true? Well, we mean exactly what the title says: *instant emotional healing.* When you master the skills presented in this book, you will be able to heal, often in one session, long-standing, troubling issues from your past: grief over a divorce, a phobia about freeway driving, a long-festering anger over a business deal gone sour. You will have a set of tools to help you immediately handle the day-to-day stresses of your life: a bumper-to-bumper commute, a critical boss, the remodeling of your kitchen, your anxiety about paying the bills or the presentation you have to make at work next week. You will work more productively and perform at a higher level.

Instant healing? Even from lifelong problems? From fear and anxiety, anger and jealousy and phobias? These seem like extraordinary claims. But all of the people mentioned earlier were treated in our offices, typically in one to three sessions. To give you an idea of how the methods of ESM can be used for a wide variety of emotional issues, from minor irritations to major traumas, we are going to share with you a few cases drawn from our experiences. (Names and incidental details have been changed to protect the confidentiality of our clients.)

Nearly three weeks after he escaped his kidnappers, Gunther continued to be withdrawn and frightened. When he arrived at my office, he seemed like a broken young man, his shoulders hunched into the upturned collar of his leather jacket, his eyes darting nervously around the room. Nightmares plagued his sleep; he was unable to leave the house without breaking into a cold sweat. It had been a horrific ordeal for the whole family, as they worried about Gunther and negotiated the terms and logistics of the sizable ransom for his release with the nervous and off-balance kidnappers. By the time Gunther came to see me, I had already treated his mother and sister for their own stress and sleeplessness. "How often do I have to come here?" he asked. "I don't know how many times I can come back." At first I thought Gunther was so disoriented that he was worried about the expense that his family would incur. But, I soon learned, he was terrified of being taken captive again. When I told him that what was upsetting him now would be gone by the time he left in the next hour, he didn't believe me.

We quickly went through the protocol for trauma, repeating the sequence for a couple of particularly terrifying memories of his time in captivity. He recalled the day when his skittish and alcohol-fueled captors bound and blindfolded him and moved him from place to place four times in the trunk of a car; a morning when they thought they were being tricked by Gunther's family and threatened to kill him right then and there. By the end of the session Gunther's whole demeanor had changed. He relaxed in his chair, where before he had been stiff and watchful. For the first time, he was able to speak about his ordeal without his heart pounding. Although still subdued, he smiled and thanked me.

The Gunther who returned to see me a few days later seemed like a different person. He was again the confident and renowned financier, making plans for a major new project. The nightmares had not returned since the first treatment. He reported that since our meeting, after the weeks of stoicism since he escaped his captors, he finally had been able to cry. He had spent many hours during the past few days talking with his family; they learned every detail of his captivity, and they told him about their ordeal and their fear for his life when it looked like the ransom dropoff had been botched.

There was more healing work ahead for Gunther and for his family. We continued to work together for three more sessions, as the layers of guilt, fear, and anger surfaced. But Gunther was himself again. He was no longer being held prisoner by feelings and memories that were blocked from his awareness.

* * *

A business friend sent his secretary to us for help. For three years Amanda had been unable to get over her breakup with a boyfriend who had left her for another woman. She thought about him obsessively and found it nearly impossible to concentrate at work. (Hence the recommendation from her boss.) She wasn't dating and slept poorly due to recurrent dreams about her lost love. In the past year she had become progressively reclusive and depressed. In short, Amanda was suffering from a broken heart.

I taught Amanda how to self-administer a simple sequence of tapping on specific meridian points while she focused on her problem. (That was easy for her to do.) I watched as Amanda's anxiety level dropped, and her jaw relaxed. Within a few minutes she said, "I feel like a weight has been lifted off me. I haven't been able to stop thinking about him for three years."

Amanda called the next day to report that she still felt as good as she had in the office, and she'd gotten a good night's sleep for the first time in a very long while. A week later she called again to say, "I can hardly believe it. I feel like I've gotten my life back again. I don't know what happened, but I'm not thinking about him like I was. In fact, I can't understand now why I was so obsessed. He was really a jerk. Thank you for helping me live again."

*   *   *

Marisa's mother brought her to see me because she was anxious and afraid of spending the night away from home. Every time she'd go for a sleepover to a friend's house, she'd become nervous and frightened as darkness descended and would have to call her parents to come and get her. For a twelve-year-old, this was embarrassing. Marisa was sure her friends were laughing at her behind her back.

As I taught Marisa the procedure for anxiety, she began to laugh, and gave me a "high-five" as we progressed through the tapping sequences. We made progress quickly, and I showed Marisa a special tap she could use if any problems came up. When we were finished, Marisa smiled and said to her mother, "I'm not scared thinking about it." She looked puzzled for a moment, then announced, "And I want to go to Amber's this weekend."

I also showed Marisa's mother how to use these techniques to help her infant son, who, as they were leaving the office, began crying inconsolably. The following week Marisa's mother called to say her daughter had had a wonderful sleepover and could hardly believe the problem was gone so quickly.

*   *   *

Joleen was terrified of flying, one of her many anxieties, but now she was planning to visit relatives in Europe. She arrived at the office in a cold sweat. So intense was her fear that she could not even carry the airline tickets in her purse. Her husband was out in our reception area holding them. Joleen asked dozens of questions and demanded explanations about the treatment before she would let me proceed. Finally she calmed down and let me administer the protocols for fear of flying and flight turbulence. As her fear subsided, her astonishment showed on her face. But she wanted to test the results. "Can I go out and get the tickets?" she asked. She went out to the reception area to retrieve the tickets from her husband and came back beaming. "This is amazing. Look at me, I feel fine. A little while ago these tickets made me so anxious, they were like holding electricity in my hand."

A few weeks later Joleen called to say that her flight to Europe was comfortable. She also reported that while she was there she had learned of a death in the family and, in spite of that upsetting news, her flight home was as free from fear as the flight over.

* * *

Ben had a lifelong inability to swallow pills, a major problem for a weight lifter and "health nut." A thirty-five-year-old engineer, he gagged and choked on even the tiniest tablets. Either he had to find vitamins and medications in liquid form, or he went through the time-consuming process of grinding them into powder, which often tasted disgusting.

Ben came to the office prepared to test the therapy, with a liter of water and a couple bottles of vitamin pills of varying sizes. After going through the thought-focusing and tapping procedures, Ben stared at the bottle of vitamins and said, "I think I can swallow one now." He placed a pill in his mouth and took a gulp of water from the plastic bottle. For a moment he held the water in his mouth and held his breath, preparing himself to gag, as he'd done in the past. He swallowed. The deep furrows of anticipation smoothed from his brow and he grinned. "It was all right," he said. "I didn't feel like choking, and my throat didn't close. I can do this." His confidence improved as he continued to swallow more "test" pills in the office. Two weeks later Ben called to report that he was doing fine swallowing his vitamins.

* * *

Sandy, a successful executive at a software firm, was consumed by anger and frustration over divorce negotiations for custody of her children. Her rage at her ex-husband was undermining her ability to arrive at a reasonable solution. Even her attorney thought she was wasting money and that the intensity of her anger was keeping her from having realistic expectations. It was her lawyer who convinced Sandy to come to our office.

Sandy didn't know what to expect but told me she was prepared for me to talk her out of her anger. Instead, I asked her if she would be open to trying a new technique to help her feel more composed and comfortable. She rolled her eyes to signify her low expectations and resignation. As I corrected for polarity reversals, Sandy was still skeptical. Every step of the way, she'd say "How can this possibly help?" I asked if she felt any change. She shrugged her shoulders and said she wasn't sure, but gave me permission to go ahead. I could tell Sandy was watching the clock and anticipating no change. I applied the formula for anger, which took about seven minutes. Sandy experienced some mild relief as her anger subsided. But then, to her surprise, guilt about the amount of time she was spending at work came up, guilt about not spending more time involved with her son's activities. We continued, applying the protocol for guilt. When the guilt lifted, Sandy began to feel grief and hurt at her husband's rejection. Layer by layer during the session, we treated the distressing emotions covered by the initial anger and rage.

The referring attorney called a few days later to say "I don't know what you did with Sandy, but when I saw her she was calm and able to stay focused on the process of custody arrangements in a way she'd never done before. She did seem sad about the situation, but the negotiations were more productive than during any other meetings in the past."

Ten Amazing Facts About ESM

We have many more stories like these to share with you. Meanwhile, here are ten amazing things about the process we call Emotional Self-Management.

1. *ESM works for virtually any emotional issue*—and, by the way, for jet lag, nasal congestion, hiccups, and premenstrual syndrome (PMS).

2. *ESM works for essentially any issue of productivity or performance,* from taking tests, to public speaking, to playing better hockey.

3. *ESM is a do-it-yourself therapeutic tool.* No therapist required.

4. *The processes take anywhere from fifteen seconds to fifteen minutes to administer.* When you are done, in many cases the problem will be gone forever.

5. *ESM is totally portable.* You can do it anywhere, without tools or equipment.

6. *You don't ever have to talk about what is bothering you.* Privacy is guaranteed.

7. *You don't have to understand the cause, or source, of the problem.* ESM will work, even if you do not know why you feel the way you do.

8. *ESM processes are effective with children, even infants; and you can teach ESM to friends and colleagues.*

9. *ESM is reliable and predictable.* If you learn the techniques and practice them correctly, you will see results.

10. *ESM has no negative side effects.* No one has ever been harmed by these practices.

We ourselves are still amazed at the power of ESM. Although between us we have nearly forty years of clinical experience, nothing before has produced the immediate and powerful results of ESM. At the end of the first week after we began using these techniques, our secretary said, "You've got to stop curing people so fast. You're seeing so many patients for only one or two visits, what's going to happen?"

It's true that ESM has radically changed our practices. We still use a variety of tools in our work—cognitive therapy, hypnosis, and other traditional techniques, plus Eye Movement Desensitization Reprocessing™ as well as the ESM techniques, depending on the particular problem. We continue to work with clients who are dealing with serious and complex issues, whom we see for longer periods. But these days we have a very high client turnover rate, and we see a large number of people for anywhere from one to four visits.

We still have a client waiting list, though. When people hear about this amazing instant self-help therapy, they want to learn it for themselves. Some clients come reluctantly, with little hope of solving problems they may have had for decades. When they see how miraculously it works, they want to deal with *all* their accumulated problems, big and small. Soon they're saying "Hey, can you do something for my golf game?" (Yes, we can. See Chapter

11.) Next they send their spouses, and friends, and bring their children. The reality is that we are delighted with our rapid patient turnover.

We continue to be excited about ESM. It is thrilling when our clients leave the office without the problems that have, in many cases, haunted them for years, and with skills that give them a sense of mastery and confidence. It is a great feeling to be able to offer these life-changing skills, to see our clients break free of needless pain and suffering, once and for all. To be themselves again after so many years. To be *happy*.

Why Not Be Happy?

The pursuit of happiness is considered an inalienable right, but for many people its capture remains elusive. Although we want to be happy, and although we spend a big chunk of our lives, and our time and energy and money, doing everything we can think of to find happiness, it remains out of reach. Often we are anxious, angry, frustrated with our jobs, bored in our relationships, envious of others. We get tired of trying so hard and yet feeling so bad, and are disappointed that things have turned out as they have. We've worked hard. We do the right thing by our friends and families, as best we can. But still there are problems and conflicts and disappointments. The new car, the cruise vacation, the new face cream, the season tickets to the ballpark or the opera haven't done the trick. Most frustrating of all, even the years of therapy and the dozens of self-help books have done little more than help make life tolerable and perhaps more understandable.

We want to be all that we can be. But we've lost the way, or never found it, and our dreams feel increasingly out of reach. We feel powerless to change, unable to make our lives work in the way we envisioned. So we resign ourselves to a sort of half-life, a pale shadow of what we expected and hoped for.

Restoring Emotional Balance

What we don't often recognize when we are caught in our problems is that, despite our efforts to seek happiness, we are locked in old patterns—old beliefs, old ways of thinking and doing things, old wounds, old memories—that unconsciously undermine our conscious desire to be happy and free of suffering. We are at the mercy of our past history. The deeply entrenched patterns and beliefs of our past are like an anchor sunk in the mud of the sea bottom, slowing our every move. We feel off balance, reacting out of habit and fear, rarely in control. We may not be completely stuck, but the powerful undertow sure slows us down.

Our emotions set us apart from most other creatures and are as much a component of our "intelligence" as our intellectual prowess. Psychologist and author Daniel Goleman, Ph.D., uses the term "emotional IQ" to compare our emotional intelligence to our cognitive IQ. When our emotions are not in balance, we get the same results as when our brains are not operating well: We do stupid and unproductive things.

All organisms seek to maintain health and equilibrium. When the system is working efficiently, the organism's natural tendency is for intense emotions to arise and then to dissolve, so that calm and balance are reestablished. It is a natural corrective procedure. We get angry, our tempers flare, the storm passes, and we calm down. We see a snake, our adrenaline surges. Then reason kicks in, we realize it is harmless, and we breathe deeply again. Stalled in traffic, we're irritated because we are already late for a meeting; but then we realize there's nothing we can do about it, and we calm down.

Sometimes, though, the stressful emotion persists. Angry with our daughter for not cleaning her room again, we storm around the house for days, unable to talk with her about our frustration. We can't go for a walk in the woods because the very idea of a snake makes our heart beat wildly and our palms sweat. Try as we might to stay calm, the frustration of crawling along in stalled traffic leaves us limp and exhausted at the office.

Strong, unrelenting emotions that don't subside deplete us. They waste energy that we could spend having fun and enjoying our lives. They color our relationships and undermine our performance. We want to stop blowing our top, or being jealous, or being frozen with anxiety, but we don't seem able to break the habit, despite our best intentions. Like the song that we can't get out of our mind, automatic response patterns become locked into our minds and bodies. They just keep going around in circles, seemingly without an escape route. Always with the same message, always eliciting the same reaction, ever waiting to spring out at us. Like puppets on a string, we are trapped in these knee-jerk responses.

THE PREMISE OF thought energy therapies is that these emotional loops are embedded in the mind/body energy system. Whenever that experience is activated, even just a tiny aspect of it—via a thought, the sight or sound of something reminiscent of it—the memory of the whole experience comes flooding back, with all the unpleasant and disturbing emotions and physiological sensations associated with it. A woman who has been raped can develop a panic reaction to any man wearing a striped shirt like her attacker wore. A Vietnam battle veteran hears the slamming of a door as a bomb dropping behind him. An angry expression on our lover's face calls to mind the full weight of our parents' disapproval. When traumatic emotional experiences are blocked from being dissipated, they can show up as anxiety and sweaty palms and a pounding heart, as nightmares or obsessive rumination.

ESM to the Rescue

Energy managed well is productive; energy out of balance is a source of stress, for ourselves and for those around us. Emotional Self-Management works by unblocking the trapped emotional feedback "loops" so that the flow of energy is restored and the body returns to its natural state of physical and emotional balance. Based on the premise that mind and body are one intelligent and fully communicating system, ESM procedures involve a combination of tapping with the fingers on emotion-specific energy meridians in the body that are associated with acupuncture. These acupuncture sites have been found to be associated with particular emotions. Don't worry; as with acupressure, a similar technique, there are no needles involved! While doing the tapping sequence, you will actively think about your distress and will in some cases repeat specific statements of intention. The tapping adds energy to the system at the proper place at the proper time—when the problem is brought to mind and envisioned—and enables the blockage or disturbance to be dissolved. The energy of the ESM procedure dislodges the trapped thoughts and allows the natural balance and flow of energy to resume, bringing immediate—instant—relief.

Another core principle of thought energy therapies is that the body has a polarity, a north and south pole, just like a battery or a magnet. Stress and many other circumstances cause our polarities to get reversed and prevent us from healing, even when we are trying hard to make changes. Just as when an electronic device is plugged in the wrong way, when our polarities are reversed, normal operation is affected. Polarity reversals can interfere with thought, emotion, and behavior. Before dealing with the emotion-specific issues, an ESM exercise corrects these inhibiting polarity reversals.

A complete ESM treatment sequence is referred to as a *protocol*. By the time you get to the full protocols in Chapter 8, you will have learned all the auxiliary exercises and procedures you will need to self-administer them.

The ESM process does not change your knowledge of the problem and does not erase appropriate feelings associated with it. It eliminates only irrational thoughts, not natural self-protectiveness. When ESM cures your fear of heights, you will not be tempted to jump off a cliff.

> Gina's fear of heights was so intense that she was not able to spend the weekends with her boyfriend, a devoted outdoorsman. But the day after we treated Gina for her acrophobia, she hiked several miles up a steep ridge. "It was a glorious day," she reported, "and I was so thrilled to be standing on top of that mountain, looking out over the lake. I haven't been able to go on hikes like that for over fifteen years. We were standing at a roped-in outlook spot and I was completely comfortable. But when I tried to step foot over the rope, I immediately felt scared, until I stepped back to a safe place and felt at ease again. I guess I still have a healthy fear and I won't do anything reckless."

The speed with which ESM procedures solve problems mystifies many of our clients. ESM brings instant relief because, in removing the longstanding disturbance, it puts an end to the vicious circle of emotional reactivity attached to the thought. The endless loop is broken. Whether the problem has been there for a day or a decade, it dissolves; the disturbance is not stronger because it's been there a long time.

The disturbance, or blockage, can be compared to a boulder in a stream. Water will flow around it, but the boulder causes turbulence and slows the water down. Remove the boulder, and the water flows freely. ESM removes the boulders impeding the smooth flow of your emotional energy.

You've Got to Be Kidding!

By now you may be saying, "Tapping on my meridians? Thought energy? You've got to be kidding." Well, we are not kidding, but we can understand how bizarre it may sound. ESM is a nontraditional approach, very much outside the box of conventional scientific and medical understanding. When people have trouble believing that this treatment can work, they are experiencing what is called a paradigm problem: Their understanding of the way the universe operates has no way of explaining the likes of ESM. Often people just filter out that which doesn't fit into their worldview.

If this is what you are experiencing as you read this, recognize that you're not alone. Many of our clients had a hard time believing the results they were getting, even when they'd just experienced ESM themselves. They too had no frame of reference with which to understand it. Now they say, "I can't believe this works so well. Why didn't I know about this?" Paradigm blindness also explains why you don't see energy therapies written up on the front pages of the paper—yet.

But with understanding and exposure, things change. Not so many years ago, we were at the you've-got-to-be-kidding stage ourselves, and sometimes we are still astounded at the rapid cures that ESM produces.

Brave New World

In our fast-moving world, we are used to seeing major changes, new developments, and whole new technologies come and go with the speed of e-mail. As the world becomes smaller, more easily and quickly accessed, East is truly meeting West. When senior citizens are loosening up with T'ai Chi, and American Buddhism is the topic of a *Time* magazine cover, you know you're not in Kansas anymore. A loss of faith in the miracles of conventional medicine and skyrocketing costs have led many people to seek alternative or complementary therapies. It's an informed—and open-minded—public that has pushed for the acceptance of alternative treatments and that spends more money on these modalities than on conventional treatments. Today we're seeing wider acceptance of herbs and biofeedback and even massage therapy. (Of course, there are still practitioners who refuse to acknowledge even the efficacy of vitamins in health and wellness.) Chiropractic, another complementary approach to healing and relief, endured its share of derision before establishing a place in clinical practice, with most insurers now offering coverage.

We all owe a debt to people like Herbert Benson, M.D., Deepak Chopra, M.D., Norman Cousins, Ph.D., Andrew Weil, M.D., Carolyn Myss, Ph.D., Ernest Rossi, Ph.D., Larry Dossey, M.D., Norman Shealy, M.D., Ph.D., Joan Borysenko, Ph.D., Bernie Siegel, M.D., and many others, whose research and books have introduced millions of people to mind/body approaches to healing and health. In 1997 the National Institutes of Health finally gave the green light to acupuncture as a treatment for pain and nausea. Now this meridian energy system therapy can be used in mainstream clinical settings such as veterans hospitals and is reimbursable by Medicare and other conventional healthcare delivery systems. The once-controversial Eye Movement Desensitization and Reprocessing (EMDR) has demonstrated its effectiveness in controlled studies and has received significant coverage in the media, including a feature segment on the television program *20/20*. The recognition of such therapies paves the way for the visibility and credibility of thought energy therapies, on which ESM is based.

ESM is at the leading edge of a whole new approach to healing that combines elements of cognitive therapy with the latest thinking in everything from the mind/body connection, to subtle energy theories, electromagnetism, polarity, neuropeptide chains, acupuncture, and quantum physics. It is not necessary that you fully understand or believe in the theoretical foundation of ESM. The techniques will work whether you believe in them or not. You don't have to understand radio waves to listen to an FM station.

But there are a couple of good reasons to learn more about how and why ESM works. One, it's fascinating information; learning about how ESM works is a drug-free way to expand your mind. Two, and most important, understanding how ESM works will give you confidence in its ability to work for you and likely will increase its effectiveness because we tend to more frequently use the methods that fit within our view of the world. Chapters 2 and 3 are all about the theories behind ESM.

Emotional Power Tools

Self-management is the key to emotional well-being, and ESM is the most powerful self-management tool we have ever come across. ESM breaks the emotional gridlock that keeps our emotions from rebalancing and that keeps us from using our emotions intelligently and productively. When you have learned the ESM procedures and tried them out on a few of the issues you are dealing with, you will feel confident that you can cope with anything that comes up in your life. You won't have to suffer needlessly, and you won't feel exposed and vulnerable. Just feeling that you have more control in your life brings its own sense of comfort and relief. When problems come up or stresses recur, you can treat yourself in minutes.

You will find that as you use these methods, you will build a base of confidence and emotional stability that makes your life run smoother. By reducing or eliminating the emotional distress surrounding the issues of everyday life, you will be able to think more clearly and productively.

A good example of this is a woman who came to us who had just taken the bar examination for the second time to become an attorney. She couldn't concentrate on her work and couldn't sleep, worrying about whether she'd passed. She didn't know how she'd get through the two months until the results were posted. Immediately after we treated her, *seconds* after, she said, "You know, I don't know why it didn't occur to me sooner. I've gone through this before. I can just let go. In two months I'll know the results. So like I did last time, I'll just put it out of my mind. It's not doing me any good to worry." Now why couldn't she do that ten minutes before? Because an encoded emotional loop was preventing her from thinking clearly. Once the disturbance was broken up, she had access to information that wasn't available to her just a few minutes earlier.

Learning to Use ESM

First of all, we want to reassure you that ESM procedures are absolutely safe. You cannot do any harm by performing the procedures incorrectly, by doing a procedure for an incorrectly identified issue, by doing an exercise you don't need, or by doing it too frequently. Can you eat too many vegetables? The body seeks calm and balance. It's almost as if, like some wind-up toys that allow the coil to slip if wound too tightly, we have a built-in safety mechanism that self-corrects. If you do the procedures as directed, you *will* get results, virtually instantly. In fact, the procedures are quite forgiving; you don't have to do them perfectly for them to work.

But here's the catch: While the procedures themselves take only a short time to perform, we strongly recommend that you spend some time learning how to do them properly. Because these skills are so unfamiliar, there's a learning curve involved in mastering them. Try to remember the last time you tried to learn something new—golf, tennis, sewing, Italian. Even if it was a simple skill, chances are you felt awkward at first. And then the time came when it was easy and natural. So be patient with yourself, and have reasonable expectations.

You may have purchased this book because you have a pressing problem, and you want help *right now.* We will be showing you a Balanced Breathing exercise and a Rapid Relaxer that you can do quickly, at any time, on their own. But even if you are tempted to skip right to the exercise instructions, we suggest that you first read through the book, to become familiar with the theoretical foundation of ESM and to learn the skills correctly. We want you to get great results on your first attempt at ESM, so that you will develop confidence in its ability to help you. The learning process itself provides a foundation for competence and self-acceptance. The more prepared you are the first time you try ESM, the greater your chances of immediate success. Don't sabotage your chances by jumping ahead too quickly. The extra time—and restraint—will pay off.

As you try the ESM procedures, you may feel silly doing the tapping and talking (and on occasion, rolling your eyes and humming!). But remember, no one has to see you; no one has to know what you're up to. When you see results, the process won't seem silly at all. With practice you will be able to do the procedures quickly and quietly, so you can use them almost anywhere. We ourselves use ESM in a variety of ways, to relieve emotional tension and to be as effective as we can. Even to play and have fun. But you aren't likely to see us tapping on the streets of La Jolla.

If you are wondering whether you can get the kind of results we discuss in this book, outside of a clinical setting, the answer is yes. In a clinical setting we are able to take into account all relevant factors of our clients' histories, and we have some sophisticated tools with which to diagnose the problems that need solving. Also, at times a combination of modalities offers clients the best chance of full recovery. Sometimes, for example, it is important that people talk about what has happened to them. One woman, for example, who had only recently seen her husband die a violent death, needed to recount her experience fully before she could put the ESM techniques to use. Sometimes we use ESM to better facilitate another treatment approach, such as hypnosis or EMDR.

But we also teach our clients how to apply these procedures on their own, and they report the same high level of success. We have worked over the telephone with people we have never met. Others have learned these procedures from our audiotapes or from written instructions. It does not seem to matter how a person learns ESM for the methods to work.

ESM tools are useful in all arenas of life—in work, play, and love—and with everyone, from your spouse to your accountant. You will find that, using ESM, you are less reactive, and can handle whatever comes up in your life. Kids also love this method, they don't just tolerate it. Normally, children are not too thrilled about coming to a shrink's office. But when they try ESM, especially when we show them "proof" that it's working with muscle testing (more on this in Chapter 2), they are amazed. Adolescents, especially, find it very cool. The sense of self-control and independence is empower-ing. It's fun, it's different, it's not just sitting and talking; they are doing something important.

We want *Instant Emotional Healing* to give you the benefit of everything we have learned in our years of practice, teaching, and research. Consider us your coaches as you learn this new skill. Our goal is to provide you with not only the tools and the techniques but the encouragement and intention to achieve emotional well-being. If you apply the techniques of ESM, we are certain that you will clear a path to the freedom and happiness you seek.

Paradigm and Pedigree

The Road to ESM

If in the early 1960s you'd been asked to name the country most famous for its watches, you would likely have answered "Switzerland." At that time Switzerland, maker of three-quarters of the world's watches, had been the leading watch producer for over a century.

Then, in the mid-1960s, an engineer for a Swiss watchmaking firm discovered that a small electrical current put to a certain type of crystal would cause it to vibrate at a constant frequency. When he realized that the frequency was so steady and reliable that it could be used to calibrate time, he brought it to the attention of his employers.

"Does it have gears?" they inquired. "A mainspring? Bearings?" His discovery bore no resemblance to any timepiece with which they were familiar. Sure that no one would be interested in such a deviant device, they didn't even bother to protect the idea with a patent.

At a trade show soon thereafter, the engineer set up a table to demonstrate his invention. Hundreds of people passed by his small display, but two attendees stopped to talk: one from Texas Instruments and one from Japan's Seiko Corporation. The rest, as they say, is history. By the mid-1970s Switzerland's share of the watch market had shrunk to 10 percent, and tens of thousands of Swiss watchmakers were looking for a new trade.

What happened? There was a paradigm shift—a change in the framework of understanding of how things work. The Swiss watchmakers were so caught in their outdated worldview that they had no way to grasp this new vision for their product.

The inability to see outside the box of our prejudices—for ultimately that's what they are—has always been a factor in the acceptance of new ideas. When, early in the century, the Wright brothers began demonstrating their flying machines, neighbors showed up to laugh as their strange contraptions skimmed and bumped across the grassy slopes of Kitty Hawk. Scientists at that time concluded that the machines were at best impractical, perhaps even a hoax. Military leaders who showed up could see no application for these clumsy craft. The New York *Herald* scoffed at the bicycle-mechanic brothers, and the prestigious *Scientific American* magazine derided their claim that a heavier-than-air machine could fly.

It is our good fortune that every era has had bold researchers and thinkers willing to explore the unexplained, even the irrational, in order to bring rational understanding to what was once a mystery. Many new inventions and technologies—from the wheel, to the combustion engine, to the microchip—have revolutionized our lives. Yet many of these discoveries have brought ridicule and ostracism for their discoverers and champions.

A Subtle Energy Crisis

Discoveries having to do with subtle energies—barely detectable and difficult to measure, the kind of energy involved in ESM—have had a rocky road to legitimacy. In the 1840s the German scientist Karl Reichenbach, known for isolating paraffin oil for use as a fuel, was introduced to a young woman who appeared to be able to identify a magnetic field, or what he called "vital forces." He also found four other women with similar abilities to perceive these fields. A contemporary of Reichenbach, the Scottish surgeon James Braid, concluded that these women were experiencing nothing more than the effects of hypnotic suggestion. Since this explanation was more understandable to their contemporaries, Reichenbach's studies were discounted.

About fifty years later, English physician Walter Kilner was experimenting with the newly invented X-ray machine, using a special blue filter over photographic film. He detected an unusual radiation around living people, which he called "the human atmosphere," as a way of dissociating himself from the hoogly-boogly world of the occult and the tainted word "aura."

So much for his career. The *British Medical Journal* of January 1912, in reviewing his book, *The Human Atmosphere,* concluded that "Dr. Kilner has failed to convince us that his aura is more real than Macbeth's visionary dagger." Kilner resigned his position at St Thomas's, London's leading teaching hospital, and retreated to a small-town private practice with his brother.

Physician Wilhelm Reich didn't fare any better. His exploration of "bio-energy" earned him the rare distinction of having his books banned twice, first in the 1930s by the Nazis, who condemned him as a Jew, a communist, and—big mistake—for talking too much about sex and orgasms.

Reich fled Germany for America, where he proposed that what he called "orgone" energy existed throughout the universe in all living things. Reich soon got in trouble for having his patients spend time in his "Orgone Accumulator," a roomlike container he claimed would increase their vital orgone energies. Again, the sexual overtones were too much. First the Food and Drug Administration (FDA) banned the device in the 1950s (the FDA seemed to be on a scientific witch hunt, concurrent with the McCarthy hearings), saying it had no effect. Then it banned his books and all reference to his work, a ban that continued until 1960.

Meanwhile, in Russia in the 1960s, scientist Semyon Kirlian invented a camera that seemed to show energy emitted by living tissue in the presence of high-voltage, high-frequency electronic cycles. His photographs reveal a fascinating pattern of electron energy radiation that appears, well, like an *aura,* on the photographic plate.

Perhaps the most incredible aspect of Kirlian's work is what is known as the "phantom leaf" effect. An ordinary leaf just plucked from a tree shows a distinct radiation pattern, with what seem like flares of light emanating from all around the edges of the leaf and the stem. As the leaf dies, the flaring diminishes.

Here's the amazing part. When a fresh leaf is cut and only a part of a leaf is photographed, *the resulting photograph also shows the missing portion of the leaf.* Because Kirlian's work is off the charts, there has been little interest in following up on his research. The only good news is that while Kirlian has not won any Nobel Prizes, neither has he been cast to the science sharks or ridiculed into obscurity. Critics merely dismiss his findings as "not really all that important."

Chapter 3 will look at new evidence indicating that these subtle energies are really quite important and powerful after all.

Is Science Leading or Following?

The inability of people to grasp a new paradigm, even one that could explain formerly mysterious phenomena, has kept them from pursuing irrefutable findings. Prevailing viewpoints blind many scientists to truths that exist outside their model for explaining even what is right before their eyes. The annals of science and technology are littered with "false predictions" and discredited researchers:

- In 1893 Berlin physician Carl Schlik was laughed out of the auditorium at a medical conference when he proposed that local anesthesia was possible.

- In 1899 the head of the U.S. Patent Office, Charles Dowell, urged in a letter to President Grover Cleveland that "everything has been invented already. Let us close down the patent office." He must have been pretty well convinced; it's the rare bureaucrat who will voluntarily put himself out of a job.

- Robert Milliken, who was awarded the 1923 Nobel Prize in physics, declared that "there's no likelihood that man can ever split the atom."

- And in 1977 Kenneth Olsen, the president and founder of Digital Equipment Corporation, was convinced that "there is no reason for any individual to have a computer in their home."

Paradoxically, scientists and researchers, who should be at the forefront in exploring new discoveries, often are least equipped to do so. The very knowledge and the rigorous investigative methods that they have worked so hard to acquire and pursue can be an impediment to seeing anything that doesn't fit in. The scientific method is based on the ability to make observations, isolate variables, and repeat those observations under the same set of circumstances. Measurement is the Holy Grail. Many scientists pride themselves on their adherence to the scientific method, which they interpret as making everything fit the existing hypotheses, no matter how fast new developments and ideas are pushing the envelope of knowledge. There are skeptics who make a career of their rigidity and refuse to even consider promising new findings.

In his thought-provoking book, *The Structure of Scientific Revolutions,* Thomas Kuhn, Ph.D., professor emeritus of linguistics and philosophy at the Massachusetts Institute of Technology, discussed the ways in which science sometimes ignores, distorts, or totally misunderstands discoveries that fall outside the prevailing paradigm. He uses the discovery of oxygen as an example. During the late eighteenth century, before it was concluded that oxygen was a gas existing within the air, several different theories about oxygen's function and properties were accepted before new ones arose to challenge them. Oxygen was first thought to be air that had something removed from it. Later the theory had to do with some principle of "acidity" related to heat. Before oxygen could be fully understood, the paradigm had to expand to contain and explain the evidence.

The sad truth is that, in many areas, the biosciences are seventy years behind the learning curve. Many scientists are reluctant to study the phenomena of energy and consciousness not only because their belief system doesn't encompass these things but because they can't measure them effectively. They don't want to admit that there is any such thing as consciousness or self-awareness that exists outside the brain. No hypothetical bridge enables them to see that observations in quantum physics might explain something about human behavior.

Not that new discoveries are never put to use before they are understood. There are many widely prescribed drug treatments about which that bible of medications, the *Physician's Desk Reference,* notes that "mechanism of action is unknown." The analgesic and fever-reducing effects of aspirin, the wonder drug of the 1950s, were a mystery for many decades. We still don't fully understand how some current antidepressants alleviate symptoms. However, medications themselves fall within the scientific paradigm, so it is easier for the FDA to approve a drug that appears to be effective, even if how it achieves its effect remains a mystery.

There's no question that investigating the unknown with tools that do not operate within the accepted framework of understanding presents a conundrum. Not to mention that research funds are rarely available for hypothetical research that can't be quantified. But as physicist turned science fiction writer John Campbell, Jr., observed: "If Science exists only when there is engineering know-how and logical interrelationships, then a scientist cannot deal with the unknown, with the not-yet-logically related. Like Logic, Science is necessary but not sufficient." Keep in mind that much of what we once thought of as science fiction has now come true.

Making Psychology Respectable

New psychological practices and research have always met with skepticism. Psychology, the study of human thought, emotion, and behavior, is considered part art and part science—although some would argue there's very little science involved. Psychology's struggle for legitimacy and respect is certainly due in part to the problem of measuring human consciousness. Unlike medicine, which adheres to standardized procedures, and where treatment dosage can be measured precisely and replicated easily, psychology is difficult to study using the usual tools of the scientific method. In the arena of human emotions, standardizing treatments often misses the point, the essence, of what makes a treatment truly effective.

The idea of spending years on a couch unearthing the source of one's psychological distress seems quaint today, but at the turn of the century it was downright radical—or crackpot. Sigmund Freud's methods may in some ways seem outmoded now, but he was truly a pioneer, risking his reputation to break societal barriers with regard to human behavior. Faster and more efficient ways of dealing with psychological problems—including sophisticated pharmacologic solutions—have burgeoned in the last twenty years. Freud would be flabbergasted by Prozac and EMDR and Thought Field Therapy. But he was a bold and broad-minded thinker. In his later writings, he predicted that the day would come when knowledge of the mind and body's workings would make psychotherapy obsolete.

Where Did You Get That Paradigm?

Each of us views the world through our own unique lens, and the characteristics and scope of that lens governs what we are able to see and know about the world. That lens is our personal paradigm.

Paradigms are not born; they are made. They are handed down first and foremost by the culture in which we live, globally and locally. They represent the collected attitudes and beliefs of what Carolyn Myss, Ph.D., calls our "tribe." What you believe about how the world works is very different from what your great-grandfather believed, and it is different from what someone living in the rain forests of Borneo believes. You, your great-grandfather, and the Borneo tribesman have very different explanations for, say, an airplane, or a computer, or a fertility fetish. A kid who grows up in a deeply religious churchgoing family interprets experiences differently than do children of the atheists next door. Quakers and Hindus have a different understanding of the world, literally a different perspective.

The way you see the world around you is profoundly influenced by what your family believes and how it acts. If your parents were always worried about what might befall them or you, you may have come to believe that the world is unsafe or unpredictable; you may live in a state of constant fear and anxiety. If family conflicts were resolved with screaming and yelling, it's reasonable to believe that anger is the only tactic that works. You may respond by spending your life avoiding intimate relationships entirely. If, on the other hand, your childhood was smooth and serene, you are likely to trust that the world is an OK place.

Of course, not everyone responds in the same way to education, neighborhood, or the class bully. Your personal paradigm reflects not only your culture, family, and life experiences but the ways that you, because of your unique temperament, have interpreted and responded to your environment. Our openness to what's new affects our view of the world. Research has shown that some people are inherently more adventurous and less conservative than others, hence more open to trying new things.

Just keeping up with our fast-changing world can be overwhelming and exhausting. We've all had that feeling of breathing hard just to keep up. There's so much information, so much news from so many sources, so many new products and whole new technologies. We don't know where to begin. And the rate of change is ever accelerating.

The buzzwords of the world in which we live are "faster, newer, better," and no one can really take it all in. It's a world of specialists, with each person trying to master a fragment of our vast body of knowledge. All of us make our choices about what to specialize in and what and how much to keep up with. Do we try to see the latest movies? Check out each new restaurant that's written up? Buy the latest alloy tennis racquet that promises to improve our game? Try the latest antiaging potion? Upgrade our computer? Get a faster modem or the latest digital video equipment?

For some people, the easiest thing to do is to stop trying to keep up and just run in place. They haven't heard any decent music since Benny Goodman; they won't buy or learn to use a computer; they just got around to accepting that talk therapy is OK—for other people. When it comes to psychology, there is an "instant" paradox in our society. Always in a hurry, we demand fast food and instant cold remedies. We are offered "one-hour" eyeglasses and ten-minute lube jobs, which we pay for with instant cash from the ATM. We revere speed. Yet somehow we still believe that, in the area of human emotions, it takes time to get over it. No pain, we think, no gain. The very idea of instant emotional healing is suspect.

A hundred years ago running in place was a workable choice. Life moved more slowly; people didn't have to know about many major changes or master new skills immediately. Little was likely to happen to you or your neighbors that was earthshaking or out of the ordinary. But in this day and age, being a Flat Earther is no longer an option. The whole wide world is right in our face. Somehow or other, we've got to keep up. The trick is to figure out what's worth keeping up with. If you want to live up to your highest personal potential, you've got to open your eyes and see all that there is to see, so you can make good choices.

Tunnel Vision Can Be Harmful to Your Health

In our clinical practices, we have seen how the new energy theories of ESM challenge our clients' dearly held worldviews. For example, a client has a very positive outcome using the techniques presented here. In a telephone follow-up, or on her next visit to the office, she will acknowledge that her problem is gone—she reports she is no longer angry, or anxious, or jealous. But since we last spoke to her, she has come to believe that the reason for the improvement is something other than the treatment—even when she acknowledges that she felt better immediately after. "I don't think that was what helped me," she might say.

Some clients guess that they feel better because they talked about their problem with a friend—even though they had done so many times before, with no improvement. Or they conclude that they feel better simply because of the passage of time—even though they had suffered for years up to that moment. Others have imagined that their improvement was due to a hypnotic suggestion that we implanted. Or that the ESM process distracted them from their feelings and it was *that distraction* which produced the relief. Some people who felt better for the first time in years could not shake the feeling that it was "just coincidence." Most surprising are the people who began with a very serious level of distress but later report that "it really wasn't that big a problem in the first place."

Some of the explanations were pretty inventive. Why? Because each of us is determined to make sense of our experiences while holding on tight to our comfortable frame of reference. This is what Dr. Roger Callahan, one of the founders of Thought Field Therapy, calls the apex problem: There is no apex or connecting juncture between what is known (the usual) and what is experienced.

We recognize that the premise behind Emotional Self-Management strains credibility. How can your "polarity" be reversed? Does it make sense that merely tapping on your body while thinking about your fear of heights can cure your fear forever? Of course not. It just doesn't fit our picture of how the world works.

No one completely understands why Emotional Self-Management works, although theories, hypotheses, and supporting evidence abound.

Your belief about the way the world works is powerful. We invite you to read on to learn about ESM and try out the techniques. As you do, remember the paradigm problem and keep an open mind. If you do not recognize the problem, you may believe that ESM is not responsible for the change that results, and you may not use it to help you in the future. Thus your beliefs can hurt you.

The Road to Emotional Self-Management

The concept of emotional healing has leapt forward in recent decades. Traditional talk therapy, which focused on unfogging your perceptions, has given way to a broad range of mind/body therapies, from cognitive and behavioral approaches, to biofeedback, hypnosis, and EMDR. Acupuncturists, homeopathic practitioners, psychologists, and a growing number of physicians who work with the body's energy systems know that physical and emotional symptoms are related and often intertwined. We are not going to elaborate on the mind/body connection, since many of the writers and researchers mentioned in Chapter 1 have done that quite eloquently. If you have any doubt about whether your mind and body are connected, however, think about this: Have you ever worried yourself sick? Does thinking about a slice of apple pie make your mouth water? Have your eyes ever teared up at a touching movie scene? Case closed. Let's look at the path that leads up to Thought Field Therapy and the new energy therapies that include ESM.

Cognitive Therapy

Cognitive therapy has evolved over the last thirty years as a mainstay of psychotherapy. Its premise is that our thoughts, even though we may be unaware of them, precede our emotional responses, and if we can exercise control over our thoughts, we can change dysfunctional emotional patterns. Cognitive theory says that our automatic thoughts stem from fundamental attitudes that we hold at the edge of conscious awareness, and they in turn evolved from core beliefs that have developed from our interchanges with our environment, others, and ourselves, from the moment of birth. The most powerful of these beliefs are thought to become entrenched early in life, as deeply embedded patterns of response. Cognitive therapy works to change the negative thoughts in order to bring about change in unproductive behavior. ESM incorporates cognitive therapy's use of intentional thoughts to bring about change. There's more about cognitive therapy in Chapter 5.

Biofeedback

Biofeedback therapy acknowledges the power of the mind to affect physiological processes. Biofeedback is a tool for teaching people how to control symptoms of stress and pain, using the power of their thoughts and awareness literally to change the body's responses. The remarkable thing about biofeedback, and probably what enabled its acceptance into mainstream medicine, is that it actually detects and measures the interaction of mind and body along certain dimensions. This is an interaction that yogis and those experienced in meditation practices have taken for granted for millennia. Attached to electrodes that measure skin conductivity, subjects can track their physiological responses on a screen and learn how to use their thoughts to moderate those responses. The myograph measurements of the electrical voltage produced by muscle tension and the electroencephalograph measurements of brain activity are themselves the means for patients to monitor and to change physiological responses.

Hypnosis

Hypnosis, which we have both worked with for decades, is another mind/body process rediscovered in the 1800s, that has struggled for acceptance as a legitimate therapeutic technique. Hypnosis was finally recognized by the American Medical Association in the 1950s as a legitimate course of study to be offered in medical schools. The process involves installing a suggestion for behavior in the unconscious mind while the mind and body are in a state of highly focused attention. In this state a person's critical judgment of suggestions is reduced and receptivity is increased. Hypnosis is difficult to study using strict scientific methods, since the most effective approach is to tailor the treatment to the individual. In standardized formats, hypnosis loses the personalized nuances that make the treatment most effective.

We still use hypnosis when appropriate in our practices. But folk tales and movies have perpetuated the misconception that hypnosis always works immediately and that its effects will last indefinitely. We blame the Roadrunner cartoons: For example, as the story opens, Wiley E. Coyote is seen reading the *Acme Hypnosis Book*. In the next scene he is sending spiraling wavelike rays in the direction of the Roadrunner, who cleverly holds up a mirror and bounces them right back at Coyote, which causes him to fall into a stupor and then off a cliff. Hypnosis can be pretty impressive, but, of course, it doesn't really work this way.

The ESM procedures employ some of the visualization and imagery elements of hypnosis. Interestingly, many people who were not highly successful with hypnosis in a clinical setting were able to get better results on their own using self-hypnosis techniques. The same elements of privacy and self-control over the process also seem to be factors in the appeal and success of ESM.

Eye Movement Desensitization and Reprocessing

Most people have some understanding of hypnosis. But only recently has Eye Movement Desensitization and Reprocessing become known outside the psychotherapeutic community. Its very impressive techniques, which we have been using to great effect in recent years, operate outside people's expectations of the clinical experience. Although its mechanism is still not fully understood, EMDR has demonstrated phenomenal ability to resolve emotional issues, in particular posttraumatic stress disorder. Shell-shocked battle veterans, victims of rape and abuse, and survivors of natural and man-made disasters have experienced quick and permanent relief with EMDR, often in cases where numerous other therapies, including hypnosis, have failed. EMDR is proving effective for the relief of more common disturbances as well.

With EMDR, clients are asked to focus on the disturbing experience— images, physical sensations, thoughts. As the therapist moves his hand from side to side in front of the client's face, the client follows the movement with the eyes. For reasons not fully understood, these lateral movements seem to foster a reprocessing of the distressing events, circumstances, or perceptions. EMDR procedures sometimes incorporate other methods of side-to-side lateralization (tones in alternating ears, tapping on alternate sides of the body) to activate hemispheric interactions.

The second phase of the EMDR procedure seeks to instill a positive thought process in place of the negative one that was associated with the distress. For example, the person who has lived through an earthquake might go from thinking "I am vulnerable" to recognizing that the danger is past and that "I am secure and comfortable."

Francine Shapiro, Ph.D., explains the effects as the breaking of a "neurological loop," installed at the time of the traumatizing event, that has not allowed the complete processing of emotional distress. The EMDR process appears to activate a natural mechanism for its dissipation, enabling clients to integrate difficult life experiences and get past them, so that thinking about the events no longer distresses them.

We were attracted to EMDR's rapid action and also to the fact that you could see if you were getting improvement in a matter of weeks rather than months, as could be expected with traditional therapies. We have incorporated into ESM methods the concept of self-evaluating one's distress and rating one's belief in a positive thought.

EMDR is highly structured, with a uniformity of procedures that lends itself to comparative studies. Most areas in the mental health community now accept it as a workable modality. Of course, in the scientific community, it's still in the questionable stage. But EMDR is ten years ahead of where thought energy psychotherapies are with regard to scientific legitimacy.

The Road Less Traveled . . . So Far

So now we come to Thought Field Therapy, which incorporates energies outside our current understanding of the mind/body mechanisms, outside the paradigms of physiology and neurology.

The modern application of subtle energy therapies began in the mid-1970s, through the combined efforts of three men: chiropractor George Goodheart, psychiatrist John Diamond, and psychologist Roger Callahan.

Dr. Goodheart developed the concepts and practice of Applied Kinesiology, which employs manual muscle testing, a fascinating, seemingly magical way to tune into the inner wisdom of the body. In order to understand how this fits into Thought Field Therapy, let's look at how muscle testing works.

In manual muscle testing, the subject typically stands with one arm extended straight out to the side, palm down. While the subject holds her arm in a rigid "locked" position, the clinician applies downward pressure on the wrist, while the subject resists. The clinician takes a "reading" of the subject's strength. Then, while the clinician again presses down on the wrist of the subject's outstretched arm, the subject will touch a part of the body that the clinician feels might be causing problems, or the subject may hold a substance suspected to be unhealthy. Unless there is something wrong, most people can meet that downward arm pressure with substantial resistance. However, if there *is* something wrong, their muscles will weaken. When the clinician presses downward, the arm muscle will give way in the presence of a distressing thought or a substance that is toxic to that person.

Applied Kinesiology has become a standard diagnostic tool for many chiropractors, nutritionists, and homeopaths. A study by Daniel Monti, M.D., and his colleagues conducted at Jefferson Medical School and published in a reputable scientific journal demonstrated the validity of muscle testing. Their research was able to show the effect of true and false statements on muscle strength.

Thought energy therapies use the same "wiring" as acupuncture—the meridian system—an intricate network of tiny pathways that conduct electrical energy. Dr. Diamond made an extensive study of the body's acupuncture system to achieve emotional balance. Using muscle testing, Dr. Diamond identified many of the acupuncture sites associated with specific emotions, which have become the "tap sites" of thought energy therapy procedures.

A key discovery in Thought Field Therapy was psychologist Roger Callahan's finding that muscle testing can reveal hidden self-sabotaging thoughts and beliefs, which he calls "psychological reversals."

For example, it would be expected that someone who says "I want to be happy" would be able to show considerable arm strength during muscle testing, since most all of us profess, and consciously believe, that we want to be happy. But some people test weak on this statement, which would seem to reveal an incongruity between what the mind says and the belief the body harbors. Dr. Callahan discovered that manual muscle testing can be used to identify an unconscious block, or what might be called an "internal disagreement."

The next step was his discovery that the self-sabotaging pattern could be corrected. Bringing the thought to mind while activating a specific acupuncture site through tapping would *reverse* the negative effect. Voilá! Thought Field Therapy!

Today there are many hybrid technologies based on the meridian systems of the body combined with cognitive approaches, among them Acu-Power, Emotional Freedom Techniques™, Energy Diagnostics™, Thought Energy Synchronization Therapy™, and now Emotional Self-Management. (See the Resources appendix for details about the various approaches.)

Dr. Callahan, whose initial application of these discoveries focused on the removal of phobias, persisted in the face of tremendous pressure from the American Psychological Association and other mainstream organizations of which he had been a member. His discovery of the effect of reversals of conscious intention on psychological processes had no precedent within

39

existing psychological models. But polarity reversals, as we call them, are a cornerstone of Thought Field Therapy. Chapter 4 presents an exercise for correcting polarity reversals, an important foundation step in clearing emotional problems.

We have adapted and added to elements of thought energy therapies to arrive at the process we call Emotional Self-Management. We use muscle testing to test the underlying beliefs—the polarity reversals—of our clients, so that we can fine-tune their treatment. And it is muscle testing that has enabled us to verify, through trial and error, the effectiveness of the emotion-specific "tap sequences" in the protocols.

Unlike some energy therapies, ESM is self-administered. In a full treatment sequence, or protocol, a Balanced Breathing exercise is first administered, to align the body's polarity, followed by a Polarity Reversal exercise to address any reversals of our thoughts. We incorporate imagery and visualization techniques from hypnosis and employ the thought-focusing component of cognitive therapy to activate the thought field during the process. There's even some right-brain/left-brain humming and counting and eye movements. We've taken the best from many methods. Since we believe that all the body's systems communicate, our objective is to engage them all in the process of healing. ESM gives you the full Monte.

ESM on the Energetic Level

These are exciting times for science and the field of health care. With advanced technologies expanding our ability to observe, collect, and analyze data, new discoveries are reported almost daily. The exchange of information is global and instantaneous. As more and more is learned about our world, a detailed picture is emerging of how we function as biological beings. Discoveries in diverse areas—neurology, aeronautics, pharmacology, engineering, quantum physics—add to our understanding of the universe.

What we have is a grand and giant jigsaw puzzle, a puzzle of the whole cosmos, really, with bigger and bigger pieces falling into place. We don't have all the pieces; many mysteries continue to elude us. Even the mapping of the human genome, a vast, complex, and astonishing accomplishment, represents but one piece of the larger puzzle. Going inward to the mysteries of genetic chemistry is as complex as looking outward toward distant galaxies. But enough pieces are in place that we are getting an idea of the grand scheme of things, from the subatomic to the cosmic, from the global to the personal.

It is fascinating how the pieces fit together and how, each time a new fact falls into place, it adds to our understanding of both the whole and the individual components. Many new observations, or even old ones revisited, require a shift in our perceptual filters. This is where an open mind comes in handy. The larger the screen on which you view the world, the better you can see the overlapping information and connections.

Here we focus on the pieces of the puzzle that help us understand how thought energy therapies and ESM work. We've already discussed some of the established components of ESM—the mind/body connection, the workings of the brain, and cognitive psychology. But ESM is fundamentally about subtle energies, the kind that are hard to detect and measure, the kind that are still kept outside the walls of science's inner sanctum. To us, part of the excitement is that there is so much still unknown, still so much to be discovered.

The fact is that ESM works. We think we know some of the reasons why, and that is what we want to explore with you. Research including our own and discoveries from diverse disciplines seem to offer clues to the inner workings of ESM. As we look at some of these clues, hypotheses, and speculations, you may feel, as we do, that each one opens another window of understanding. Each provides an alternative prism through which to examine another aspect of the same underlying phenomenon: *energy.*

Are You Ready to Change Your Mind?

Imagine that we are living in a sea of energies. Just as a fish doesn't know it's in water, often we are unaware of the forces surrounding us—atomic waves and particles, thermal and chemical and electromagnetic energies. Our species is programmed to receive, like a radio certain of these energies. Other species, with different physiological and biochemical makeups, are attuned to other frequencies, sensitive to other energies. We humans tune in, both consciously and unconsciously, to the energies available on our broadcast band and make use of them, often without recognizing their presence or effect.

However, certain energies are available to us that we don't make use of. Sometimes it's a matter of ignorance: We don't know that the information is available, or we've been conditioned to discount it. Sometimes our refusal to believe keeps us from tapping into power sources that we might use to our advantage. A common example of this is the inability, or refusal, to take advantage of our "gut feelings" and hunches or intuition, which can be highly valuable sources of information, when we know how to access and apply them.

Understanding the unity of mind and body has led to powerful new ways of healing physiological and emotional ills, including biofeedback, cognitive therapy, and hypnosis. Growing understanding of the workings of subtle energies brings us to energy therapies. There is powerful energy out there, available to us at any moment, and we are not taking full advantage. For the most part, it's not a shortcoming in our equipment. We're just not tuned in.

Tuning In

Thought Field Therapy may seem far out, but energy therapies are as old as recorded history. For thousands of years there have been civilizations whose healing modalities were centered around the understanding of the body's energy systems and of the importance of working with those energies. The concept of energy balance is the foundation of nearly all the world's healing systems. Western medicine speaks of homeostasis, the state of equilibrium and constancy of the body's systems. In traditional Chinese medicine, the physician's central objective is to balance the "chi," or "Qi," energy. Ayurvedic traditions speak of "prana." Physician and author Deepak Chopra says "the life energy, or Prana, is channeled throughout our bodies by a 'wind' known as Vata. . . . When Prana Vata is out of balance, there is general disruption throughout the system." By any name, these energy systems have been central to our understanding of healing for a very long time.

In the past couple of decades, instruments have been developed that can explore the inner workings of the brain. Although the mapping of our most important organ is far from complete, a convincing case has been made that the brain is the seat of who we are as individuals and is responsible for generating our sense of reality. Neurosurgeon Richard Restak points out that "no creature, including ourselves, can ever know any other 'reality' than the representations made by our brain." Essentially what he is saying is that we are boxed into knowing only what our instruments—including our brain—can measure.

But in our view of the world, the brain is not the be-all and end-all of human consciousness. As we see it, information is not merely stored in the brain; rather, information is contained in a *field* of energy. We do not need to be conscious of that energy field for it to affect us. Traditional medicine and scientific research have largely overlooked the role played by barely detectable electrical and electromagnetic energies.

The subtle energies of thought exist in a realm beyond the biochemical and bioelectrical ones we are able to measure. However, we can measure the *effects* of thought energy. Studies by Larry Dossey, M.D., have shown that prayer can be a healing agent, even prayers over very long distances, directed to people unknown to those praying. Some hospitals now recognize the value of therapeutic touch in healing, and train nurses to use it. Parapsychological effects—remote viewing (the ability to "see" something at a distance), precognition (the ability to know something before it happens)—have been demonstrated repeatedly (albeit largely ignored by conventional science). In other words, although we cannot yet measure a specific thought energy field or examine its substance until it reaches the neurological system, we can detect the effects of thought energy.

Electromagnetic Influences

We understand some types of energy better than others—meaning, usually, that we can detect and measure them. Electromagnetic energy is one. Many people are familiar with electroencephalograph (EEG) readings, which measure brain activity. Specialists can identify alpha (relaxed), beta (awake), theta, and delta wave (unconscious) frequencies, and associate each with a different level of consciousness. Right now, reading this book (assuming it's keeping you awake), you are probably in a beta-wave state of consciousness.

These brain waves can be compared to the AM radio band. The entire AM band can be recognized, and with precision equipment (a radio), we can tune in to specific frequencies along that band. In much the same way that alpha or beta waves indicate different kinds of activity, each frequency, or what we call a "station," carries different information—rock or country or classical music, baseball or talk shows.

According to energy therapies, thoughts are tangible aspects of reality that exist and eventually will be cataloged, just as many brain activities are graphed and plotted today. What we cannot do—yet—with our instruments is further break down that beta wave band and measure the specific electromagnetic frequencies of *different kinds* of thoughts—anger and sadness, happiness and anxiety. But the effectiveness of thought energy therapies in linking meridians in the body with specific emotions indicates that there is indeed an interaction between thought energies and the meridian system. The interaction of the thought energies with the meridian energy system is believed to be the source of emotions, or emotional distress. In other words, emotions are believed to be the result of the effect of thought energy on the body's meridian system. Each type of thought seems to vibrate at a specific frequency and affect specific meridians in the body.

Thought fields created by strong negative emotions appear to deliver a shock to the system, causing blockages in the meridians. The energy of that thought field is believed to become trapped, creating an emotional loop that cannot escape or dissipate. Whenever that thought loop is reactivated, through any reminder even tangentially related to the original experience or emotion, the whole encoded memory is reexperienced as an unpleasant and disturbing sensation throughout the body.

Thought energy therapies balance the energy channels, thereby eliminating the power of our thoughts to affect the body's chemistry and thus to disturb us. To illustrate: If you were thinking about how you were recently overcharged at an automotive repair shop, you might develop tension in the hands or abdomen, a flushed face, and the clouded judgment that often accompanies anger. When you're not thinking about this incident, you feel fine. There is something about the thought itself that triggers the physical and emotional symptoms.

In the normal course of events, the memory of this incident fades, the emotional energy dissipates, and the body returns to a state of equilibrium. Memory of the event no longer has the power to disturb you. But if your energy system is blocked in its ability to dissipate anger, if your personal history is dotted with incidents of unresolved anger, this incident will just be added to the pile. Trapped in the system, the wound will continue to fester, sometimes for years. It is precisely these disruptions of the meridian system that are the target of the ESM processes.

It has been noted that cognitive therapy operates on the premise that thoughts affect our emotions, and that by controlling and changing our thoughts, we alter our emotions and eventually our behavior as well. This approach, like medications or behavioral therapy, can be effective, but ESM takes a more direct route. Here's an analogy that illustrates the difference. If the drain lines in your home were partially clogged, you could solve the problem of the water and sewage backing up by decreasing the intensity of the water flow by, for example, avoiding running the dishwasher, taking a shower, and flushing the toilet at the same time. But the more effective solution would be to put something in the drain line so that it opens to its normal capacity.

That is what ESM techniques accomplish. They clear away blockages, opening the meridian system to its normal capacity, allowing trapped emotional energy to flow freely. It is believed that thought energy therapies work with the disturbed electromagnetic field, adding energy into the emotion-specific meridian using direct stimulation: tapping or rubbing at specific acupuncture sites. At the same time statements of intention are made that activate thought energy fields. The combination of tapping and these deliberately created fields have a balancing effect on the meridian energies, and the disturbing emotions are unblocked.

Acupuncture and the Meridian System

The idea that the body possesses an unseen energy stream has been a fundamental tenet of traditional Chinese medicine for a very long time. Although they work with the presenting physical symptoms, acupuncturists don't separate the mind/body. They assume they are dealing with the emotional component as well. Stimulating specific acupuncture sites has been shown to be effective in blocking pain signals. While needles are the traditional means of stimulating acupuncture sites, they also can be activated through heat, massage, direct electrical stimulation, and tapping. In this country the focus of acupuncture generally has been quite narrow, emphasizing the relief of physical pain. But whatever the underlying disease or the nature of the disruption, when the flow of chi energy is restored, the body heals itself. As the famed humanitarian physician Albert Schweitzer remarked, "We are at our best when we allow the doctor that resides within to work."

Acupuncture sites have qualities that make them unique. One of them is a difference in electrical conductivity compared with surrounding tissue. Ordinarily the sites have a significantly lower electrical resistance compared to surrounding skin locations. Ordinary dry skin has a resistance of between 200,000 and 2 million ohms (a standard measure of electrical resistance). At an acupuncture location the skin resistance is significantly lower. Within TCM, there are over 360 acupuncture sites on the body; some acupuncture models put that number closer to 1,500. However, ESM procedures use only fifteen of these sites.

Why does tapping with the fingers on an acupuncture site work? One component of its effectiveness is believed to have to do with the "piezoelectric effect." When certain crystals are struck sharply, causing them to vibrate, they bend and then snap back to their original shape, generating an electrical charge. The piezoelectric effect ignites a modern gas range—that "clicking" sound you hear is the ignition. The speculation is that calcium in the bones provides the mineral crystals for this piezoelectric effect when tapping an acupuncture site.

Pinning Down the Meridian System

The meridian system cuts across every single one of the traditional Western medicine systems—the nervous, circulatory, and lymphatic. Until recently, the existence of the meridian system was purely speculative, an almost metaphoric subtle energy network. However, there is evidence of its physical existence. It was the Korean scientist Kim Bong Han who several decades ago discovered that the meridians are a network of microtubules. Examining rabbits and dogs, he found that a vast network of microtubules (about 0.5 microns in diameter; for comparison, a human hair is about 1.5 microns) passes through the walls of veins and arteries as well as around and through various organs. He also discovered circulating within the microtubules a rich concentrate of DNA, RNA, and a variety of neuropeptides and other chemical messengers that are also known to wash over the brain.

More physical evidence of the meridian pathways can be found in photographs taken at University of Paris Hospital in 1985–86. Physicians and researchers Jean Claude Darras and Pierre de Vernejoul injected radioactive isotopes (technetium) into meridian and nonmeridian sites. At the meridian location, the fluid flow is coherent and can be traced along a known meridian pathway; at the nonmeridian site it dissipates locally.

Researchers recently have developed techniques to measure meridian activity. The Apparatus for Meridian Identification (AMI), developed by Hiroshi Motoyama, Ph.D., founder of the California Institute for Human Science in Encinitas, California, uses a sophisticated detection method that measures the electrical conductivity of the meridians. The AMI applies calibrated low-voltage impulses into acupuncture points at the tip of the fingers and toes and uses that information to infer the flow of chi. When the energy flow in the meridian is not as expected, the theory is that something has distorted the measurements. One explanation is that negative emotions affect the free flow of electromagnetic energy. The AMI is being developed as a diagnostic device.

University of California at Irvine physicist Zang-Hee Cho, Ph.D., is credited with inventing the prototype of the positron emission tomograph (PET) scan and was a pioneer of magnetic resonance imaging (MRI). When his back was injured some years ago, he found relief through acupuncture. Ever the inquiring scientist, he began using MRI technology to explore how acupuncture works. He found that the MRI was able to identify the effects of an acupuncture treatment administered at the site of the little toe upon blood flow to the brain, where no direct nerve, blood, or other connection existed.

Dr. Cho's findings were published in the Spring 1998 *Proceedings of the National Academy of Sciences,* providing further scientific evidence of the existence of energy systems that have been used for thousands of years by physicians in other cultures. Dr. Cho is expanding his research to better understand the effects of acupuncture on brain functioning.

Polarity and the Electromagnetic Field

Most people have seen the effect of iron filings in the presence of a magnet, how they align themselves according to the field polarity of the magnet. It's a typical grade-school science experiment. Well, we humans are similar: We're polarized. As early as the 1940s Yale University School of Medicine professor and researcher Harold Saxton Burr discovered that all living organisms have a top-to-bottom electrical polarity as well as lateral polarity, left to right. Other researchers following in Dr. Burr's footsteps found that specific organs have a north/south polarity and that the polarity was reversed in 80 percent of a group of breast cancer patients. The implications of those findings have yet to be fully realized.

A central tenet of Thought Field Therapy is that the body's energy has a polarity, a positive and negative pole, much like a battery, or the north and south poles of a magnet. A reversal of the usual polarity can interfere with thought, emotion, and behavior. The electrical currents that deliver power to the receptacles in your home are polarized. Modern sockets have one slot slightly larger than the other so that the plug can go in only one way—with the positive and negative poles properly aligned—because today's sophisticated electronic gadgets are particularly sensitive to misaligned polarity. Plug them in the wrong way, and they'll be out of phase; you'll get an ominous humming sound, and they won't work properly. Polarity reversals have an effect on all known energy systems. The reversal of magnetic energy has a profound effect on whatever it's operating on. Since we humans are more sensitive than your average stereo system, it figures that we need to be properly plugged in as well.

On an individual level, many factors besides the generalized effects of electromagnetic fields can cause polarity reversals. It has nothing to do with our volition or any conscious process over which we have control. Causes might include environmental factors such as certain chemicals or electromagnetic radiation from a television or computer screen. Certain foods and stressful situations can be a factor, and other people's reversals can essentially "rub off" on us. In magnetic or electrical induction, a wire carrying a current close to another wire induces the same current or a resonance of it in the second wire. We have all had the experience of being brought down by another person's depression, agitated by their anxiety, or feeling that another's happiness was contagious. Sigmund Freud noted long ago that anxious individuals can benefit from being in the presence of a calm therapist. We believe he was observing the effects of one aspect of the inductive quality of human electromagnetic energy.

What makes us so sensitive to electromagnetic fields? Geobiologist Joseph Krichvink and his colleagues at Caltech Institute may have another clue to understanding the effects of the electromagnetic field on humans. Magnetite is the crystallized form of iron and thus is responsive to both geomagnetic and electromagnetic fields. It is known that animals with navigational and homing abilities—homing pigeons, migrating salmon—show significant concentrations of magnetite. In humans it is found mostly in the pineal gland, which is located approximately in the center of the brain. The function of the magnetite is not understood, yet it must have some purpose. Its presence seems to indicate we can be influenced by magnetic fields.

Planetary Polarity Reversals

There is convincing evidence of polarity reversals on a planetary level. Although it was once taken for granted that the earth's magnetic poles are fixed, research indicates that the earth's magnetic poles have reversed at least six times in the course of history. James Hayes, Ph.D., held a conference in 1971 to report his findings regarding the earth's polarity reversals at the Lamont Geophysical Observatory at Columbia University. Upon examining core samples from the ocean floor, Dr. Hayes found that tiny dust particles that settle on the water and then sink to the sea bottom tell a fascinating story. Some of these particles contain magnetite. As they settle to the depths of the ocean, these particles act something like tiny compasses, aligning themselves with the earth's geomagnetic field. They form layers on the ocean floor, leaving a record of the earth's magnetic polarity through their alignment with magnetic north. Hayes discovered that these global reversals take place over spans of about 10,000 years, with millions of years of relative stability in between.

Also, Hayes found that tiny sea animals called radiolarians, experienced tremendous "die-offs," as documented by their hard exoskeletons that remain after they die, that coincide with the earth's polarity reversals. One of those reversals coincides with the extinction of the dinosaurs. Additional evidence suggests that other mass extinctions coincided with global polarity reversals.

It is theorized that polarity reversals occur when the earth's magnetic field is very low. When only a weak geomagnetic field protects the earth from solar wind and ionizing radiation, huge numbers of animal and plant species die. Currently, the comet-impact theory is favored as an explanation for the extinction of the dinosaurs. However, the theory of a decreased magnetic field offers a plausible alternative. It is possible that both events occurred at about the same time, geologically speaking.

Studies indicate that the earth's magnetic field is now in a period of decline, which may have a variety of unhealthy effects on living creatures, including behavioral changes, negative influences on reproduction, and defects in offspring. The observations of how electrical polarity effects animal cells was explored by Robert Becker, M.D. (developer of bone growth stimulators used in orthopedic surgery) and others, who found that if a weak negative polarity can be created at the site of damaged tissue or nerves, it will promote healing and growth.

These speculations regarding the effects of planetary polarity and the observations of polarity on physical healing help us understand more easily the effects polarity reversals can exert on an individual's electromagnetic field. The reversal of a person's energy polarity can sabotage attempts to make cognitive, emotional, and behavioral changes. Corrections of reversals are immediately detectable using manual muscle testing.

Valerie Hunt, Ph.D., professor and researcher at the University of California at Los Angeles, has demonstrated evidence of human sensitivity to electromagnetic (EM) fields using a spectrographic process. Dr. Hunt's UCLA lab contains a specially constructed room in which ambient electromagnetic (EM) and magnetic energy can be controlled. When sensitive individuals, such as healers, were placed in the room and deprived of EM energy, they reported diminished mental and physical capabilities and increased anxiety. When EM energy was raised above normal levels, however, the subjects reported feeling well, highly conscious, with positive excitement and physical acuity.

When electrical radiation levels in the room remained norma magnetic fields alone were decreased, the subjects experienced consi lack of coordination. They had a difficult time with balance and eve forming basic tasks such as touching a finger to their nose. With a magnetic field increased above normal, high levels of balance and coordination were reported; subjects were able to lean over at steeper angles without falling. Findings such as these indicate that we are physically and emotionally affected by ambient electromagnetic and magnetic fields, both positively and negatively. Certainly there is a great deal more to learn about the effects of EM fields.

The Molecules of Emotion

Georgetown University professor and researcher Candace Pert, Ph.D., in identifying the chemicals and molecules responsible for activating the body's complex responses to emotional arousal, describes another pathway for the physiological effect of emotion on the body. This electrochemical pathway travels by way of the limbic system, which is the brain's emotional interpreter of incoming information, and down into the body by way of the adrenal glands and the autonomic nervous system. In this process, specific brain cells are activated to produce complex formulas of amino acid and peptide and neuropeptide chains of molecules that communicate with various parts of the body. The firing of certain nerve cells dispatches specific neuropeptide chains, which find built-in receptor sites throughout the body that control physical processes. These amino acid neuropeptide chains are able to activate or deactivate specific biological processes that are involved in emotion and behavior. Dr. Pert calls these "the molecules of emotion."

At the cellular level, positive and negatively charged neuropeptides form the information link among the blood, the lymph system, and digestion. Polarity shifts that occur at the cellular level are responsible for the uptake of material through cell walls. Here again are polarities, positive and negative charges within the nerve impulses on the surface of the skin.

Another confirmation of the existence of polarity in the human organism is provided by MEG (magneto-encephalography), a relatively new technique that measures the tiny magnetic fields produced by electric activity in the brain. While still an evolving technology, the sophisticated electronics of MEG can identify the polarity of brain activity at given moments in time. The ability to measure electromagnetic polarities in the brain may one day help to explain the underlying mechanism of how thought energy influences polarity reversals.

Neuropeptide chain theories do not contradict thought energy therapies. But what's missing in the molecular view of emotional events is an explanation of how thought energy activates the nerve cells in the first place to produce the chemical messengers in the body. We have to go back up that neuropeptide chain, to look at what triggered the neuron to fire and create that peptide in the first place. Dr. Pert talks about a very interesting phenomenon that may offer a clue. The receptor sites on a nerve cell vibrate at a certain frequency. However, when the neurotransmitter locks onto a receptor site, the frequency changes. Something is going on at the energetic, or vibratory, level. Our thesis is that the energy flowing in the meridians activates certain cells to trigger the manufacture of the neuropeptides.

We propose that thought energies interact with the meridian system to activate an electrochemical cascade, which triggers particular nerves to fire, in turn generating electrical and chemical signals throughout the body. Meridian and thought energy in harmonizing frequencies do not disturb the electron balance that would trigger the cascade effect on the nerve cells. This proposition is based on the theories of quantum physics and experiments conducted with thought energy.

The Quantum World

The world of quantum physics suggests yet another way of looking at the effects of thought on subtle energy fields. The rules of the world of things, the macroworld, do not always apply at the quantum level.

Energy fields are not composed of matter. They do not contain "material" in the ordinary sense; they contain *information*. Yet these fields affect the material world, just as iron filings are affected in the presence of a magnetic field, and just as all objects, animate and inanimate, are affected by gravitational fields. Although unseen, the effects of these fields are visible.

According to relativity theory, energy and matter are equivalent and interchangeable. Or, as Einstein put it, $E = MC^2$—energy (E) equals the mass of an object (M) multiplied by the speed of light (C), squared. Energy can exist either in wave or in particle form. A wave is essentially energy in motion, whereas a particle takes up space. One fascinating phenomenon of the subatomic world is that the observation of an electron has the effect of changing it. The laws of quantum physics say that when we observe a sub-atomic particle—once we "see" it—we alter it. Its mass and density are changed by the act of observation, and its next orbit location will be unpredictable. Once we observe an electron, we no longer can predict what will happen to it. Where will it appear next? As things get smaller, the observer has a greater influence on the outcome. Remember, this is at the quantum level; the chair in your living room will remain unaltered no matter how long you stare at it. Could the basis of cognitive psychology be that the very act of observing our thoughts is the key element that creates change?

An experiment conducted by Stanford University engineering professor William Tiller, Ph.D., vividly demonstrates the powerful effect of intentional thought on matter. Dr. Tiller constructed a sensitive electrical capacitor that could be discharged by a minute electrical influence. He found that ordinary people, with no special abilities, could cause the capacitor to discharge merely by focusing their thoughts on the intention to do so. The magnitude of influence on the capacitor from these intentional thoughts was enormous. Intention alone apparently triggered the capacitors' discharge thousands of times within a few minutes. When the same subjects directed their thoughts elsewhere, there was no effect; the capacitor did not discharge. Dr. Tiller also found that having his subjects hold their hands near the capacitor was helpful but by no means necessary. Even when the subjects were at great distances, or when they could not see the capacitor, it could be made to discharge.

How information is communicated through "thin air" is another mystery illuminated by the quantum paradigm. How do our thoughts "travel" from one place to another—from our brain to our emotional reactions, from here in our mind to there in our body? Do they travel some sort of path from point A to point B? At the subatomic level, something can go from one point to another without ever having to be anywhere in between. The example of "jumping" of electrons from one orbit around an atom to another, theorized by Nobel Prize–winning physicist Niels Bohr, is the classic "quantum leap." According to the rules of quantum physics, there is no way of knowing where an observed electron will turn up next; there are only probabilities. The notion of predictability evaporates at the quantum level.

In 1997 a remarkable scientific observation followed up on earlier findings that subatomic-size photons could communicate instantly over large distances. Researchers at the University of Innsbruck put photons into an optical device called a beam splitter. The beam splitter divided the photons of a single atom, which then traveled in different directions. Researchers found that when the spin of one paired photon was deliberately reversed, the other photon, a considerable distance away, reversed its direction as well. Information was instantaneously communicated from one place to another. Here is proof of what is called "nonlocal" effect: that what happens in one place can have an effect—seemingly across time and space—on what happens in another place.

Thus it seems clear that thoughts exist independent of physiological stimulus or aside from a response to our internal or external environment. We can generate a thought intentionally that has nothing to do with survival or merely stimulus and response. Our human capabilities of abstract thought are not just the by-product of biochemical processes, as some scientists would have us believe. It's never "all in your head." The thought that you have right now, whatever it is, is vital to all parts of you and exists all through you and around you. Quantum physics explains how that can occur.

Mutator Genes

No one theory seems adequate to answer all the questions about the human organism, not even genetics. The mechanistic model for understanding biological behavior based on DNA blueprints is grossly inadequate.

Genetic theory states that the genes are fixed. According to Darwinian theory, genes are mutable only over time, by way of accidental mutations caused by random factors in the environment. If the mutations are survivable or improve the survival level of the species, the new characteristic will persist. If not, it will die out.

But in 1988 research by geneticist John Cairns, Ph.D., at Harvard's School of Public Health, turned up genes in bacteria that can respond deliberately to environmental factors. This discovery of mutator genes, genes that can modify other genes, is revolutionary. It means that an organism can change its own genetics in response to the environment. Essentially, what Dr. Cairns and others have found is that organisms do not need to wait for random mutations in order to adapt and survive. *They can mutate on their own under stress and cause other genes to change and better respond to the environment.* This discovery is quite startling. It means that genes are not a preordained blueprint; they can be altered through an *intention* to change. Not surprisingly, the paradigm police, as science and technology journalist Richard Milton calls some scientists, have been unenthusiastic about the findings of Dr. Cairns and others who have replicated his research. But Dr. Cairn's observations are supported by molecular biologist Alexander Rich and his colleagues, who in 1999 published evidence of what they termed "editor" molecules of RNA, which may be the genetic material that allows for self-directed change to occur.

Dr. Cairns's discovery gives us another insight into thought energies. It indicates that there is a consciousness at work, an intentional intelligence that responds to undetectable information sources. Mutator genes might explain how bacteria are developing immunity so quickly to antibiotics and how these mutations are occurring, seemingly simultaneously, in bacteria all over the world. The question becomes: How is this information transmitted?

Morphic Fields

Here is a tantalizing theory: Perhaps bacteria are transmitting information synchronously throughout the world via what the English biologist Rupert Sheldrake calls morphic fields. The information in these fields may be expressing itself in genetic changes. A Cambridge University researcher and professor, Dr. Sheldrake theorizes that a morphic, or forming, field surrounds every organism and contains information about its form and function. It may provide the catalyst for some thought activity and could even be involved in memory and other information storage. Sheldrake provides the example of how spiders of a particular species are able to know instinctively how to spin complicated webs without having seen any other members of their species do it.

Morphic fields also explain, far better than any other theory, the remarkable behavior of a certain species of cuckoo birds. These birds smuggle their eggs into their nests of birds of other species, which hatch and raise the young cuckoos. Raised apart from others of their kind, they eventually migrate independently to another continent where they finally meet up, and congregate with, others of their kind. How do they know where to go?

When a salamander loses a limb, how do DNA molecules know precisely where the limb has been lost? Where is the information that informs the cells to begin forming new bone, nerves, blood vessels, and skin tissue, to regenerate exactly what is needed and nothing more? This is a task significantly more complex than closing a wound or repairing a broken bone. To say that the genes contain all the information is woefully inadequate.

Dr. Sheldrake thinks that we may be looking at the brain backward. In his model, the brain acts as a receptor device and interpreter of information available in the morphic field of our species. The brain is a *link* in the communication process rather than the generator of information. The brain could be a receptor organ that receives and interprets information, even information beyond the five senses. Talk about tuning in.

If this is hard to grasp, here is an analogy. Imagine a world in which we had no instruments to detect radio waves that were broadcast from some unknown place, but we had radios (think of them as gifts of nature or of God), little boxes that produced different sounds as you turned the dial. In that world, scientists might examine the radio to determine how it created all those sounds.

Unaware of the existence of unseen and undetectable radio signals, we might conclude that *the radio* produced all the programs. Scientists examining the radio might conclude that electrical energy flowed into and out of microchips and oscillators and into speakers. Researchers would correctly identify that an electrical frequency was conveyed from the radio to the amplifying system and eventually to speakers that convert the electrical energy into sound we can interpret as music or speech.

Now suppose that one of the functions of the brain is to receive information from the morphic field and interpret that information into neural and chemical responses. The unseen broadcast station would represent the morphic field, the radio would represent the brain.

Morphic fields explain a good deal that genetics leaves unanswered. The morphic field is essentially an information field, composed of unknown forms of energy, which contains information about and available to a certain species. There is circumstantial evidence that morphic fields exist, as indicated by the salamander, spider, and cuckoo bird. On a theoretical level, such fields explain significantly more than mechanical or genetic models.

Perhaps the morphic field helps to store or record the emotional loops that wreak so much havoc in our emotional lives. When a thought is generated related to a particular emotional loop, it also creates, or "forms," the disturbance in the body's meridian system and activates the whole emotional response. It's like a hologram. One part re-creates the whole entity.

In his research on the variety of human expressions, Paul Ekman, Ph.D., professor of psychology at the University of California at San Francisco, found that when people "faked" an emotion by mimicking the associated facial expression, such as sadness, they experienced some of the emotion they were faking. It was as if the expression carried some information, some fragment of an emotional state, that could be recovered—perhaps from the holographic information stored in the morphic field. University of Iowa neurologist Dr. Antonio Damasio reports the case of an opera singer who said that it took tremendous effort to remain separate from the extreme emotions of the characters she played. Once, while playing in Tchaikovsky's Queen of Spades, she merged so closely with her character in an intensely frightening scene that she actually became terrified herself.

The existence of morphic fields also may offer insight into the mechanisms of cognitive therapy. Cognitive therapy starts with the premise that changing our thoughts produces a change in behavior. What it cannot explain is how that change in thought creates the change in emotion, or how the thought interacts with the body. It may be that the incoming stimulus interacts with the patterns of information contained in the individual's morphic field; Dr. Sheldrake would say that that morphic field is influenced by the trend of all other organisms of the same species. In other words, each species has some native preprogrammed response or pattern possibilities. The incoming signal, unique to that individual, interacts with those existing patterns and in that action a core belief is encoded.

Morphic fields bear an uncanny resemblance to what pioneering psychiatrist Carl Jung was describing when he spoke of the collective unconscious, an informational field created by, and accessible to, everyone. Jung would have understood this concept in a nanosecond.

No Easy Answers

We have presented a number of tantalizing clues to the workings of the emotions and of energy therapies. We have looked for links between electromagnetism and acupuncture, neuropeptide chains and morphic fields, quantum theory and cognitive therapy. However loosely tied together, these divergent theories and observations provide a foundation for understanding how thought energy can interact with the body's electromagnetic frequencies to cause emotional disturbances.

No single theory or line of inquiry tells the whole story of how emotions work. Although new findings continue to shed light on these mysteries, there is as yet no "Theory of Everything" to explain all the observable effects of ESM and other energy therapies. That these methods of resolving emotional distress work is clear, even if the mechanisms are not.

Are you running out of energy from all this discussion? Try the following Balanced Breathing exercise. It will balance and enhance your body's energy systems.

BALANCED BREATHING EXERCISE

Proper polarity alignment of the body is a key to emotional health. The Balanced Breathing exercise, based on a two-thousand-year-old meditation, is a tried and true method for allaying anxiety that also rebalances the body's polarity. We have added elements of intentional thought and visualization in order to engage all systems in the process and amplify its effect.

The physiological design of the human being is vertically symmetrical. With the exception of certain lone organs, like the stomach, spleen, liver, and pancreas, we have matching left and right sides. The electrical polarity of the body operates on both north/south and east/west axes—or what we might term plus and minus, top and bottom, left and right. The posture used in the Balanced Breathing exercise corrects the body's overall polarity balance. The Balanced Breathing exercise is the preliminary step in all the emotion-specific protocols. In Chapter 4 you will learn to correct for polarity reversals of your *thoughts*.

Balanced Breathing takes about two minutes. The photos will help you to get into the right posture for the exercise. Once you are in position, relax and breathe comfortably. Sitting in a straight-back chair is best, but Balanced Breathing can be done while lying down or in a standing position.

1. Cross your left ankle over your right ankle.

2. Extend both arms straight out in front of you.

3. Cross your right arm over your left arm at the wrist.

4. Rotate the palms of your hands so that they are facing and interlock your fingers.

5. Rotate your hands down toward your stomach.

6. Continue rotating inward so that you bring your hands up close to your chest. At this point you have crossed the center line of your body with your hands, arms, and legs.

Note: If it is more comfortable for you, you can reverse the order—right ankle over left, left wrist over right. It doesn't make a difference, as long as they are opposite.

Once in the proper position, inhale through your nose while touching the tip of your tongue to the roof of your mouth. Exhale through your mouth, resting your tongue on the floor of your mouth.

Focus your thoughts on the concept of *balance*. It might be the idea of the balance of mind and body, or just the word "balance." At the same time picture in your mind, if you can, an image that represents balance. This could be the image of a scale, or a see-saw, or standing on one foot. Throughout the approximately two-minute process, breathe comfortably. Don't worry if you are not always able to hold the thought or image; come back to it if you drift away. If you have trouble estimating two minutes with your eyes closed, you might calculate the number of breaths you take in fifteen seconds, and repeat that cycle eight times.

. . . .

You may feel surprisingly relaxed and clearheaded after doing the Balanced Breathing exercise. It's a good way to start the day and to use any time you feel out of sorts. We know from the work of Harvard researcher and physician Herbert Benson and others that slow deep breathing initiates a relaxation response, but this procedure also properly polarizes the electromagnetic energy of your body. Don't worry, if your body is already properly aligned, you won't do any harm with this exercise. At the very least you'll feel more relaxed, and you have ensured that your body's electromagnetic energy has proper polarity and organization. Now you're ready for the next level of thought and body energy corrections—polarity reversals.

Energy Alignment

Correcting Polarity Reversals

The purpose of this chapter is to get you plugged in properly, so that your intentions align with your unconscious thoughts. According to thought energy theories, blocks to our intentions to change and release negative emotions are due to unconscious reversals in the polarity of our thoughts. Dr. Roger Callahan's pivotal discovery was that these reversals could be corrected. The Polarity Reversal exercise that you will learn here accomplishes that correction.

Chapter 3 introduced Balanced Breathing, an exercise for aligning the body's electromagnetic polarity. Now you're going to straighten out the polarity of your thoughts. The Polarity Reversal exercise, an ingredient of all ESM protocols, is a foundation for doing the emotion-specific tap sequences. If the polarity of our underlying beliefs and thoughts is not correct, the process will not work. In our clinical practice, we have found that about 40 percent of emotional problems are blocked from being released due to polarity reversals. When they are corrected, some problems resolve themselves.

We believe that the phenomenon of polarity reversals may explain why therapies that should be effective do not work, or are only partially or temporarily effective, and may explain why medications are sometimes ineffective. Underlying polarity reversals are likely to inhibit the effectiveness of any treatment.

Internal Disagreements

Polarity reversals exert a powerful pull. Most people have had the experience of feeling like they were undoing their own best intentions. We might resolve to eat less, exercise more, or be more organized. Yet somehow when the time comes to convert the intention into action, we get sidetracked. One minute we had decided, *definitely,* that we were going to take a walk every day . . . and the next thing we know, it's bedtime and we've only walked as far as the kitchen. Somehow we've finished the whole box of doughnuts before we remembered our diet resolutions. At the moment when our behavior ought to have been in concert with our intention, it went in a different direction. There are many ways in which we experience self-sabotage.

> Leslie is a good example of the way the mind can say one thing while the body operates on a different wavelength. Leslie had been in a rocky and sporadically miserable relationship for several years and recognized that her unreliable boyfriend was not good marriage material. It was as if her mind knew that the relationship wouldn't work, but her emotions kept her from taking action. Fear of being alone, fear of being hurt, and anxiety about the future kept her from leaving him. She felt that everything she was doing was the opposite of what was good for her. Every time she thought about leaving Carl, her fear of loneliness rushed in.
>
> As soon as Leslie did the Polarity Reversal exercise, she became calmer and more relaxed. Clearly something had already changed. We then went through the Tap Sequence for disappointment. Her disappointment in Carl was the source of considerable emotional pain. But in just a few minutes time it became clear that a big factor for Leslie staying in the relationship was her unwillingness to see that she had made a mistake in choosing to be with him. Using the sequence for guilt, we targeted those feelings. Next she targeted her fears about the future and applied the formulas for fear and anxiety.
>
> It was like peeling back the layers of paint on a building, each a different color, each revealing different emotional hues of the past. In about twenty minutes Leslie's distress level had dropped from what she felt was a 10 on the Subjective Units of Distress (0 to 10) scale, when thinking about living on her own, to a level

of about 3. After further polarity corrections and another round of tapping her distress level dropped to 0. Leslie knew she still had to make some important decisions. The difference was that she was now able to consider options that she had not been able to see earlier. That clarity empowered her to move forward in her life with new strength and focus.

We do not understand why and how these reversals of our intention occur. We mean to do what we said we were going to do, but somehow we get tripped up. Correcting the reversals in thought and body polarity alone may relieve some distress or bring a sensation of relaxation. Some people do not notice any difference, although when we muscle test after this exercise, we find that the muscle that was weak is now strong. After her session, Leslie said that she was now able to think clearly about the future. Leslie left Carl a few months later and began a new life for herself. It wasn't easy to make the break, she reported, but she felt much stronger, and in control of her life and her emotions.

What Are Your Intentions?

Leslie's story tells us a great deal about an important element of ESM, intention. Intention is the focusing of thought. It is the way to organize thought energy to serve our goals. But in order to have our conscious thoughts get to their destination and have the effect we desire, we need to clear away the underlying blocks in their path. This is what the polarity reversal exercise accomplishes.

Leslie's tale also demonstrates that the underlying reversals are not conscious. We are not always aware of hidden saboteurs. Our conscious thought is that we want to be happy or that we will benefit from getting over our distress. But we may be unaware of the hidden reversals, lurking in our minds and bodies, that foretell a different outcome. These hidden messages keep us from getting what we want or doing what we say we want to do.

It is possible for polarity reversals to self-correct. In the normal course of life, this is often what happens. If we think about our problems, talk about them with friends, even process them in our dreams, deal with them in therapy, or just with the passing of time and with distance from the original provocation, they may resolve themselves. It's the ones that become fixed and enduring that we can get rid of with the Polarity Reversal exercise.

The Twelve Polarity Themes

There are twelve standard polarity reversals. One is global in scope, one addresses the possibility of a uniquely personal reversal, and each of the remaining ten focuses on a particular theme or motif. Through trial and error we have found that these twelve themes cover just about all the unconscious undermining motifs of our lives. The twelve polarity themes are:

- *Global*—this reversal, which is used by itself in many ESM processes, concerns everything in one's life, the whole ball of wax

- *Keeping*—refers to keeping the problem or releasing it

- *Future*—addresses whether the problem will continue

- *Deserving*—addresses the fundamental issue of deserving to be over the problem

- *Safety of Self*—refers to the issue of personal safety should the problem be resolved

- *Safety of Others*—considers the impact on others of getting over our problem

- *Permission*—concerns whether we feel entitled to get over the problem

- *Allowing*—focuses on whether we allow ourselves to get over the problem

- *Necessary*—pertains to the ability to do what is necessary to get over the problem

- *Benefit of Self*—considers whether getting over the problem will be a benefit

- *Benefit of Others*—considers whether getting over the problem will benefit others

- *Unique*—takes into account most uniquely personal blocks or themes

The body naturally seeks balance, equilibrium. If the polarity of the underlying life theme is reversed, the stimulation of a specific meridian site while simultaneously holding two opposing thoughts (a positive statement of self-acceptance and the negative verbalization of the theme) will effect a correction. If that theme is not reversed, the polarity will remain properly aligned. Correcting for a theme that is *not* reversed will not *cause* a reversal. There is no downside risk. In its infinite wisdom, the system won't correct what doesn't need fixing.

Even though you may not have underlying reversals connected to all of these life themes, you will correct for all twelve possible reversals, as a precaution. In a clinical setting, we muscle test and use other diagnostic tools and information to isolate the specific undermining reversals that a client may have. Here, because we cannot muscle test you, and because self-testing involves fairly sophisticated skills, we will have you correct for *all* possible reversals. The whole exercise only takes a few minutes.

Intention Statements

As you do the Polarity Reversal exercise, you will tap or rub specified acupuncture sites on your body as you repeat, three times, a statement having to do with each polarity theme. We call these Intention Statements. These statements are similar to what are commonly called "affirmations," positive statements about desired goals or self-image. But there is a significant difference. Affirmations don't acknowledge the persistent underlying negativity that is the source of the problem in the first place. And so they don't always work.

Sometimes people keep pumping at their affirmations, feeling that if they just say them loud enough and often enough, or write them down enough times, the change will have to happen. Affirmations alone can take people down a dead-end road. On some level, people recognize this internal conflict. "I can't say that I deserve to get over my guilt," they admit. "I just don't believe it." Well, they are right. Wishing won't make it so, and, in fact, in repeating affirmations they may be digging a deeper trench for the negative underlying thought to cycle around in. But they *can* say "I totally and completely accept myself, even if I don't deserve to get over my guilty feelings." There's a big difference. The "even if" assuages the nagging doubts at the back of the mind. Intention Statements are a way of stating your intention with self-acceptance while acknowledging the counterproductive thoughts that may lie below the surface. Such statements are more likely to resonate with the inner truth. They are not lying; they are not jarring.

Polarity reversals have nothing to do with our conscious beliefs. To our conscious mind, they may not even make sense. We may feel that we do, in fact, deserve to get over our problems, or that it is safe to do so. Intention

Statements compensate for these hidden contradictions and acknowledge our unconscious difficulty in believing the positive part of the statement. By linking the positive statement of self-acceptance with the negative theme that may sabotage it, and by tapping to release the blocked energy, we allow the reversal to correct itself. The "even if" is a bridge between the positive and the negative aspects, between the conscious and unconscious, between the polar opposites. It equalizes the positive and negative.

Intention Statements set up an intentional "verbal polarity," in that opposing thoughts are included within each statement. Each statement contains an intentional polarity, a north and south pole. The exercise properly orients the polarity of our thoughts about each polarity theme.

Self-esteem is vital to health and wellness. It is from a position of self-acceptance that we are grounded to move toward change. The analogy of weightlessness in space helps to illustrate the point. When astronauts on the space station or shuttle are adrift in the center of the cabin, they can move their arms and legs about but go nowhere. Yet when they are grounded to a stable structure like a wall, they can push off and easily float to a new position. Self-acceptance is the grounding that allows us to move toward personal change.

Action is implicit in Intention Statements. They are mission statements about what we want to accomplish: the complete and total acceptance of ourselves in spite of, or in the event of, some negative influence or circumstance. Ultimately, the message of the polarity reversal exercise is: "I accept myself, *no matter what!*"

"It's the Thought That Counts"

The electromagnetic energy of thought is believed to be the causal agent of emotional disturbance. For the most part, the disturbance is present only when the negative thought is activated. When the thought is not there, we feel OK. That's why distraction works, that's why we do all the things we do to avoid dwelling on our problems. Eventually, though, if we don't address what's bothering us, no amount of distraction—no amount of drink or drugs, no spending spree, no amount of aggressive weight training—will hold those feelings at bay. We need more.

When you do the Polarity Reversal or any ESM exercise, you are asked to focus your thoughts. Focused thoughts resonate throughout your system. Like the strings on a guitar, resonance adds texture and depth. Focusing our thoughts amplifies our intentions, enriching the energy field and amplifying the effect. If your thoughts drift too far from your problem, you will not generate enough energy to create a thought field.

It is easy to say that it is important to keep our thoughts aligned with our intention. But with all the energy and emotion spent dealing with life's daily necessities and intrusions, we do not have much time or stamina to focus on our intentions. The statements you'll make while tapping on the acupuncture meridian sites are a way of focusing your thoughts. The mere act of repeating the statement three times will create the appropriate thought field. It is not absolutely essential for you to believe what you are saying. Even faking some enthusiasm or belief will amplify the effect of the treatment. Merely going through the motions *will* put energy into the system. More important than the words is your sincere conviction that you want to resolve your problems. Your sincere desire to get better is a powerful expression of a deeper intention toward balance, healing, and stability.

Following the Rules

As you learn the polarity reversal procedure, you will use a very general theme in your intention statements. You will refer to "my problems." Later, when you are doing the Polarity Reversal exercise as part of the emotion-specific ESM protocols, your statements will focus on the target emotion you are addressing. You will state the issue you are working on more specifically: "my anger" or "my fear of heights" or "my jealousy of Anna." As you will see in Chapter 9, specific intention statements also will be incorporated into the tap sequences of certain protocols.

As you tap or rub the designated spots, you will repeat each intention statement three times. We have found that if you verbalize a statement at least three times, you *cannot avoid* creating a thought field associated with that statement. You have actively focused and given energy to that thought.

There is nothing magical in the particular words of the twelve Intention Statements that you will make in the Polarity Reversal exercise. It's the concepts that are important. But we have found that this structured set of polarity reversals covers nearly all bases. As you work with the ESM system, you may find that you want to tailor the statements so that they sound exactly right to you. "Deserve" may not feel like quite the right word for you. "Safety" may not feel like an issue that concerns you. But indulge us and stick to the script.

For now, repeat the statements just as they appear. Words have power, and you are using words to help organize and produce certain thoughts. At this stage, tinkering too much with the wording may undermine the effectiveness of the exercise. The effect of polarity reversals is so crucial that if there's even one reversal left, it will sabotage the entire sequence. We want you to succeed the first time you try the ESM procedures.

As you become familiar with these procedures, you'll find that there is ample flexibility in the process. Pretty soon you'll be an old pro and can custom tailor intention statements that resonate with the exact feeling you want to convey. Chapter 8 will give you some guidance with this.

A Note About Polarity Disorganization

We want to mention another issue with regard to polarity. In our clinical practice, in the course of administering thousands of ESM treatments, occasionally we have found people with what we call polarity "disorganization." They seem to have no detectable polarity, or their polarity is chaotic, like a jumble of forks and spoons turned every which way in a drawer. While uncommon, such disorganization can keep you from getting the results you anticipate. Chapter 10 provides explanations for polarity disorganization and ways to correct it.

TAP LESSON 1

Tapping Tips

Now you're going to learn how to tap on the ESM meridian sites. Because this is the first time you will be doing the tapping procedures, we want to give you a few pointers. Tapping is part of all ESM procedures except Balanced Breathing.

First we want to reassure you that there is a broad spectrum of effective tapping techniques. Even though we demonstrate tapping techniques to our clients, and model the exercises for them as we go through the procedures, they often can find their own unique tapping style.

Tapping with two fingers (usually the index and middle fingers) seems to be comfortable and efficient for most people. And it ensures that you're covering the target site. Some people use three fingers or the flat of all four fingers at certain tapping sites, in particular at the underarm spot, the rib site, and for the Back-of-Hand Tap. This is the can't-miss strategy. The first time you try the Polarity Reversal exercise, tap firmly. Err on the side of firmness, then back off as you develop confidence in the predictability of the method. It doesn't matter which hand you use, and feel free to change hands at any point in the process. Most locations exist in pairs, one on each side of the body, face, or hands. The two solo locations are Under Nose and Under Lip.

Four taps per second is about the right speed and comfortable for most people. Three taps per second is fine. (But not less; there seems to be a threshold level for effectiveness.) If you exceed six taps per second, you might consider a career as a drummer.

The three tap sites shown here are used for the Polarity Reversal exercise. You will learn the rest of the tap sites in Chapters 5 and 8.

Chest: Wouldn't you know it, this is the only site that employs *rubbing* instead of tapping. The chest spot is located above the heart, about three inches off the center line of the body. It is sometimes referred to as the "sore spot," because in many people the spot is tender compared to the surrounding area. To locate the site, probe in that vicinity until you feel a tender spot. Using three or four fingers, rub in a tight circular motion, about one revolution per second, outward toward your shoulder and down toward your heart. It is important to maintain a *firm* steady pressure as you rub, as if you were massaging oil deeply into that spot.

Under Nose: Tap with one or two fingers directly in the center between the nose and upper lip.

Under Lip: Tap with one or two fingers directly in the center on the chin just below the lower lip.

POLARITY REVERSAL (PR) EXERCISE

Begin by doing the Balanced Breathing exercise to align the body's polarity. Then, sitting comfortably, tap or rub the designated point while saying each Intention Statement three times. It does not matter how quickly or slowly you speak each statement; do whatever feels right to you.

Global PR. While rubbing the Chest spot:
Intention statement: "I deeply and completely accept myself, even with all my problems and limitations."

Keeping PR. While rubbing the Chest spot:
Intention statement: "I deeply and completely accept myself, even if I want to keep this problem."

Future PR. While tapping under the nose:
Intention statement: "I deeply and completely accept myself, even if I will continue to have this problem."

Deserving PR. While tapping under the lower lip:
Intention statement: "I deeply and completely accept myself, even if I don't deserve to get over this problem."

Safety of Self PR. While rubbing the Chest spot:
Intention statement: "I deeply and completely accept myself, even if it isn't safe for me to get over this problem."

Safety of Others PR. While rubbing the Chest spot:
Intention statement: "I deeply and completely accept myself, even if it isn't safe for others for me to get over this problem."

Permission PR. While rubbing the Chest spot:
Intention statement: "I deeply and completely accept myself, even if it isn't possible for me to get over this problem."

Allowing PR. While rubbing the Chest spot:
Intention statement: "I deeply and completely accept myself, even if I will not allow myself to get over this problem."

Necessary PR. While rubbing the Chest spot:
Intention statement: "I deeply and completely accept myself, even if I will not do what is necessary to get over this problem."

Benefit of Self PR. While rubbing the Chest spot:
Intention statement: "I deeply and completely accept myself, even if getting over this problem will not be good for me."

Benefit of Others PR. While rubbing the Chest spot:
Intention statement: "I deeply and completely accept myself, even if getting over this problem will not be good for others."

Unique PR. While rubbing the Chest spot:
Intention statement: "I deeply and completely accept myself, even if I have a unique block to getting over my problems."

. . . .

Putting the Polarity Reversal Exercise to Work

After doing this exercise, you may feel relaxed, even tired or sleepy. People sometimes yawn when reading the statements—perhaps as much from the boredom of repetition as relaxation! Perhaps you will not notice any effect at all. Women with PMS mood swings often notice an immediate lifting of spirits, a more positive perspective. Men who are prone to feeling "down in the dumps" also may be experiencing cyclical swings in body chemistry that temporarily produce reversals.

The Balanced Breathing and Polarity Reversal (PR) exercises are the preparatory organizing and clearing processes for the main tapping sequence of each protocol. They also have enduring value as everyday skills for maintaining emotional balance.

In certain situations you may be asked to do one or more of the corrections (usually the Global Polarity Reversal) daily for several weeks as part of a treatment program for particular problems. Chapter 12 will give you suggestions for incorporating this exercise into a regular ESM maintenance program. For now, you may find it helpful to do the Balanced Breathing exercise, then the Global Polarity Reversal each day (all of which takes about four minutes), to maintain a generalized polarity balance and for its calming effect.

At this point you may be grumbling to yourself, "But I thought this was supposed to be *instant* relief." Stay with the learning process. The instructions may seem complicated, because we want to give you all the guidance that we give our clients in person, but the actual processes take only a few minutes. Relief for your emotional distress is developing in stages. When the key that unlocks your distress is turned, you *will* experience the relief you seek, virtually instantly.

PART II

Understanding Our Emotions

FIVE

. . . .

ESM

The Remedy for Emotional Gridlock

Imagine a world without emotions, a place without love, anger, or fear. In this strange land, no one gets excited about baseball games. Come to think of it, no one plays games, because there's no pleasure in playfulness or competition. Ice cream is a dull affair. Art does not exist. And stories? No one bothers to tell them; without the complication and intrigue of emotions, who cares what happens? There's no joy in sex, no pleasure in work, no desire of any kind, no incentive to create, no dreams, no meaning in experience. It's a good thing we're not there.

Emotions are a quintessential element of our humanity. Our lives are bathed in emotions, ranging from the relaxed contentment of a conversation with a good friend, to the slow-boiling frustration of waiting in a supermarket checkout line behind someone whose credit card won't go through. Virtually no human thought or experience is unaccompanied by emotion, whether or not we are aware of it.

We humans exhibit an impressive range of feelings. According to Dr. Paul Ekman, there are more than one hundred unique facial expressions reflecting distinctly different emotional states, and they are found in practically every culture throughout the world. Richly diverse emotions are a hallmark of the human condition.

Our thoughts, senses, and emotions are the infinitely colorful and variable fibers of awareness and meaning of which our lives are woven. Our emotions serve us in many ways. At the most fundamental level, they enable us to survive: Fear alerts us to danger and activates the fight-or-flight response.

Anger fuels the ability to persevere in difficult circumstances. Desire assures the continuation of the species.

Beyond survival, our emotions play an essential role in our continuing health, safety, and well-being. They give us vital clues to our character, behavior, needs, and the quality of our relationships and experiences. They inspire us to take action, to evolve, and to learn. Even emotions we tend to think of as "negative" serve natural and useful regulating roles in our overall functioning: Frustration, impatience, disgust, and anger can spur us into productive action. Anxiety and irritability let us know when we've been pushing too hard and can remind us to slow down and relax. Loneliness can lead us to a deeper understanding of ourselves. Grief helps us heal from loss. Guilt keeps us honest. Our own *particular* set of emotional responses sets us apart as individuals, forming a vital part of the pattern we call our personality. Without our emotions, we would not be ourselves.

And yet our culture has tended to view "rational" thought as more valuable and "enlightened" than our emotions. Emotions are often seen as messy; they "get in the way" of making good choices. A worship of rationality was probably a natural turn of events as humans discovered their power to exert mastery over the environment and began to understand the workings of the world and the mind. During much of human history we have grossly underestimated the tremendous positive role emotions play in our lives. The Age of Reason wasn't all it was cracked up to be.

Emotions Count

Today we recognize the complex interplay between emotion and thought, and we understand that bringing our emotions into play in our lives is just as important as engaging our intellect. In the nineteenth century, psychologist William James recognized this when he noted that "the union of the mathematician with the poet, fervor with measure, passion with correctness, this surely is the ideal."

As the high-tech twentieth century comes to an end, Daniel Goleman, Ph.D., again points out the value of "the dance of feeling and thought." "The emotional faculty guides our moment-to-moment decisions," he writes, "working hand-in-hand with the rational mind, enabling—or disabling—thought itself."

Goleman calls the ability to manage and use our emotions "emotional intelligence," a capacity that allows us to learn better, create successful careers, establish more meaningful relationships, and enjoy improved health. According to Goleman, emotional intelligence includes such skills as self-awareness, impulse control, altruism, self-motivation, empathy, and the ability to love. Only when we learn to manage our emotions, and bring them into play in all aspects of our lives, are we making full use of our faculties.

Goleman makes a striking point about the ability of our emotions to enable or disable thought. When our emotions are out of whack, we can't think clearly. If we were applying our emotions intelligently, we wouldn't have many of the problems that we do. We wouldn't be wounded and suffering and wouldn't be inflicting pain on others. How is it that our emotions become so reactive and unbalanced that they hurt us rather than help us? When we look at the ways in which our emotions undermine our happiness and our best interests, it's puzzling. Why do we react in ways that clearly are not in our best interest, or that clearly do not make us or those around us happy?

No Bad Emotions

The appropriateness of our responses is a key indicator of our emotional intelligence. There is no such thing as a wrong emotion, only the wrong amount of the emotion at the wrong time. Aristotle put it this way: "Anyone can become angry—that is easy. But to be angry with the right person, to the right degree, and at the right time, and for the right purpose, and in the right way—that is not easy."

In love, work, and family relationships, unproductive emotions can lead to poor communication and an inability to work through and solve problems. Relationships are improved when we are able to think about other people and respond to them without being what Dr. Goleman calls "emotionally hijacked." When our emotions hijack us into overdrive, we react to others without the benefit of reason. By managing our emotions more effectively, we are able to dissolve distressing emotions, which allows us to think more clearly and to use our emotional intelligence to make better decisions.

When our beliefs about ourselves or our world are out of kilter, our reactions are bound to be out of proportion to the provocation. Forgetting to pick up a quart of milk, we fume and curse and tell ourselves over and over, "I'm just a big idiot." Twenty years ago we lied to a girlfriend about another woman, and in our mind the nagging thought is still, "I'm a lowly, unforgivable weasel." Since the time in the fourth grade when we weren't chosen for the softball team, we've been convinced that people think we're incompetent. Ever since we've taken jobs well below our abilities, so that we never again have to feel that we don't measure up. Although we have a job and a savings account, we worry about ending up as a bag lady dumpster-diving on the cold streets of Poughkeepsie.

Using Emotional Information

To one degree or another, we all have innate emotional intelligence. In the normal course of our lives, we use emotional information as part of our decision making on such a routine basis that we're hardly aware of it. However rational we think we are, however practical, there is no decision we make that doesn't have an emotional component. To make successful decisions, we depend on emotional responses to modify, inform, and balance our rational and logical thinking. Our hunches and "gut feelings" offer emotional input. Gut feelings, which come literally from the stomach and abdomen, may be, from an evolutionary standpoint, the first brain we ever had. The stomach contains some of the same neurotransmitter receptors as the brain; the most primitive organisms experience much of the world through the stomach. People with emotional intelligence trust their intuition. They consider it a natural part of the decision-making process. *Really* smart people cultivate their intuitive abilities. They make use of any information they can tune in to, including their physical reactions.

Antonio Damasio, M.D., professor of neurology at the University of Iowa College of Medicine, and his colleagues set up an experiment to demonstrate how important the ability to use emotional information when making decisions is. In the experiment, gambling was used to represent the risks and rewards inherent in everyday decision making. Half of the subjects in the study had suffered brain damage to their frontal lobes (the thinking part of their brain) and were hampered in their ability to make sense of emotional information. The other half were judged to have "normal" emotional makeup.

All the "players" were given $2,000 in realistic-looking play money and told that their objective was to lose as little as possible while gaining as much as possible. To play, each player selected and turned over one card at a time from any of four decks of cards stacked in front of him or her. Each card revealed an amount of money won or a penalty to be paid.

What the players did not know was that a pattern was built into the system of rewards and penalties. Two of the decks were arranged to yield small rewards and small penalties. The other two decks offered large rewards and even larger penalties. The decks that offered small rewards and penalties work far better to achieve the stated goals of the game.

What Dr. Damasio and his team found was that the subjects who had suffered damage to the frontal lobe areas could not seem to figure out the internal system. In trying to isolate what was blurring these subjects' judgment, the researchers connected them to biofeedback instruments that measure skin conductivity, which is associated with emotional arousal. They found that both groups showed emotional arousal when making good decisions and when costly cards were turned.

However, as the game went on, the non–brain-damaged subjects began to experience emotional arousal *just before* they turned over a card from the decks that were likely to produce a penalty card. And that anticipatory arousal increased as the game progressed. They were getting emotional information as they played and were able to recognize a pattern. To the degree that they were able to interpret this emotional information, it benefited their play. They learned which decks to play, and which to avoid, by a measurable margin. The brain-damaged subjects were not able to process the emotional information through the frontal lobe and therefore couldn't benefit from its powers to integrate, compare, and organize that information. The study offers more evidence that there is a biological advantage to having access to emotional knowledge; it serves a vital purpose in our growth, and success.

Crossed Wires

Our thoughts and emotions do not live in different neighborhoods. They share information on what is essentially a two-way street. Our emotions affect our thinking and our thinking affects our emotions. If you have any doubt about that notion, simply close your eyes for a moment and recall a happy memory—the best birthday party you ever had, hugging someone you love, savoring your favorite dessert. Are you smiling? Do you feel good? Then your thoughts are influencing your emotions.

When our thoughts and emotions are in sync, the natural ebb and flow to our responses affects every aspect of our experience and every choice we make. Most of us find strategies for managing our emotions that help us to understand and utilize what happens to us, to self-soothe, and to release them. When something unpleasant happens, we reflect on it. We mull it over. Perhaps we get right on the phone and hash out every little detail with friends. For some of us, it helps to keep a journal. We may turn to drawing or music to explore our feelings. Or we run five miles. We might dream about what happened, perhaps even revisit it in our imagination, until we arrive at a point when it no longer bothers us. There are many ways to cultivate a feeling of mastery over the events of our lives and to integrate our experiences in some adaptive way into our worldview. Ideally, after we cross the bridge from agitation to acceptance, we take whatever benefit we can from the experience and discard what is useless: unproductive beliefs, distressing emotional and physical reactions, and inappropriate behaviors.

Of course, this is not always what happens. Sometimes an experience is so troubling, perhaps so rooted in old, unprocessed emotional wounding, that we cannot shake it. These feelings become trapped in an emotional loop that replays itself whenever we think about the event or whenever we are in any way reminded of it.

If Lee hears a sound during the night, he is paralyzed with fear. His automatic thought is "Someone is in the house," even though there is no evidence to support that conclusion. The doors are locked, he lives in a neighborhood where break-ins are uncommon, and his neighbor's dog, which barks at the slightest provocation, is quiet.

What sets this disturbing pattern in motion? Lee grew up in a violent, inner city housing project. Shootings and robberies were everyday occurrences. Walking home from school, getting on the elevator to his apartment were fraught with danger. A sound in the night was a warning to take cover. Where Lee grew up, fear was an intelligent response.

Now it is not. Nevertheless, any stimulus, no matter how mild or seemingly unrelated, that calls up the traumatic circumstances of his childhood forces him to experience the world as unpredictable and unsafe. Lee's experiences have left him with a core belief that he is not safe from harm. He has developed a pattern of hypervigilance and is ever on guard, certain he is in imminent danger. Although Lee is aware that his fear of an intruder is irrational, he cannot seem to break this automatic pattern of pervasive and unproductive thoughts and reactions.

A trapped thought loop can become so stubborn that you can't put it out of your mind. Sometimes nothing is able to distract you from your poisonous thoughts—no amount of work or exercise, food, or drink. You have trouble eating and/or sleeping, you aren't working well, and you're behaving badly. Sometimes controlling our thoughts is not that easy.

It All Comes Down to Stress

On some level, the end product of our unproductive emotional responses is stress. Stress in and of itself is not bad. It can be a motivator; if we weren't stressed we might sleep late and get little accomplished. It's large quantities of badly managed stress that cause problems. Our stress is a combination of cultural and personal factors. Culturally, we're often bowled over by the unrelenting pressures of modern living—the speed at which technology advances, the longer hours we need to work in order to keep up, the pervasive feeling that there's not enough time in a day to do what needs to be done. It's hard not to feel that everything is moving too fast and that we're being left in the dust. All this, on top of the emotional burdens we carry on our backs.

The current epidemic of anger is a by-product of the cumulative and unresolved stresses of modern life. We've become so inured to pervasive images of violence that we barely react to them on the evening news. The newspapers are jammed with news stories of drive-by shootings, road rage, random violence, gang wars, and machine-gun killings in schoolyards. Movies thrive on violence choreographed in slow motion or with riveting special effects. Out-of-control anger is being held up as the norm. Dr. Ekman notes that "in prehistoric times, when you had an instantaneous rage and for a few seconds wanted to kill someone, you couldn't do it very easily—but now you can" because we have the technology to act on our emotions.

Information overload can overwhelm our ability to respond to our experiences correctly or wisely, leaving us in some ways like the brain-damaged subjects in Dr. Damasio's study, unable to organize and fully use our emotional intelligence. Irrational or impulsive behavior that disregards consequences is often the fallout of excessive, poorly managed stress.

It is instructive to see how people respond differently to stress. Say two passengers in an automobile get into an accident. Suppose neither one is at fault, and neither is injured. Yet one develops an intense fear of driving and the other does not. It's not clear what causes the divergent response. Each seems to have processed the incident differently; in each case, it may have run through the body's systems via different circuits. For one person the experience never got past the primitive, fight-or-flight brain. It never made it to the neocortex, where it could be reasoned with. Somehow—by nature or nurture—the person who developed the driving phobia had a lower threshold of tolerance for stress and had an insufficient mechanism in place by which to dissipate the emotional intensity of the accident.

> On January 17, 1994, an earthquake devastated the community of Northridge, on the outskirts of Los Angeles, causing extensive damage to roads, buildings, and other structures within a twenty-mile radius. At magnitude 6.7, the quake caused fifty-one deaths, injured more than 9,000 people, and racked up billions of dollars in damages. The vast majority of survivors went on with their lives, rebuilding their homes or perhaps moving to another area. They can talk about the earthquake with little emotional distress. Unfortunately, that is not true for everyone.
>
> The Northridge quake lasted only fifteen seconds, but for some people it continued to reverberate. Jamie was one of those people. Jamie and her husband's home shook so badly that parts of it collapsed. Her husband, Allan, suffered minor cuts. Although he was saddened and frustrated by the loss, there were no lingering aftereffects. Jamie was another story. Although she was physically uninjured, she was terrified of returning to evaluate the damage. Even from a safe distance, she could not view her house without breaking out in a sweat and suffering from a pounding heart. With Jamie disabled by her trauma, Allan had to return alone to salvage what he could and rebuild. Jamie's distress continued to escalate in the months after the quake. She got to the point where she could not travel anywhere in her community where there were signs of the earthquake. Eventually she ended up staying at her mother's home, fifty miles away.

Jamie had developed a psychological condition called posttraumatic stress disorder (PTSD), a cluster of symptoms that linger after a trauma, disrupting work, social, and/or family relationships. PTSD is characterized by a certain set of symptoms: sleeplessness, anxiety, memory loss, the feeling that one is reliving the experience, avoidance, and other disabling effects. Jamie was still trapped in the earthquake. Trauma of this type responds well to treatment with ESM. When Jamie finally came to our office, we were able to break its hold on her.

What causes an overwhelming emotional reaction like Jamie's to develop and not abate with the passage of time? The answer is not clear. Learning theory would suggest that a powerful single exposure to a conditioned response might create such an effect, particularly in people who already are anxiety-prone. While that concept may account for some of the dysfunctional behavior, such as avoidance, it cannot explain the wide range of distressing symptoms that can occur even in the absence of any stimulus or cues from the original event. It is as if some process that ordinarily allows for a dissipation of the emotions becomes blocked and prevents a resolution of the experience, so that the mere thought of the trauma brings on symptoms of anxiety. Francine Shapiro, who developed Eye Movement Desensitization and Reprocessing (EMDR), has a theory about why people become stuck in an emotional response well past the point of its being productive. Like Drs. Goleman and Damasio, Shapiro recognizes that powerful negative emotions can serve an adaptive role, such as impressing upon us how to avoid danger. Shapiro believes that our information-processing systems provide a natural method for integrating distressing events, allowing us to maintain mental and physical balance and to function effectively. However, she believes that strong emotional events can overwhelm our natural mechanisms and cause the processing to become stuck in the nervous system.

While PTSD is an extreme example of an emotional loop, it does fall at one end of a continuum of symptoms. The most trivial incident may precipitate an emotional loop, so that added experiences build up around it, the way a pearl forms around a grain of sand. We are all inherently different, and each of us has traveled a different path to where we find ourselves today. What bothers one person is no problem for another. A daredevil race car driver may be literally terrified to tell a woman that he loves her. A mother may be assertive with her children yet is afraid to speak in public. But whether we are overreacting to a criticism from a coworker or avoiding a trip to the dentist, we are stuck in an unproductive way of reacting to life events.

Cognitive Therapy: What Was I Thinking?

The first step in changing maladaptive responses is to become aware of what we are feeling. That is easier said than done. Especially as children, our natural tendency is to repress emotions that are too painful to bear or for which we might be ridiculed or punished. If our feelings were repeatedly ignored or invalidated, we bury them. Eventually we are not even aware of their presence, although our behavior betrays our inner feelings, even when they are deeply buried.

It is also necessary to develop a sense of when our emotions are appropriate and helpful and when they are not. Clearly someone who punches his boss in a fit of anger is behaving inappropriately; his emotions are so unmanaged that *they* control *him*. Whenever the type or intensity of our emotional response does not match the circumstances that provoked it, we will respond inappropriately. Some people experience a buildup of emotion as physical discomfort—muscle tension, racing heart, shortness of breath. Others experience hurt, heavy feelings and disturbing thoughts. The response might show up as the inability to get out of bed or the uncontrollable urge to spend money. We may feel stuck, rough, raw, congested, out-of-sync, and jangled.

Sometimes our thoughts and our emotions don't seem to be connected. The mind says one thing and the body does another, as if the brain's chemical and electrical messengers are scrambled. We know, for example, that the person we are dating is no good for us, but we continue to see him or her. Or we desperately want to save money for a new car but are forever squandering money on useless gadgets. We feel abused by a critical and neglectful friend, yet we never confront the person and can't seem to break away.

Like many therapies, cognitive therapy seeks to help us manage our emotions by working backward toward out belief system, seeking to alter it so that it is more productive. A basic precept of cognitive therapy, which is a mainstay of modern psychology, is that our thoughts precede our emotional responses and that, to the degree we can control our thoughts, we can control our emotions. Rooted in the work of psychologist Albert Ellis, Ph.D., and psychiatrist Aaron Beck, M.D., cognitive therapy maintains that how we think about an event—how we interpret it—changes how we experience it emotionally. If we change our thoughts about it, we change our emotional response.

Take, for example, the situation of a woman who is terrified of dogs, to the point where she makes inconvenient detours to avoid them and is continually scouting for escape routes along her way in case she is attacked. In the course of therapy, the woman might reveal being viciously attacked by a dog long ago. A cognitive therapist would help her examine the evidence of her current experiences. Together they might look closely at her reaction to one particular dog that had scared her just that day. Was it growling? Not really, just whimpering. Was it threatening? No, it was behind a fence. Where then, the therapist would ask, is the evidence that the dog was a threat? The therapist would help this woman make rational sense of her experience, prompting her to change her thought about the unlikely threat presented by the dog and move her toward composure. If she kept reinforcing this new way of thinking about dogs, then, when she encountered another barking dog, she would be able to evaluate the situation rationally. With new thoughts that this particular dog is no threat, she would react calmly.

Wrestling with Core Beliefs

Cognitive therapy ultimately changes our emotional responses by changing our core beliefs. Our core beliefs are formed by early experiences with our environment. When we are young, we learn ways of managing our emotions and responding to the world through all the many avenues by which we are socialized—school and church and community, and, these days, the media barrage that informs us all. But our primary influences were close to home, through the example and guidance of our parents, who in turn learned from their parents and their own lives. We interpret these experiences according to our age, our temperament, and our circumstances. It is not only traumatic experiences that distort our thinking. All our experiences, from the moment of birth, shape the core beliefs that affect our patterns of behavior. Our earliest experiences—when we have little ability to understand or influence them—are thought to make a powerful imprint, even if we have no conscious memory of them. Sometimes in the formation of core beliefs, what really happened is not as important as how we perceived what happened.

Core beliefs are the inner instruction manual we unconsciously refer to in order to determine our responses. They are the source of the ingrained automatic thought patterns that dictate our responses to daily events and circumstances. Our automatic thoughts trigger our responses so quickly that we often register only the emotion, and not the thought that provoked it.

Many of our automatic responses are highly intelligent. When we face new situations and challenges, our ability to recollect how we felt about comparable past experiences helps us to make better choices in the present. If we didn't have some system in place to help us process the events of our everyday lives, we'd have to start at square one to respond to every circumstance without the benefit of what we'd learned in the past. *I lied to my parents and they are upset; should I do that again? That person is making a scary face; what does it mean, what should I do? Is the person telling me she likes me telling the truth? How can I tell?* Stored response patterns come in very handy.

Changing thoughts through cognitive therapy is not for sissies. It is kind of like bending steel, mechanically shaping, through sheer will and effort, the way a person thinks about a problem. Cognitive therapy does work. It takes the unproductive thought and slowly but surely bends it so that it's altered. You've altered the disruption because you've altered the thought process; you've shifted it. To the degree you can keep that bend going, it works. But one problem with cognitive therapy is that automatic thoughts and unproductive behaviors have a tendency to spring back. It is not so easy to reason with our emotions. It's difficult to "just say no" to established thought loops. They have a life of their own; they don't just go away because you tell them to.

If you think about it, the very idea of reasoning with your emotions is an oxymoron. With effort, of course, you can make a dent. If we make a serious and dedicated effort to root out the wrongheaded thinking and replace it with a more productive thought, eventually we will bypass the trigger for the emotional response. But emotions are powerful; working this way takes diligence. We lead busy lives. Many of us don't have the stamina or dedication to do what needs to be done.

Alex, the fifty-three-year-old manager of a travel agency, worked for almost three years with a cognitive therapist to try to manage his obsessive fear of illness and his debilitating belief that he had a serious undiagnosed medical condition. Alex's problem is not plain and simple hypochondria, because he does have some health problems. He has a minor heart condition called mitral valve prolapse and he suffers from low back strain.

Alex spends a lot of time with doctors—about eight visits each month—checking out his symptoms and fears. His primary care physician calls him a "high utilizer." No one can find anything seriously wrong with Alex. What's happening is that the chronic worry has taken over his life, and in the long run, it's liable to make him sicker.

The challenge for Alex, and for his therapist, was to learn to be *appropriately* concerned about his health, to sort out what was a legitimate concern for worry and what aspects of his concern were self-sabotaging. As part of his therapy, Alex learned to pay attention to his automatic response patterns. Assiduously observing and cataloging his responses, he learned to recognize his cognitive distortions. He came to see how he twisted incoming information to fit his own perceptual filter. As he became aware of the ways in which he distorts reality, Alex was able to formulate more constructive and realistic internal statements or thoughts to counter the negative ones. He learned to refuse to give in to negative thinking and to use reason to examine the tangible evidence of his health issues.

This was hard work. It required daily monitoring of his thoughts, moods, and behavior. Alex had to remind himself constantly to tune in to his thinking process, to see where it was leading him astray and to replace the fearful thoughts with constructive ones. He had to learn to stop obsessing about every ache and hiccup. By the time Alex came to see us, he was doing much better, but to him the effort sometimes seemed just a substitute obsession, and sometimes he felt like it was a losing battle.

With the first round of muscle testing in our office, it was clear that Alex had polarity disorganization, which would interfere with almost any therapy. The first step was to remedy the disorganization with the Five-Step Breathing process and then to correct for polarity reversals. By periodically correcting these reversals and administering the anxiety protocol, Alex was able to more easily control and eventually eliminate his nerve-wracking worry.

ESM: Operating at Full Power

When we learn to trust our feelings, when we have learned that they are a reliable source of information, we ratchet our emotional intelligence up a notch. But not all of us are lucky enough to have had good models, non-traumatic childhoods, or a resilient temperament. We have to work to change, to overcome past hurts and experiences. To the degree that we can do this and install productive patterns in their place, our emotional savvy increases. We develop a clear lens through which to interpret our experiences that can be relied upon to help us. We are less reactive, no longer at the mercy of our knee-jerk responses.

A big step in this process involves uprooting patterns that cause us to respond in unproductive, self-defeating ways. As anyone who has spent years in therapy can attest, it's hard work. But ESM is a powerful ally in this endeavor. The great advantage of Emotional Self-Management is that it has the power to instantly break up long-standing emotional loops. ESM is like instant cognitive therapy. John's experience is a good example of what we mean.

John and his wife came to see me the day after returning from a visit with his family. The minute they came in the door, Trisha slumped in the chair like a deflated balloon. John was fit to be tied, pacing up and down the office, ranting about his family and practically foaming at the mouth. His face was red and his shoulders were cinched up. He looked like he might have a heart attack. The visit with his parents and brothers had been the usual fiasco, one in a long and unending history of unpleasant and frustrating family gatherings.

I wanted to use the ESM techniques on John right away, before he had that heart attack right there in my office, but he was fussing and fuming so much, and so sure that nothing could help him, that it was impossible to get him to sit still and listen.

So I asked Trisha if she by any chance had any fears or phobias. "Claustrophobia," she replied immediately. "So bad that I can't drive with the windows up in the car." She confessed that she was feeling claustrophobic right there in my office. So we went through the claustrophobia protocol, which took just a few minutes. She felt immediate relief; the boxed-in feeling was gone.

John was still venting his anger and frustration toward his family, but he couldn't help but notice the change in Trisha. I said I thought I could help him with his anger, the same way I had helped Trisha with her claustrophobia.

One of the great things about ESM is that you don't have to dwell on the problem or even know exactly where it came from. In John's case that was a good thing, since stewing about the problem was already driving him crazy. John consented to the treatment that, again, was very brief. The fuming stopped, and his color, I was relieved to see, returned to normal.

Calm and relaxed now, he sat down next to his wife. I said, "How are you feeling?" Without any other prompting from me, he offered the most astonishing insight. He said, "You know, I realize that I can't change them. I can only work on feeling better about myself." He experienced this insight and awareness—this clarity of thought about something that had dogged him for decades—after one ten-minute process. The elimination of anger completely restored and balanced his view of the world. Trisha's jaw had dropped. "Has there been an alien abduction?" She laughed. "He always seems to be in a snit about his family. I've never seen him this calm while talking about them."

ESM's magic is that it makes quick work of rooting out stuck, unproductive patterns and responses. People who have experienced an emotional trauma in the past may avoid focusing on that memory because of the pain involved. The avoidance prevents them from exploring and understanding what they could have done differently or how they could avoid the situation in the future. With ESM, they don't have to go into the details of the past experience. However, after ESM treatment, it is often much easier for people to face that past event and process it. *And learn from it.*

The way ESM works, the nature or source of the disturbance doesn't much matter. It could be the original wiring, or inherent sensitivity. It could be learned sensitivities or personality or upbringing or biosocial factors. It's not so much why it happened but how we intervene that makes the difference. We are not working to change the stubborn thoughts themselves. We are clearing the disturbance in the body's energy that keeps them trapped and produces the physical stimulus that leads to emotional distress. We are clearing a path by which they can exit.

ESM processes dislodge the interference to the free flow of the body's energy, or *chi*. If the disturbance persists, we can't completely process certain emotions. ESM instantly dissolves the stuck point and releases the negative emotional load, opening the floodgates for the trapped energies to flow freely and self-correct the imbalance. In breaking the loop, ESM restores the balance of thinking and feeling.

People using ESM techniques often report that afterward they are able to think about the situation more clearly and productively. John's sudden insight that he could not control his family is one example of that. John always knew this; it's basic wisdom. But somehow he couldn't get to that place while the old pattern stood in the way. When we are in the grip of emotion, seemingly simple decisions can loom large.

A self-described "nervous wreck," Evelyn came to us in a welter of fear about asking her boss for a raise. For nearly a year she'd been consumed with this issue, to the point of losing sleep thinking about it. She was wearing down the patience of her husband and friends, constantly spinning detailed scenarios about what she might say and when would be a good time to talk to her boss. Then there were the what-ifs—what if she were fired, what if she couldn't find another job, they might lose their house, the kids would suffer—a nightmare of fantasized outcomes.

A few days after we treated Evelyn for fear and anticipatory anxiety, she wrote a note to say that she had asked her boss for a raise, adding "Now I can see that my request was reasonable and based on all the hard work I have done. My boss may or may not agree, but I know that I am not unreasonable in asking. For some reason I couldn't see that before. It felt like I was being greedy, or at least I was afraid that's how she would see me." This seems like a logical, no-brainer insight. But when we get enmeshed in strong emotions, we cannot think—or feel—straight.

The ability to work with your emotions is a major life skill. ESM lays the groundwork for profound changes. When you begin to use ESM techniques, you will notice incremental improvements in your ability to handle the everyday stresses of life. Once you get the underbrush cleared away, you immediately begin to manage emotions better, and your problem-solving ability improves. As time goes by, you will notice that you do not have as many disturbing problems. When troublesome issues come up, you find you are able to handle them without undue worry. With all available sources of intelligence working for you, you may finally feel like you're running on all cylinders—and the following exercise will help you to do just that.

THE RAPID RELAXER

Note: The Rapid Relaxer will be most effective if you have already corrected for polarity reversals.

The Rapid Relaxer is the secret weapon of ESM, a simple but very powerful technique that instantly reduces stress and tension. Once you've learned the steps, the Rapid Relaxer takes only about thirty seconds to do and provides a calming effect that lasts about half an hour to an hour. It's not a permanent treatment—that is, it won't remove phobias or undo emotional loops—but it will relieve tense, stressful feelings, cutting your emotional distress in about half. You can repeat it as often as needed for further relief. In our stressful lives, it's a handy tool to have. For this technique, the focus of your thoughts can be on your present physical or mental sensations of tension or stress.

The Rapid Relaxer combines tapping with humming, counting, and eye movements. This combination of activities may seem peculiar—a bit like hopping on one foot while juggling. But there is a method to this madness. The process involves all of you; it gets all systems communicating while it balances your energies.

All the procedures involved help to integrate the energy of your thoughts through various regions of your brain. Humming stimulates right-brain activity, while counting stimulates left-brain activity. Eye movements activate regions within the visual cortex and integrate both hemispheres of the brain, activating both the cerebral and visual cortex while the distressing thought is present and active. While the tapping treatment adds energy to the meridian at an acupuncture site, the eye movements balance the thought energy more completely throughout the brain.

The Rapid Relaxer combines two ESM procedures, the Eye Roll and the Bridge, with tapping at a new site, the Back-of-Hand spot. You'll use these two elements of the Rapid Relaxer separately in the emotion-specific protocols. Here we will teach you the two exercises separately and then show you how they go together to make the Rapid Relaxer. But first—the Back-of-Hand Tap.

TAP LESSON 2

The Back-of-Hand Tap

Do you remember your first tap lesson from page 68 in Chapter 4? Now you are going to learn the Back-of-Hand Tap, which you will do steadily throughout the Rapid Relaxer.

To locate the Back-of-Hand spot, make a fist with one hand. On the back of your hand, locate the indentation, or valley, between the knuckle of your pinky finger and the knuckle of your ring finger. Now trace back about an inch in the direction of your wrist in the indentation formed between the tendons of your pinky and ring fingers on the back of your hand. Now that you've found it, you can release your fist.

To perform the Back-of-Hand Tap, use the flat of four fingers (that's how most people do it; you may feel more comfortable using fewer fingers) of your opposite hand and tap—or lightly slap—the Back-of-Hand spot. You'll be making about four taps per second, but don't worry about precise speed; this method is forgiving. Practice the tap now, so that you can keep up a steady rhythm.

THE EYE ROLL

The Rapid Relaxer begins and ends with a continuous eye roll which is done while tapping the Back-of-Hand spot. Before adding the tapping, let's run through just the eye movement. Throughout the exercise, keep your head level, facing straight ahead. *Move only your eyes, not your head.*

Begin with your eyes closed. Open your eyes, look down (at the floor if you're standing, or into your lap if you're sitting), and with your eyes, slowly trace an imaginary line straight forward across the floor to the wall in front of you. Continue slowly rolling your gaze up the wall to where it meets the ceiling and then back toward you across the ceiling, until you are looking above you; stop there. Give it a try now. It's not a race; the whole sequence should take about eight seconds.

Once you feel comfortable doing the Eye Roll, add the Back-of-Hand Tap, keeping up a steady tapping rhythm all the way through. The Eye Roll sequence consists of this eight-second eye movement while continuously tapping the Back-of-Hand spot.

THE BRIDGE

The Bridge consists of a series of eye movements, humming, and counting, all the while keeping up the Back-of-Hand Tap. The Bridge is part of every emotion-specific protocol. In the Rapid Relaxer, the Bridge is like the filling in a sandwich in which the Eye Roll is the bread. As you did with the Eye Roll, practice this set of activities (eye movements, counting, and humming), as shown in the illustrations below, until you can do the sequence easily. When you feel comfortable and confident doing these nine steps, you can add the continuous Back-of-Hand Tap as you go through the process. It will only take a few minutes of practice to get the hang of it.

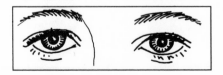

1. Start with your eyes open.

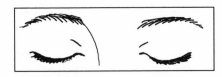

2. Close your eyes.

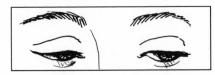

3. Open your eyes and glance down toward the floor to your right.

4. Glance down to your left.

5. Rotate your eyes in a full circle in one direction. *Make sure you are not skipping any part of the circle. It may take a little practice to be sure you are making a complete circle.*

6. Now rotate your eyes around in a complete circle in the opposite direction.

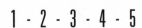

7. Hum about five notes. *This might be a familiar tune, such as "Happy Birthday," or just make up a few notes of your own.*

1 - 2 - 3 - 4 - 5

8. Count from one to five.

9. Hum a few notes again.

Try this a few more times. Practice so that you can do the nine steps from memory or with the aid of the visual prompts provided. Then continuously tap the Back-of-Hand spot as you go through the whole sequence. Got it? That's the Bridge.

. . . .

Putting It All Together

Finally, you get to do the whole thirty-second spectacular, the Rapid Relaxer: Eye Roll, the Bridge, and another Eye Roll, tapping the Back-of-Hand spot all the while. Practice the whole sequence a few times, until you can move through it rapidly. Be patient with yourself as you move through the learning curve of these procedures. Mastering the Rapid Relaxer will not only bring you rapid stress relief, it will give you confidence in Emotional Self-Management. At first you may need the visual instructions, but soon it will become second nature.

Now you have the secret weapon. Use it in good emotional health!

Getting Ready for Change

Labeling and Rating Your Emotional Distress

C hapter 5 discussed the importance of managing your emotions, which, as its name implies, is at the heart of Emotional Self-Management. This chapter will guide you through the preliminary self-diagnostic steps of the ESM process, vital prep work for administering the emotion-specific protocols. Your task is first to identify as best you can the feelings or issues that are distressing you and then to evaluate the intensity of your feelings. Monitoring your distress level during the course of the treatment enables you to measure your progress. Identifying multilayered problems is another preparatory matter. You will learn how to administer sequential treatments that peel away the layers of emotional distress as they arise.

Labeling Your Emotions

In many instances we are crystal clear about the nature of our feelings. We are clearly angry, definitely grief-stricken, most certainly anxious about an upcoming mammogram, absolutely terrified of flying. At other times, it's hard to label just what is distressing us.

When we are caught in our emotional experience, we normally don't pay attention to exactly what it is we're feeling. In the middle of a temper outburst or crying jag, we don't pause to reflect "Now, am I being angry, or am I feeling rejected? Is it shame I'm feeling, or embarrassment? Am I sad or regretful?" Sometimes our emotions pile up in such rapid succession that we can't keep up. At one point we're frustrated, then angry, then we become unexpectedly sad. Or we're confused about what we feel—we don't know whether to laugh or cry.

When it comes to choosing an ESM protocol, these distinctions are important. The ESM protocols can have a laserlike accuracy; each is effective for a specific category of emotional symptoms. Through observation and manual muscle testing over the thousands of applications conducted in our clinical practices, we have developed and refined the unique formula, or Tap Sequence, that works for each emotion or issue listed.

For example, the Tap Sequences for anger and jealousy are different, and choosing the wrong one to address your problem can affect the outcome of the treatment. Of course, if one sequence doesn't work, you can always try another. For example, if the protocol for anxiety doesn't work, you can administer the sequence for fears and phobias. But the more accurately you label your feelings, the greater your chance of immediate relief. For maximum benefit, hitting the bull's-eye with your self-diagnosis will pay off.

This is not meant to let you off the hook in the self-diagnosis process, but there *is* a fallback position. In Chapter 9 you'll find a Comprehensive Tap Sequence that often provides relief when specific protocols have not worked. Because it includes elements of many commonly overlapping emotions, it is significantly longer than most of the specific sequences.

Activating the Thought Field

When you apply the ESM protocols, you will hold in mind the problem that you are working to heal. This is the cognitive component of the process. Thinking about the problem, and verbalizing it, creates a "thought energy field." Once you are clear about the emotion, you will be asked to hold in mind the issue, or some aspect of it, as you go through the procedure. Keeping your focus on the problem keeps the thought field active. As you administer the Tap Sequence, you may want to say "the guilt" or "the anger toward Jim" or "the fear of snakes" as you tap at each site. One way of tuning into the thought field relating to your distress is to imagine the object of your emotion, such as the pastries you want to stop eating or the snakes you fear. Or you might focus on the person or situation that provokes your emotional response. Some of our clients have wondered if ESM works because all the tapping and repeating intention statements and humming distracts them from their distress. ESM works not on distraction but on focusing our thoughts.

What if it is painful to think about? You may be dealing with something that is very painful to think about—a trauma from the past, such as an accident or a deep grief over the death of someone close to you. There is no need to relive that pain or call up in full force the stress it often provokes in order for the procedure to work. Just a thought about the problem will suffice. In many cases of emotional trauma, the person is constantly thinking about or aware of the memories and no special "tuning in" is necessary.

If a problem has a long and complex history, it is usually sufficient to focus on just one aspect of the larger problem. You do not need to recall every screaming battle at the dinner table or the day-to-day deprivations of your family's poverty. In a case of abuse that took place over a period of months or years, it is not necessary to recall all past incidents. One or two will suffice. Typically, ongoing past trauma will have generalized in the memory, so one incident will bring up "all of that." Turn to Chapter 8 for more on this topic.

Note: If you are feeling overwhelmed by a traumatic incident, it is important for you to seek professional help to overcome this distress. Resources in the appendix can help you find a professional who utilizes energy psychotherapy methods.

Travis's story illustrates the way the memory generalizes to past events and how change can occur when our emotions are healed. Travis wanted to be free of a nagging sense of guilt over not being a better father to his son and daughter. While his children were growing up, he had deserted the family for many years because of marital conflict. Eventually Travis reconciled with his wife. But by that time he had missed out on a multitude of family activities, irretrievable birthdays, graduations, and Christmases. Travis had made amends and had essentially been forgiven. Yet his unremitting regret and guilt was interfering with his ability to enjoy the time he spent with his now grown-up children. Although he should have been able to feel some level of peace, he was still torn by guilt.

As Travis went through the sequence for guilt, he did not need to focus on each memory for which he felt guilty. He tuned into one particularly troubling memory about his son's high school graduation that provoked strong emotion. When the intensity of emotion associated with that memory decreased, another more recent memory came to mind, so he went through the procedure again. Travis went from an initial distress level of 8 on the 10-point SUD scale to a 1 level (see the evaluation chart that follows), which he considered a success, far exceeding his expectations. The treatment transformed his ability to enjoy the company of his children and grandchildren without the held-back feelings of love that he had feared to express because of his guilt.

Following is the list of emotions and symptoms that are treatable with ESM. If you are unclear about what is troubling you, scanning through the list may help you to put a label on what you are feeling. Once you have read through it, sit quietly for a few minutes as you reflect on your feelings. Relax and take a few deep slow breaths. As a feeling comes up, try to give it a name. Keep "trying on" labels until one fits. If, after tuning in, you are still struggling to pinpoint just what it is that's troubling you, turn to Chapter 7, which provides a more detailed discussion of emotions and symptoms. In situations where similar emotions might cause confusion or where emotions overlap, this information will help you to decide on the correct ESM protocol to use.

Sometimes it is impossible to call up any level of distress in the absence of the stimulus that typically provokes it, such as fear of flying or freeway phobia. You may have to wait to administer the treatment until you are in the presence of whatever (or whoever) it is that makes you anxious. More about on-site ESM in Chapter 8. The protocols appear in Chapter 9.

ESM TARGET SYMPTOMS AND EMOTIONS

- Addictive Urges: (page 153).

- Anger: (page 154).

- Anticipatory Anxiety: (page 155).

- Anxiety (Generalized or Free Floating): (page 156).

- Awkwardness: (page 183).

- Bitterness: (page 154).

- Chronic Pain: (page 171).

  Clumsiness: See Five-Step Breathing (page 183).

- Negativity: See Balanced Breathing (page 58) and Polarity Reversals (page 61).

- Obsessional Thinking: (page 170).

- Pain: (page 171).

  Phobias, General: (page 173).

  Phobias (Spiders, Claustrophobia, Air Turbulence): (page 172).

- PMS Symptoms: (page 174).

- Procrastination: (page 175).

  Rage: (page 176).

- Regret: (page 177).

- Rejection: (page 178).

- Remorse: (page 163).

- Resentment: (page 154).

  Revulsion: (page 158).

- Sadness: (page 162).

- Shame: (page 179).

- Sorrow: (page 162).

- Stress (Generalized): (page 156).

- Tiredness: (page 160).

- Trauma (Emotional): (page 180).

- Worry: (page 155).

The SUD Scale: Rating the Intensity of Your Emotions

Naming your emotions tells you *what* you feel. The SUD scale tells you *how much* you feel. In the 1950s psychiatrist Joseph Wolpe developed a scale to help patients rate their discomfort or distress in increments of 0 to 100. This measure, known as the Subjective Units of Disturbance Scale, or SUDS, has become a standard means of self-evaluating individual experience. We use a simplified version of the scale, with increments of 0 to 10. Considering that what brings people to seek out mental or physical help is their subjective experience of distress, it makes sense to give their personal report a voice in evaluating improvements or change. Diagnosis of physical problems frequently relies on patients' own reports of how they are feeling. Often an examining physician will ask, "Does this hurt?" Or, "Is it a burning sensation or does it feel like a sharp pain?"

The SUD scale is used in ESM procedures to monitor the change that occurs during the course of the process. At the beginning of the procedure you will rate your level of distress on the SUD scale while thinking about the problem you are working with. You will write down the number, from a 10 (the highest imaginable disturbance) to a zero (indicating neutrality, or an absence of any disturbance).

By tuning in to your discomfort, you will become more aware of the effect of your emotions on your mind and body. Your symptoms may include mental obsession, agitation, or fogginess. There may be physical tension or pain in a certain area of the body. Take into consideration all dimensions of your distress when you rate your level of distress.

The changing distress level is your personal measure of treatment effects. At several points during the course of the treatment, you will reevaluate the level to monitor your progress, to measure the changes in emotional intensity, and to see whether additional treatment is needed. The periodic tuning in to the 0 to 10 measurements in ESM also serves to keep your thoughts focused on the target emotion or problem. After tuning in to the distress to measure it, you will naturally recall part of that thought as you apply the ESM techniques. It is virtually impossible to rate your distress about a specific problem and *not* be thinking about it.

The following chart describes each level of distress on the 10-point scale.

In a clinical setting, we usually say to our clients, "If 10 is the most intense distress you can imagine, and 0 is the absence of any distress, where would you rate your distress on this scale?" We find that people are remarkably accurate in their judgments, which we verify by manual muscle testing. Of course, some people insist that their distress level is more like 12 or 20. It doesn't matter; begin at whatever distress level you are experiencing. You're on your own here, so tune in carefully to what you are feeling. Some people have a tendency to exaggerate at the higher and lower ends of the scale.

Subjective Units of Distress Scale

0   The absence of any distress. Feeling calm and totally relaxed.

1   Neutral feeling or just OK, not as relaxed as could be.

2   A mild irritation. First awareness of tension or vague stress.

3   Increased discomfort, unpleasant, but in control.

4   Noticeable discomfort or distress, perhaps agitation, but tolerable.

5   Discomfort is very uncomfortable, but I can stand it.

6   Discomfort worsens and affects my life.

7   Discomfort is severe and emotional pain interferes with life.

8   Discomfort increases and it is in my thoughts constantly.

9   Discomfort is nearly intolerable.

10   Discomfort is extreme and the worst imaginable. I feel panicky and overwhelmed.

They either overstate their feelings or pretend that they don't have them. The ability to know what you are feeling is an important self-awareness skill that improves with practice.

Sorting It All Out

Figuring out just what we are feeling can be tricky, because several issues may be active in our lives at once. When we try to tune in, all we get is a jumbled confusion of emotions difficult to sort and label. Anger may cover up the hurt of rejection, which in turn may mask sadness and grief. Anger at a friend may turn into anger about the way your parents hurt you. In the course of an ESM treatment, treating one problem may allow another to surface.

How can you tell if there are other problems underneath the one you're working on? What typically happens is that, as you move through the steps of the protocol, you initially see a reduction in the SUDS level but then seem to get stuck and are unable to reduce it any further. If you tune in to your thoughts again, often you will discover that another emotion, or another aspect of the same emotion, has surfaced, causing renewed distress.

Multiple Aspects of an Emotion

Sorting out feelings can be complicated. A single problem may have two or more aspects. For example, a person may feel guilty about his behavior toward a family member. Perhaps he refused to do a favor for a parent or sibling and feels guilty for days or longer. In addition, he might be involved in a longer-term pattern of guilt in relation to his family. What may happen is that when he uses ESM methods to treat his most recent, situational guilt, he may find that his level of distress has decreased but not gone away completely. Now he can focus on eliminating his guilty feelings related to earlier experiences with his family. Each experience regarding guilt that he recalls and thinks about represents a different aspect of the original problem. After he goes through the ESM sequence for eliminating several instances of guilt, focusing on each of these memories, the positive effects of the treatment will generalize to all similar experiences.

Layered Problems: It's Just One Thing on Top of Another

Layered problems come in many configurations. The best way to proceed in these cases is to identify as best you can which emotion is the most intense and begin with the sequence for that emotion. As you resolve one layer of the problem and notice new intensity or distress, tune in again to what you are feeling. Attempt to examine its nature and see if the theme has changed; see if you can label the new feeling.

Here's an analogy. Say you have a strained back from lifting something heavy; it becomes the focus of your distress. However, imagine that while your back is still aching you develop an abscess in a tooth. Now the tooth may be capturing the majority of your attention. As you round the corner on the way to the kitchen to fix a warm saltwater rinse to soothe the infection in your mouth, you stub your toe on a chair. Suddenly your attention is riveted by the acute pain in your toe. As you put ice on the toe you begin to feel the toothache again, and so on.

A more common possibility is that the layering has to do with different emotions piled one on top of the other. This creates a sort of perceptual masking, where one emotional distress screens out the awareness of another. When the most distressing emotion is eliminated, then another layer of the emotional distress may be revealed. In this situation the nature of the target emotion may change. For example, a woman gets angry at someone who has insulted her. She treats the angry feelings and reduces her distress somewhat. But some level of distress still remains. Now she realizes that she feels embarrassed and that the anger was covering up her embarrassment.

Melinda was struggling to finish graduate school while raising three children and dealing with a husband who had difficulty holding a job. Melinda felt like she was holding the whole family together. Her stress mounted as the bills went unpaid and turn-off notices arrived for the utilities, due in part to her husband's unreliable work history. As her usual coping skills became overwhelmed, Melinda found herself yelling at the children, finding fault and punishing them for the least little infractions. She never hit them and always apologized profusely for her outbursts, but her guilt was like a boa constrictor around her neck and shoulders, strangling her ability to relax and renew her energy. So badly did she feel about herself for being unreasonable with the children and taking out her frustration on them that in her own words, she "didn't deserve to enjoy life."

You probably can see that Melinda's issues are multifaceted. Certainly she felt guilty, but also there was disappointment, frustration, and anger at her husband. The layers of emotional "static" were hard to sort out. When her guilt over her behavior toward her children was resolved, Melinda realized how angry she was with her husband for his inability to be a stable and responsible breadwinner. She understood, intellectually, that she could not change him, but emotionally she was disappointed with him in a big way. Her anger and then disappointment were her next targets.

When Melinda's anger with her husband dissipated, resentment, another aspect of anger, surfaced. This time it was also directed toward her parents, for not helping her out when she and her husband nearly lost their home to foreclosure the year before. Her husband's parents had been the "white knights" who saved the day, while her own parents had remained on the sidelines, even though they had the financial resources to help out. She discovered that her resentment toward her parents had aggravated her feelings at her husband, for having parents who did help. Because his parents had come to the rescue, she felt as if she were not entitled to hold him accountable. Emotions can become a vicious circle when they aren't flushed out; they can back up like a clogged sewer.

In working with layered problems, it is important to identify the issues and decide just what you want to treat. Either you can work on a very narrow aspect of a problem, ignoring the more general emotion, or you can work on the whole problem. For example, you could work on your feelings of rejection or just on your rejection about a particular incident. The effect does generalize to some extent when a procedure is applied successive times to different aspects of a similar problem. But it is important to be clear about just what it is that you want to include. What you can't do is treat different emotions all at once—anger, regret, and guilt. Each emotion responds to a particular Tap Sequence, and each has its own thought energy field. You have to treat the emerging layers one at a time.

Kathy's story illustrates another manifestation of layered problems: the way that worrying about one problem can divert us from facing more difficult issues. Kathy came in to be treated for her anxiety about taking on a business project. This is usually a very simple problem to treat. But in the course of our conversation, she related that her son had died in a car accident less than six months earlier at the age of nineteen, and she also revealed that she was in a complex and rocky situation in her relationship. So she was dealing with a lot of emotional issues.

Initially we worked with the project anxiety and got some measure of relief. Kathy said she felt better. But obviously there were other things going on for her that she wasn't quite prepared to deal with. In the midst of this, as Kathy started to feel more relaxed about the new project, the relationship issue got stirred up as her live-in boyfriend was preparing to move out. She came in again, extraordinarily distressed. So we dealt with some of the relationship problems to help her feel calmer. That worked, but at the same time she was experiencing pervasive sadness and grief over the loss of her son. We did a little bit of work on that, but what she said, which made sense, was that she didn't feel OK about eliminating that stress, because it wouldn't be respectful to her son. So we didn't address her grief directly, because it wasn't out of proportion, and it wasn't incapacitating. Had it been extreme, or had it persisted for too long, she might have chosen to try to reduce it further. The point is that we may not always try to eliminate all the emotional distress, because it isn't always appropriate. It wouldn't be respectful of the person's ability to respond naturally.

Chapter 8 goes into more detail about how to work through layered emotions as they surface during the ESM protocols. You may find it helpful to make note of your emotions and their intensity level as you become aware of them. Chapter 12 offers guidelines for keeping a log of your progress, as part of an ongoing program of emotional self-management.

Now and Then: Treating Issues of the Past, Present, and Future

Often just one ESM treatment solves a long-standing problem forever. Administer the protocol, zap the distress, and it's gone. Other problems may need to be retreated periodically. It seems to depend on whether the emotion you are treating is related to experiences in the past, the present, or the future.

Surprisingly, profound wounds and long-standing problems are sometimes the easiest to correct. By this we mean phobias, like Joleen's fear of flying in Chapter 1, and the deep-rooted aftereffects of traumatic events or patterns, such as abuse, a tornado or a serious auto accident. Perhaps because these devastating problems have caused such severe disturbance in the body's energy system, the act of suddenly unclogging the blockage has a cathartic effect.

Certain conditions related to present and ongoing circumstances may require ongoing retreatment. This category includes habitual or compulsive behaviors. Addictive urges are fraught with reversals that need periodic correcting. Frequently the substance itself—the chocolate or cigarettes—is a causal agent for the reversals, acting like a toxin in the system. The very substance that is being overconsumed is what prevents the person from breaking the cycle. As the treatment sequences take effect, the person has far less contact with the substance. It becomes a more marginal part of the person's life, its influence diminishes, and the need to correct the reversals lessens. The cravings diminish, and each treatment lasts longer.

Habits seem to require monitoring and procedure readministration, because the temptation is ever present. But ESM gives new hope to people whose lives have been out of control with compulsions. The self-empowerment aspect is powerful in these instances. When people notice that their discomfort reaches a certain threshold, they can excuse themselves for a few minutes to administer the treatment, and take care of it for the day or the week. The ability to change old patterns brings a sense of mastery over urges that seemed unmanageable before. The tools to take care of their cravings are always at their fingertips.

Cases where there's an ongoing provocation also may have to be retreated. This might be a critical supervisor at work, a landlord who's harassing you, a protracted battle with the IRS, a sullen teenager (in this case it may help to share ESM with the teen). ESM can handle these chronic stressors very well, and as time passes, they have less power to disturb us.

Sometimes we get rid of a troubling feeling but changing circumstances bring that feeling back into our life, and we need to retreat it. For example, a man may use ESM to get over a long-festering heartache about someone in his past. After the treatment, where once he would become upset just thinking about the person, his feelings are neutral. But if the person reintroduces him- or herself into the man's life in some way—a telephone call, a chance meeting—those feelings may come rushing back. With a new provocation, or if some aspect of the original wound had gone undetected, the old wound may be reactivated. The solution is to go through the ESM procedure again and eliminate any residual distress.

Issues related to the future often can be handled in one session. For example, many people have tremendous anticipatory anxiety about public speaking, or taking a test, or athletic performance. These feelings can be resolved using the protocol for anticipatory anxiety and may never arise again. One complete treatment may be all that's needed. With their anxiety under control, the person performs even better than expected. Now the person is comfortable—as long as the context stays the same. If a new type of situation comes up—say speaking in front of three hundred people instead of fifteen—some anxiety could recur. In all likelihood, however, it would be far milder than what was experienced before. If needed, the sequence can be readministered as often as necessary, and the problem will be gone once again. The Optimizer Protocol for enhancing performance and productivity is often helpful for such issues. See Chapter 11.

As you can see, sorting out feelings can be tricky business. If you're clear about what's bothering you, you're ready to move on to learning the protocol procedure in Chapter 8. If you're still having trouble sorting it all out, the more detailed discussion of emotions in Chapter 7 will help.

What, **Exactly**, Are You Feeling?

If, after reading Chapter 6, you are pretty sure you know which treatment protocol to turn to, you can proceed directly to Chapter 8. However, you may still be having a hard time figuring out exactly what is bothering you, even though you are all too aware of the stressful and uncomfortable feelings that dampen your enjoyment of life. Can you distinguish between feeling anxious or just tired? Do you know if you are angry? Is your anger veering toward rage? Is it about jealousy, or failure? Do you feel ashamed, or guilty, about the way you treated your ex-husband or ex-wife?

Remember, there are no wrong emotions, only inappropriate emotions, or levels of emotion that are irrational and that interfere with normal thinking and functioning. There is a common factor in all of these symptoms and emotions: stress. All are physiologically, mentally, and emotionally taxing. With each problem that we address using ESM our stress level drops, and we reduce the wear and tear on the system. The following discussion of emotions and symptoms will help you hone in on what you are feeling and give you more detailed information about working with the treatment protocols.

Note: Terms in **bold** *are protocol designations. Terms in* ***bold italic*** *are cross-referenced to the main protocols.*

Addictive or Compulsive Urges

Addictive or ***compulsive urges*** are pervasive in our culture, a not surprising attempt to manage the stress of our complicated and busy lives. The compulsion may be for a substance—food, tobacco, alcohol, or drugs. Perhaps we turn to gambling, shopping, or sex to assuage our **anxiety.** Anything to escape our discomfort, to distract us from our thoughts and fears, to calm us down. When we can't resist the urge to smoke or drink or spend, when nothing distracts us from our psychic pain, the urge can be considered addictive.

In clinical terms, addiction refers to a physiological dependence on a substance, usually alcohol or drugs. With addiction comes physiological tolerance for the substance, necessitating an increased dosage to achieve the desired effect. Discontinuing the substance brings on a pattern of withdrawal symptoms. Addictions are accompanied by anxiety that increases until intake of the substance calms it down.

The techniques in this book are not, by themselves, intended to resolve long-standing physiological addictions to such substances as heroin, alcohol, and prescription medications. We want to emphasize that the treatment of addiction to alcohol or drugs can be complex, because the individual is likely to have formed his or her life around the addictive substance. Many of the addict's activities may center around the drug—their social contacts, places where they typically acquire or use the substance, thoughts about being high or intoxicated, or of how to hide their activity. Successful treatment addresses all aspects of addiction. ESM methods offer a powerful tool for controlling or eliminating the urge for the addictive substance. However, the choice to use that tool involves many factors that are typically part of a comprehensive treatment plan requiring professional intervention, medically supervised detoxification, clinical treatment, and long-term aftercare.

Addictive urges related to food, gambling, excessive spending, cigarettes, and other behaviors can be managed with these techniques, provided that the compulsion is not so severe that it has impaired one's functioning. ESM techniques are not a sole treatment for serious eating disorders. When in doubt, it is best to err on the side of caution. It would be prudent to seek professional help for any addictive urge that's significantly disrupting your life.

Addictive urges that are not life-threatening can be annoying, inconvenient, unsightly, embarrassing, expensive, and unhealthful. Urges for food, excessive spending, nail biting, gambling, and other habits can be controlled or eliminated using ESM techniques. Some problems can be switched off with one treatment, while others require periodic retreatment and monitoring. For example, nail biting is a *habit* that a single ESM treatment can often stop completely. However, compulsive eating or spending money usually has to be treated over time. The triggers for these behaviors are always present in our lives. We are continually faced with decisions about eating and spending. If our compulsive urges are food-or money-related, we may need to monitor ourselves carefully and readminister the protocol as needed to keep anxiety and self-sabotaging behaviors in check.

ESM treatments work by reducing or eliminating the anxiety that underlies addictive urges. Because each treatment reduces the anxiety level, the urge for the substance or behavior typically lessens rapidly, and the interval between treatments grows, often until the urge is completely gone. As the anxiety is replaced by calmness, the urges disappear and new, productive behaviors can take their place. Exercise, recreation, hot baths, socializing, reading, listening to relaxation tapes, music, journaling your feelings, volunteering, taking a class, and activities that foster personal growth can take the place of compulsive urges.

> Donna knew the location of every bakery in her community and knew exactly what calorie-laden concoctions were available at each one. As she drove about in her job as a manufacturer's representative, she found herself stopping for pastries once or sometimes twice a day. Cupcakes and strudel were Donna's way of coping with stress. These "comfort foods" provided momentary relief from tension, but had added two dozen pounds to her frame in the last year and a half. She knew what good eating was all about, and she understood the importance of exercise. The minute *after* eating a cupcake she'd be chastising herself for her weakness. When she came to see us, she knew her urges were out of her control.
>
> Donna's treatment was not a quick fix. In the early stages of her maintenance program, in addition to the Six-Week Stabilizer program (see Chapter 12), she administered the full anxiety protocol daily in order to calm her urges to stop for food. Sometimes when she felt an urge coming on, she'd pause to do the Rapid Relaxer. By paying attention to her symptoms and treating them as they arose, she was soon choosing healthful foods to keep around the house for meals and snacks. The time came when she only needed to go through the whole protocol a couple times a week, with a morning tune-up that included Balanced Breathing and the Global Polarity Reversal. As these new behaviors became established, Donna felt calmer and was able to recognize the triggers of her stress, a necessary element of maintaining long-

term change. Finally she was able to put in place positive measures: exercise and journal writing to provide an outlet for unexpressed emotions. These steps, over time, made room for new, healthful patterns to develop. Within about twelve weeks Donna was totally off the junk food, making wiser choices about what to eat, and resolving her work-related stress by working out at the gym more regularly. She was back in control of her life.

Anger, Rage, and Frustration

Anger can be a powerful motivator for us to take productive action. Anger at legal injustice, for example, can inspire us to work to bring about reform. More often our anger is provoked by everyday occurrences, as when we spill a drink or when a careless driver cuts us off on the freeway. Anger may show up in the form of **disgust** or *revulsion,* as *impatience,* **frustration,** or *bitterness.*

Anger causes our face to flush, our heart to race, and the nostrils to flare. The more intense it becomes, the less control we feel. If anger lasts more than a few minutes, it can feel very uncomfortable, as if we're jumping out of our skin. Anger and hostility have been found to be the most negative stressors of the body, particularly the heart and circulatory system.

The word "anger" derives from the Latin word *angere,* meaning "to strangle." It is the root for *angina,* the "choking" of the heart. Holding onto anger can be damaging to the cardiovascular system. Research conducted by cardiologists Meyer Friedman and Ray Rosenman in the late 1960s and early 1970s identified what they called a Type A personality as being prone to cardiovascular disease. Type A behavior was associated with physical tension, quick eye movements, fast-paced speaking patterns, firm handshakes, talkativeness, and seeking control over situations and people. Later research discovered that there were really only two features of Type A personality that predicted ill health: high levels of anger and hostility (especially if not released) and a perceived lack of control over one's life or situations. The two seem to go hand in hand.

Anger is nearly always directed outward—toward a person, a situation, or an entity such as an institution or a pesky rodent. Angry responses are often out of proportion to the provocation. They may leave those who are the targets of our anger drained, mystified, and angry in return. Anger certainly doesn't do much for our own peace of mind. It has a rebound effect. Anger directed at ourselves often turns to guilt and depression.

Most of us didn't get very good training in managing our anger and frustration. Anger isn't considered nice or polite. Many families discourage children from displaying anger and deny the validity of their angry feelings. How many of us have been told not to get upset about something, or that we "shouldn't" be angry, and have grown up choking back angry feelings? As adults, many of us have so deeply internalized the prohibition about anger that we don't even recognize our angry feelings; we're depressed or anxious instead. Others seem unable to keep a rein on their angry feelings; their anger seeps out into every nook and cranny of their lives.

Frustration is a less intense version of anger, a kind of simmering irritation with the way things are going—or not going. We feel frustrated when our efforts have been thwarted or undone, when we want things to move faster, when we feel we're not being heard, and when we're not able to get what we want. Elements of *impatience, disappointment,* and **rejection** may lurk behind frustration. Frustration may bring the same physical symptoms as anger, but to a lesser degree.

Impatience is a feeling of restlessness, an eagerness to move forward. The ode to impatience goes, "If there's time enough to fix it or do it over, then there's time to do it right the first time." Delays annoy us to the point where we feel like screaming. We grumble and pace when things—or people—are moving too slowly. The first question to ask yourself in these circumstances is whether you feel impatient and cannot wait for others to keep up, or if you hurry yourself to the point that your mistakes are delaying you more than if you'd just taken your time in the first place. The nearly **obsessional** quality of impatience is a tip-off that **anxiety** is part of it. You will notice that the Tap Sequence for impatience contains elements of the sequence for anxiety.

As anger increases in intensity it moves toward **rage,** which takes away our ability to think clearly or rationally. Rage takes us to that place where we have no perspective, no control, a furious place of dark red vision where we are blinded to reason and prone to violence.

Anger, rage, and frustration often can be remedied through the act of forgiveness. Of course, forgiveness is usually the last thing on our minds when we are angry, and it is unimaginable when we are enraged. But forgiveness benefits not others but ourselves. We do not forget what was done to us, but we let go of our anger for our own well-being. Whether we silently and inwardly forgive people or vocally and outwardly express our forgiveness, we are the benefactors of this act of letting go. Forgiveness can dissolve anger. Because many times letting go is essential to healing these emotions, these ESM protocols include Intention Statements of forgiveness or release.

Phobias, Fears, Generalized Stress, and Anxiety

Phobias, *fears,* and **anxieties** share a common bond: They are all emotional responses to future uncertainty. With the uncertainty comes the dreaded possibility of negative, painful, or otherwise awful outcomes. In our agitation, we create a fantasy catastrophe. Just as guilt, embarrassment, and grief are emotions of the past, fears, phobias, and anxieties are generally related to the future.

It is important to recognize that fear can be a productive emotional response that helps keep us safe. A healthy fear of heights keeps us safe from risky behavior that might lead to falls. Wariness about unfamiliar or strange surroundings makes us cautious and heightens our vigilance. Fear causes certain muscles to contract, which can restrict the ability to breathe freely. The tightness in the chest directs our attention and often causes an involuntary drawing in, or holding, of the breath. Paradoxically, fear sometimes causes paralysis at the very moment when we want to flee. More often, however, those muscle contractions serve as a powerful stimulant that allows us to respond with extraordinary strength and keenness of senses. It is with good reason that we respect the ferocity of a cornered and frightened animal, regardless of size. The fight-or-flight response creates a rush of adrenaline into our blood system, spurring us either to do battle or to run for our lives.

Fears and phobias exist at different levels along the same continuum of emotional reaction. While people may use the terms interchangeably, in this book we use "fear" to describe a less intense reaction. Also, fears often have a realistic component. The feared situation or object—ferocious dogs or being mugged on the street or violent thunderstorms—is often a real presence in the person's life. Phobias, on the other hand, are extreme and uncontrollable reactions, sometimes due to a past trauma, which frequently lead to an avoidance of any possibility of facing the feared situation, often at life-limiting cost. But the hidden message of *fear* is: Face Everything and Recover.

> Five-year-old Jason developed a fear of dogs after he was startled and frightened by a large and threatening Doberman pinscher in his neighborhood. He wasn't scared of all dogs, for he was still

able to play and be around small dogs rather comfortably, but whenever a larger dog was around, no matter how tame or quiet, he clung to his parents or any adult present, shaking and crying. After his parents applied the ESM treatment, Jason was able to pet large (and tame) dogs again.

*   *   *

Lucinda was terrified of snakes, although nothing in her past seemed to be the cause of her fright. It wasn't just squeamishness. She was not just disgusted by them or went out of her way to avoid them. Snakes terrified her, to the point where she declined invitations to go hiking and camping, always providing some other explanation for her avoidance. The mere photograph of a snake would cause Lucinda to shudder and look away; just the word "snake" sent shivers down her spine. But after Lucinda used the protocol for specific fears and phobias, she was able to go to a pet store and then to the local zoo's reptile exhibit. Of course she was also able to enjoy outdoor activities with comfort and enthusiasm.

Jason had a *fear* of dogs, brought on by an unpleasant and scary event. Lucinda had a *phobic reaction* to snakes, way out of proportion to the threat, apparently unconnected to any past experience. Fears and many phobias are treated with the same sequence. For a few phobias (spiders, claustrophobia, and air turbulence), there is a slight variation in the sequence. It isn't always clear why certain Tap Sequences work for specific symptom patterns; we only go by the evidence of our clinical experience.

Fear often shows itself as **anxiety.** Some anxiety is a normal part of being human. In fact, a moderate amount of excitement can enhance the performance of many tasks. However, when the anxiety interferes with enjoying life or activities, it's time for it to go. Anxiety is often specifically connected to an upcoming event, such as a speech, an athletic contest, or an exam. This is **anticipatory anxiety.** But many times anxiety and apprehension are free-floating, a generalized *worry* and apprehension that stalk us and sap our energy. We go through our days with an unsettled stomach, with perhaps a skipping heartbeat and a catch in the throat. We have trouble focusing, and little is getting accomplished. Worry is like a rocking chair. It gives you something to do, but it doesn't get you very far. We may have only a vague notion of what the problem is, we think it's just life. But worry is a maladaptive way of responding to fears we cannot identify, to anticipated nightmares we do not even acknowledge. Where cues or symbols of the target object or situation activate fears or phobias, anxiety can develop and persist even in the absence of conscious thought about any feared object.

With anticipatory anxiety, the underlying worry is often about being overcome with fear at the wrong time. Part of Robin's duties as the department head at a large clinic included conducting a monthly meeting of the physicians, administrators, and staff in her group. Ordinarily, Robin's presentations go well. She feels anxious and worried for nearly the entire month, but once she begins her presentation, she mostly forgets about her anxiety and does a fine job. No one but her closest colleagues know how distressed she becomes.

But these meetings were a tremendous drain on Robin's energy. She would begin to fret about the next month's presentation within hours after the one she'd just finished. Anticipating the next meeting would bring on awful and unmanageable discomfort. The weeks of anticipatory anxiety were like a vise, tightening and squeezing a few turns with each passing day. Robin couldn't seem to shake the anxiety, no matter how much she told herself that the meetings were always successful. Usually Robin stayed focused on keeping herself distracted from her worry and anxiety; that distraction often took the form of massive overpreparation for the meeting and her often-brief presentations. To be free of that feeling would feel like a miracle, she thought.

After using the Emotional Self-Management process, Robin was able to shift her attention to other matters at work. In fact, the shift in her awareness had so much impact that she was able to significantly scale back her preparation for the next presentation. A few weeks later she reported that not only had her anxiety not returned, her stress level had gone way down now that she was working less intensively on preparing for the meetings. This allowed more time for some other tasks that had required her attention, such as team-building activities she had neglected and even expanding her after-work social life. She felt more productive than before, with far less effort. She was able to enjoy life again.

Anxieties sometimes can be provoked again after a successful treatment, because of some new aspect that triggers a new target for anxiety. In Robin's case, it might arise if she was promoted and then had to lead meetings for a board of directors. Other times anxiety may return due to polarity reversals as negative thoughts creep back in. In some cases, merely correcting the polarity reversals on a daily basis will allow the treatment to "hold." Other times you may need to reapply the entire sequence. Anxieties related to the future are more likely to return, while emotions related to the past may require only one treatment for complete and lasting relief. In Chapter 8 you will see that there are separate protocols for generalized and anticipatory anxiety.

Embarrassment, Shame, and Guilt

While fears and anxiety are usually related to the future, other emotions have their roots in the past. One group of past-related emotions includes **embarrassment, shame**, and **guilt.**

Feelings of **embarrassment** usually stem from doing something that makes us feel foolish, like tripping and falling as we get up to speak, spilling wine on our dinner companion, or forgetting to zip our fly. We may feel embarrassed if we get caught doing something we didn't want others to see or something that we usually do in private—attending to itches in private places, passing gas, or using profanity. Many embarrassing incidents fall into the category of social faux pas. Embarrassment exposes us.

Embarrassment also can be indirect. A woman can be embarrassed by her husband's crude jokes at a social event. A man can be embarrassed by his spouse's veiled allusions to his sexual problem. Feelings of embarrassment are usually momentary and transient, forgotten by the next day. Yet our embarrassment may linger, casting a shadow over future encounters with people whom we believe are aware of the embarrassing circumstances.

Embarrassment is distinct from **shame.** Where embarrassment usually is associated with some specific behavior or action, shame stains the person all over. To feel ashamed is to feel that *you* are the object of error or mistake. Powerful feelings of shame can infect people's fundamental beliefs about themselves. Embarrassment passes; shame endures.

There is no clear demarcation between chronic or repeated embarrassment and shame. Embarrassment that becomes chronic and pervades several areas of life can lead to feeling ashamed. The younger we are when these sorts of feelings begin, and the longer they persist, the more likely they are to take root as an ingrained pattern of shame. Young people ridiculed by others for being different, for looking different, or for doing things incorrectly may grow up ashamed of who they are and the way they act. Comments by parents, teachers, or classmates that they are "stupid" or "clumsy" can become a global condemnation.

While shame can develop from childhood and hover constantly in the background, it also can develop later as a result of adult trespasses. Shame also stems from breaking a societal taboo. There are situations in which adults do something that is so deeply and profoundly against the moral, legal, ethical, or religious code of their community that they suffer shame. People who become addicted to alcohol or drugs often deal with feelings of shame as they are recovering and recognize the consequences of their past conduct. People who commit adultery often feel ashamed of their deceit and of their betrayals of trust. There are different treatment sequences for embarrassment and shame.

Guilt bears a resemblance to shame and embarrassment. Guilt arises from a feeling of *remorse* regarding behavior. It is more the product of our own self-judgment than of others (although others may go out of their way to make us feel it). Whereas embarrassment often is the result of inadvertent actions that are not usually hurtful to anyone else, guilt is nearly always related to culpability. It implies that at least someone believes you purposefully did something wrong (or would believe so if they knew). Guilt, because it assumes an offense, is the handmaiden to conscience. Guilt occurs only in the presence of some sense of conscience or inner struggle with what's right and wrong. Intention statements of forgiveness are part of the protocol for guilt.

Guilt rears its head when we violate the expectations we have for ourselves. When we behave in a way that is inconsistent with our stated intentions and moral code, we can feel guilty. For many of us, feelings of guilt were instilled early in life. Guilt is a powerful socializing tactic, used by most parents, and society in general, to help shape and control our behavior. Applied too liberally, it can corrode our sense of self-worth and cast a shadow over our every move. Guilt often is felt in the gut and stomach; bowel problems may be involved if the emotion is chronic.

We can be so torn by guilt that it keeps us from repairing the damage that brought on the guilt in the first place. Phil had been married for twenty-five years, with a twenty-four-year-old grown son, when he left his wife and soon after began a relationship with a woman in his office. His wife was devastated yet left the door open should Phil "come to his senses."

About six months into the new relationship, Phil realized he was not in love with this new woman. In fact, now that they could spend time together, he wasn't enjoying the relationship as he thought he would. Phil spent another six months dating other women, hoping to find what he felt was missing in his life. But the intellectual stimulation he thought he needed and would find in another woman never materialized. Throughout this period he remained in contact with his "soon-to-be ex-wife." As time passed, Phil came to miss his wife and missed the things they did have in common. He came to the realization that for all his dissatisfaction with his marriage, the alternatives were no better.

Although his wife had not given up hope, she was understandably cautious. Phil had not strictly cheated on her, having begun his affair only after moving out of the house, but he had violated her trust. His wife had suffered a profound betrayal. She was deeply hurt when he announced that he was leaving so suddenly, adamant that there was no room for discussion.

But this story is about Phil. His guilt for having hurt his wife was causing difficulty in reconciling and working to rebuild a relationship with her. Interestingly, she did not do much to foster his guilty feelings. Quite the opposite; she was willing to forgive. She was keeping the pace slow with Phil, however, not allowing him back into her life in a rush as if nothing had happened.

Phil's struggle was mainly within. The powerful feelings of guilt kept him from being spontaneous. They kept him focused on the past and prevented him from thinking about his wife without pity and remorse. In seeking help, he recognized the importance of resolving his guilt so that he could engage in reconstructing his marriage. Phil was not a bad person; he had made a big mistake. Certainly he had learned a lesson from his behavior. Now his guilt was no longer productive and was interfering with his desire to reestablish a bond of intimacy with his wife. He'd learned his lesson; it was time for the guilt to go.

When we first assessed his level of guilt, Phil reported it was about an 8 on the SUD scale. He openly admitted that he felt terrible and was pained whenever he looked into his wife's eyes and knew the anguish he had caused her. Although she had forgiven him, he had not forgiven himself. It was not surprising that when I tested Phil for polarity reversals, he had several, and one of them was on the theme of "Deserving." After correcting for all reversals, we applied the procedure for guilt. Guilt was the appropriate sequence, because Phil's guilt was localized to a well-defined set of circumstances with his wife. Had there been many affairs, many betrayals, or other complicating factors, we might have elected to use the sequence for emotional trauma, which includes the tap treatment points for guilt.

As Phil tapped the Index Fingernail location in the treatment sequence, he made the affirmation, "I forgive myself, I did not know then what I know now," three times. Afterward, he reported that he felt a sense of relief as he spoke those words on the second round of the Tap Sequence. After completing the entire procedure, he reassessed his SUDS as a 2 with regard to his guilt.

I asked Phil to reflect for a moment, to see if there were any other aspects that he was now aware of with this problem. Closing his eyes and tuning in again, he said yes, he was feeling sad about all the pain he had caused his wife and their son, who, like a wounded soldier in the background, had said little to his father about the separation. Feelings not expressed in words were visible to him in his son's face at each visit. We next focused on Phil's sadness, which he estimated was a 6 on the 10-point scale, and applied the procedure for sadness.

As with all the protocols, we again applied polarity reversal corrections for this new emotional layer, with sadness as "the problem" in the corrective statement. As we progressed through the tapping sequence, the change was immediately apparent. Phil's face softened; the hard lines in his forehead smoothed out. At the end of the procedure, after the final Eye Roll, Phil said his distress was only a 1. When I asked him if he wanted to eliminate even that small amount of disturbance, he said, "No, I think I want to keep just a little of this feeling to remind me of how bad it can feel. I don't want to forget what I put everyone through." If that was OK for Phil, it was OK with me. In some situations it is appropriate for a small amount of emotional distress to remain. It provides positive incentive for further learning or behavioral change.

Phil kept in contact over the next few months and reported that he had moved back into the house. He and his wife were building a new relationship based on what he had learned about himself and, more important, on what he now knew it would take to make his relationship work. The unburdening of the guilt and grief were instrumental in allowing him to be free to engage with his wife at an emotional level unencumbered by limiting and self-damaging emotions. He could now work on building a new foundation for their relationship and repair the differences that had originally led him to separate.

Feelings of embarrassment, guilt, and shame are often closely related. If you have doubts as to which you are feeling, choose the one you believe is the most relevant. If that treatment sequence does not work, you may need to try another.

Grief, Sadness, and Regret

Grief, *sadness,* and **regret** span a broad spectrum of feelings. In some situations all of these emotions are reasonable and necessary responses. Feeling the heavy hand of grief after a big loss is normal; it provides a way of coming to terms with drastic changes in one's life. Feeling regret allows us to convey remorse. If we felt no regret or ***disappointment*** at doing poorly at some task, we would not be motivated to take action to change our behavior. Prolonged sadness and grief, however, can lead to depression. Clinical depression, however, is a serious and often complex condition that should be assessed and treated by a medical or mental health professional. Any thoughts of harming yourself are clear signals to seek professional help and guidance immediately.

As with all emotions, the appropriateness of the response is what concerns us. There are times when sadness serves no productive purpose and merely holds us back in some way. Sadness can turn to **negativity,** an outlook that colors even positive events, highlighting instead the deficits and flaws. When negative thinking arises, very frequently correcting polarity reversals will resolve these feelings. Once the negative thoughts are cleared away, the target emotions can be resolved with the specific tapping sequences.

Grief arises from a *loss.* The word "grief" stems from the same root as grave, severe; heaviness and ***sorrow*** are the companions of grief. Profound grief usually is associated with the loss of a loved one who will be deeply missed. The grieving process honors the memory of the lost loved one and allows the individual to process the pain of the loss. Grief reveals the value of life and makes us aware of the bonds between people. We grieve as well the loss of a job, a good friend moving away, the loss of our health or a beloved home or pet. The **fatigue** and *lethargy* that often accompany grief reflect the body's suffering as well and afford time for reflection that can serve somehow to incorporate the loss into one's life. Grieving is a natural process for healing pain. When we do not go through the process of grieving a serious loss, we risk becoming disoriented and disconnected from life.

Most experts have found grief to follow a fairly predictable path that has been described by Elisabeth Kübler-Ross, M.D., as having six stages: denial, anger over the loss, bargaining with God to reverse the loss, depression and sorrow, acceptance, and eventually hope for the future.

The stages are not distinct. They frequently overlap, and a person may move from one to another and then back again. Gerald Koocher, Ph.D., chief psychologist and grief expert at Boston's Children's Hospital, believes that a person may grieve for the loss of a loved one for up to two years before a noticeable change occurs. The grief may continue naturally off and on for many years following, but with decreasing intensity. There is nothing pathological or unhealthy about it. However, the process of grieving is also a process of healing. If the process is halted or becomes stuck, healing is no longer taking place. We might say that the grief has outlived its usefulness.

Beyond a certain point, the level and duration of our grief is not a measure of how much we loved someone. More often it is a measure of how much the situation has disrupted our energy and balance. Grief can become trapped in the system with no way to escape, a vicious circle of pain and unhappiness. After a reasonable period of time, if grief does not show evidence of fading and diminishing, and if our lives are suffering, there can be a value in nudging the process along. As with all our feelings, normal and productive emotional responses are unaffected by the administrations of the ESM protocol.

Claudia's teenage son had been killed instantly in a car accident two years earlier. Her life had come to a standstill since Kyle's death. Claudia was consumed with her sense of loss and missing her son. Daily she would find herself frozen in the act of some simple task, daydreaming about Kyle for minutes before she caught herself. She cried often and was sensitive about discussing what happened. "I couldn't stand to hear or use words like 'Kyle was' instead of 'is,' " she reported. Claudia was so preoccupied that she was ignoring important decisions that needed to be made about her husband's offer of promotion, which would mean moving across the country. Nothing seemed to penetrate her cloud of grief and preoccupation. Claudia was stuck in the denial stage of grief after her son's death and could not move on.

When Claudia applied the formula for grief, she said she was finally able to let go of Kyle and to truly acknowledge that he was gone. Her paralyzing grief over Kyle's death became an appropriate level of sadness. At that point she realized how much anger she felt that her son had been taken at such a young age. She next applied the Tap Sequence for anger and felt relief immediately. Other aspects of her anger surfaced, and she treated those as well. The sorrow stayed with her, but she was now able to move on. She would have given anything to have her son back. But now, having faced her loss, she was in some ways able to remember Kyle better than before. There was more grieving Claudia needed to do, but at least now the process was moving. Grieving people are often angry with God for their loss, and moving beyond the anger allows them to recover their spiritual connection; that was the case for Claudia.

* * *

Julia and her boyfriend had grown apart over the past year and had finally split up six months before she came to our office. Although this was not the outcome she'd hoped for, Julia was clear that she needed to move on in her life to find someone who wanted marriage and children. Even so, she couldn't seem to get past her sadness over the unfulfilled dreams and expectations she had nurtured during their four-year relationship. Julia was feeling low, with little interest in going out and having fun and even less in looking for another relationship.

In a matter of half an hour, as Julia went through the grief protocol, she felt the burden of loss and grief lift. She was utterly amazed at how quickly her heavy heart and lethargy seemed to transform into an almost lighthearted feeling. She was still aware of her unmet expectations and hopes, but she no longer felt hopeless. "I know he's not anywhere near as upset about us breaking up as I have been," she commented. "I guess I should take my friend's advice and show up at her party this weekend. It's her birthday and she throws great parties."

Only after shedding the heavy cloak of grief and sadness was Julia able to see her situation in a new light. Strong, intractable feelings interfere with our ability to reason clearly and use all the information that is available to us.

Unresolved grief, or unrelenting and seemingly insoluble troubles, can lead to despair. **Despair** is the loss of faith that things will change, loss of the belief that there will be rescue or renewal. Despair goes beyond grief, into **hopelessness**. When the car battery has drained to the point where the lights barely glow, when there's not enough juice to start the car, when the horn has lost its voice although the radio may work—that is despair.

Regret is the if-only feeling about events in the past. It is our feeling about what *wasn't* said, what *wasn't* done—what might have been. The old saying that "hindsight is 20/20" does not diminish the feeling of regret we may experience at an opportunity missed or for having made what now feels like a poor choice.

Most of us regret something or other in our lives—the date we did (or didn't) kiss; the apology we should have made; the time and money we wasted playing the horses. Regret can serve to bring to our awareness something important from which we can learn. It can help us to make better choices in the future. But prolonged dwelling on past failures or **disappointments** brings with it a **sorrow** that can prevent us from enjoying the present moment and mobilizing our resources to create positive changes in our lives. Beyond whatever lessons we can learn initially, feelings of regret are not productive.

Love Pain, Heartache, and Loneliness

Love pain and heartache are complex emotions that usually are compounded of several forms of hurt, including **rejection, disappointment, loneliness,** or fear of being alone. Sometimes **anger** and **jealousy** are mixed in there as well. **Heartache** is the way people often describe it, a dull and relentless ache. Some people distract themselves from heartache—they go out and have a fling or two, eat too much, drink too much, exercise till they drop, or take a trip to

INSTANT EMOTIONAL HEALING

Cancun. For other people the pain pervades every activity and intrudes on their thinking; there's no escaping it. An old life is over, but there's no interest or energy to start a new one.

The pain of lost love may ebb and flow with cues or reminders of the lost lover. And often the pain is greater when the relationship breaks up for reasons beyond our control. Typically, the longer and deeper the relationship, the more intense the pain and loss and feelings of rejection. In other circumstances even a brief but intense romance can trigger a profound aftershock. Some of this is natural. But prolonged pain and **obsessional thinking** are not productive or effective in helping to develop a satisfying future relationship.

> Paul's girlfriend dumped him, telling him she just didn't love him anymore. He was completely taken by surprise. They had been dating for nearly a year, and in his estimation they had a great relationship. Paul had been ignoring the signals that his relationship was deteriorating. Devastated by the breakup, he tried desperately to contact his girlfriend, sure he could convince her to get back together. She didn't even return his calls. He felt disoriented and ruminated constantly about what had caused her to stop loving him. Was she insulted by the birthday gift he got her? Did he talk too much? Was she disappointed when he didn't get that promotion? His questions were endless, and he began to question whether she had ever been in love with him.
>
> Paul's constant brooding kept him awake much of the night and kept him from working effectively in his job as an architect. Instead of getting better as time went by, he became more tormented by his loss. He found himself driving past her home, hoping to catch sight of her and talk to her. After several months of self-torture, he realized that his agony was not diminishing and his life was suffering. His brother strongly suggested he get help. That's when he came to our office.
>
> When Paul first rated the intensity level of his pain and misery, he claimed it was 20 on a 10-point scale. After completing a series of sequences for love pain and for grief and anger, all of which took less than an hour, he rated his pain level as a 2. We asked him if he wanted to try one of the sequences again to see if he could get rid of it completely. He declined, saying that the

level of 2 felt to him about right. Sometimes a small level of distress can serve as motivation. For Paul it was the impetus to crawl out of his cocoon and, like Julia mentioned earlier, reenter life.

Loneliness is a common spin-off of a broken romance or a failed relationship. It frequently accompanies the death of a spouse or dear friend or moving to a new community. Loneliness often diminishes of its own accord with the passage of time. But while it has its grip on you, it can be devastating. The discontent or unhappiness experienced when one is isolated or feeling disconnected from others can be debilitating and frightening. Sometimes loneliness is due not to physical solitude but rather reflects a lack of close or intimate relationships.

"To be isolated is the greatest tragedy for a human being and the most generic form of stress," according to psychologist Joan Borysenko. Others, such as epidemiologist Leonard Sagan, have recognized that it is not merely the number of people around us but rather the satisfaction that we derive from our connection with others that makes a difference between perceiving ourselves as isolated or connected.

Researchers have identified five specific elements as the most common reasons for loneliness:

1. Living alone.

2. Feeling different or misunderstood and having difficulty making friends.

3. Situational isolation, such as physical limitations, hospitalization, lack of transportation, or living far from others.

4. Having no significant other, such as a spouse, close family, or companion.

5. Being disconnected by distance from family or friends, such as being away at school, frequent travel, relocation due to work or other reasons.

While the objective of ESM is to reduce the distress of loneliness, it is not meant to be the sole solution. An individual may need to make specific corrective alterations in life to prevent the return of loneliness. Such alterations can include changing one's living situation, taking courses or other training in social skills, seeking out community resources in order to connect with others who may be experiencing similar life circumstances, getting a pet, or making efforts to repair relationships that have been allowed to deteriorate.

Jealousy and Envy

The green-eyed monster, **jealousy,** and its echo emotion, *envy,* are silent killers of the spirit. Jealousy is what we feel toward someone who has the love of the *person* we want and can't have; envy is what we feel toward someone who has the *things* we want. To see a former lover with someone new can be like a searing poker to the stomach. Even the thought of someone having what we think we deserve can be galling. It is with good reason that many of our words to describe jealousy are centered on the stomach. Psychiatrist John Diamond, the author of *Life Energy,* compares the emotions of envy and jealousy to greed and the desire to have something even if we do not need or have a place for it. These are unpleasant emotions to experience and unpleasant to see in others. Jealousy and envy can be particularly tormenting because we may harbor these poisonous feelings in secret. If jealousy and envy do leak out, they can be as foul to others as a garlic belch. The sequence for jealousy and envy seeks to relieve our attachment to what we do not have.

Negativity and Obsessional Thinking

When our energies are depleted, for whatever reason, our thoughts can take a dark turn. **Negative thinking** is the proverbial wet blanket, characterized by a generally pessimistic feeling that anticipates failure or unpleasant outcomes. It is important to recognize when negative thoughts become habitual and to root them out. Until we are in a more receptive frame of mind, specific protocols are likely to be ineffective. Often a pattern of negative thinking is caused by polarity reversals. If negativity seems to be a factor for you, begin by doing the Balanced Breathing exercise and the polarity reversal corrections. If this doesn't work, you may be dealing with the more troublesome problem of polarity disorganization. The remedy for that is the Five-Step Breathing exercise in Chapter 9.

Unresolved emotional issues also can lead to a pattern of **obsessional**

thinking. When we get to this point, no amount of reasoning or willpower can shut off the repetitive thoughts, desires, or ideas that keep us awake at night. Here too we need to clear our minds with the Balanced Breathing and Polarity Reversal exercises before addressing other problems we want to heal.

Emotional Trauma

Traumatic events in the past—the terror of battle, rape, abuse, a mugging, a natural cataclysm such as a fire, earthquake, or tornado—can leave us literally in a state of shock. A deep and profound wound may stem from a single experience or from repeated exposure to the causal circumstances. Often the aftereffects of these shocking and painful events persist for years. An untreated shock to the system can manifest as posttraumatic stress disorder (see Chapter 5), a condition that warrants professional clinical attention. Self-administered thought energy therapies may be only one part of the solution for serious trauma of the type that produces PTSD.

The intense experience of a traumatic event leaves us feeling unsafe, as if our lives are out of control. Emotional trauma can include feelings such as **anger, rage, guilt, rejection,** confusion, **anxiety,** *fear,* and **grief** over the loss of our innocence and sense of safety. Emotional trauma also can stem from such losses as an important relationship, a job, or from the failure of a business. Emotional Self-Management techniques often are successful at treating obsessional thinking about a past trauma with only one application of the trauma protocol. Other times the protocol for **obsessional thinking** will need to be applied.

> Jonathan, the victim of a vicious mugging three years earlier, was referred by a local pain treatment center. After reconstructive surgery on his face, he was still disfigured and in nearly constant pain. Potent and addictive painkillers provided only brief and limited relief, and they did nothing for his emotional pain. The loss of his once-handsome appearance, forever scarred by the beating and only partially repaired by the surgeries, was a constant reminder of that day in late June when his world changed forever as he walked to his car after work. Gone also was his feeling of safety. He lived in trembling fear of another attack; he was edgy away from home. The loss of confidence and loss of control over

his life had left Jonathan with a seething frustration that he could only barely disguise. In one of the most moving experiences of my years of practice, I watched Jonathan's fears and torment drain away in one forty-five minute session.

At first, I could see that Jonathan was going through the procedures with great deliberation but little hope. But at one point a profound change came over his face. A tall and stoic man, he looked up, smiling, with tears rolling down his cheeks. It was his smile that saved me from worrying that these were more tears of sorrow. Tears of relief were streaming down his face, and Jonathan said that he felt the years of torment lifting from him. My own eyes were moist at this point, with the realization that he had made a crucial turn on his journey back to life.

Jonathan's physical pain lessened as his emotional pain resolved, and he was able to talk about the assault. The process of integrating that awful experience into his self-concept and worldview could now begin. Therapy for Jonathan was not over, but relief from the trauma freed him to face the future. ESM is sometimes both an ending and a beginning. In Jonathan's case, it marked the end of his emotional pain and the beginning of rebuilding his life.

Miscellaneous Applications for ESM

Our experience with ESM procedures has shown them to be effective for the psychological or emotional components of some types of **pain.** The chronic pain and discomfort that can accompany injury, illness, or structural disorder can put a huge kink in our enjoyment of life. In addition to the physical sensations generated through the nervous system, often feelings of misery and suffering are within the mental and emotional realms. Examples of the physical source of such pain are toothaches, tension headaches, back and sciatic nerve pain, childbirth labor, muscle strains and aches, low back pain, cancer, arthritis, and other degenerative tissue conditions. The pain protocol can provide temporary relief for the emotional component of these and other discomforts. It is not meant to replace medical evaluation for pain of unknown origin. We recommend that you first seek appropriate medical or dental evaluation. Pain is a warning; you should be examined for any medical explanations before turning down the alarm.

As we gain more knowledge about the workings of this therapy, we expect to develop sequences for additional target symptoms. For now, we offer the following remedies, in alphabetical order:

- Many of us have been beset by periods of *awkwardness* or **clumsiness** that are unrelated to neurological conditions, when we are prone to stumble and bump into things or to be forgetful and drop things. When grace seems to desert us, polarity imbalance may be the culprit. Often the problem can be corrected with the Balanced Breathing exercise. If this does not remedy the situation, turn to the Five-Step Breathing exercise for polarity disorganization in Chapter 10.

- Lack of endurance, physical or mental weariness, exhaustion, or general feelings of *tiredness* (not associated with clinical depression, chronic fatigue syndrome, or other medical problem) are often improved with Protocol #8, for **fatigue.**

- **Hiccups,** an inconvenient, sometimes embarrassing, and certainly annoying malady caused by involuntary contraction of the diaphragm, often can be remedied with Protocol #12.

- **Jet lag,** which causes a disturbance in the circadian rhythm during air travel across time zones, can lead to sleepiness, grogginess, and poor concentration. See Protocol #14.

- **Nasal congestion** or *stuffiness,* including that caused by *allergies* associated with airborne particles, can find symptomatic relief with Protocol #17.

- The feelings of irritability, hypersensitivity to criticism, negativity, diminished frustration tolerance, and fatigue associated with premenstrual cycles often respond to Balanced Breathing, the Polarity Reversal exercise, and Protocol #22 for PMS symptoms.

We hope that these fuller descriptions of the target emotions and applications for ESM have helped you clearly define the issues you want to address with the specific protocols in Chapter 9.

PART III

Administering ESM Protocols

How to Administer an ESM Protocol

So far you have visited various outposts on the ESM map. Now you are go-ing to get the map of the whole territory, so that you can self-administer the ESM protocols. Many of the steps of an ESM protocol are already famil-iar to you. You've done the two-minute Balanced Breathing exercise and cor-rected for all twelve polarity reversals. You've learned the 9-Step Bridge, with its humming and counting, and the eye movements of the Eye Roll. You have identified your emotional issues and learned to rate your distress level using the SUD scale. This chapter shows you how to put these steps to-gether with the emotion-specific Tap Sequences so that you can administer the full protocols. All of the ESM protocols are alike, except for the series of tapping points in Step 4. All the protocols are given in Chapter 9.

Here is what a complete emotion-specific protocol looks like, step by step.

Step-by-Step Through the Protocol Procedure

1. SUDS   Think about the issue or problem and rate level of distress on the 0 to 10 scale (page 102).

2. Balanced Breathing   Do the Balanced Breathing exercise (page 58).

3. Polarity Reversals   Correct for Polarity Reversals, stating your emotion or problem with each one (page 61).

4. **Tap Sequence**   Administer the specific tapping sequence for your feeling or problem. Here is an example of a Tap Sequence:

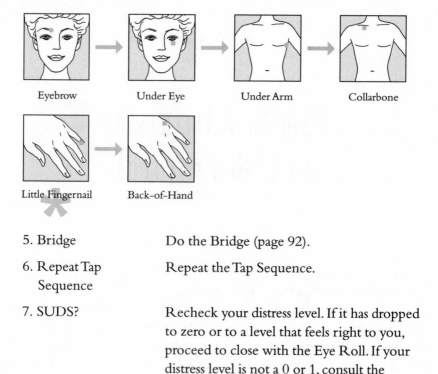

| Eyebrow | Under Eye | Under Arm | Collarbone |

| Little Fingernail | Back-of-Hand |

5. Bridge	Do the Bridge (page 92).
6. Repeat Tap Sequence	Repeat the Tap Sequence.
7. SUDS?	Recheck your distress level. If it has dropped to zero or to a level that feels right to you, proceed to close with the Eye Roll. If your distress level is not a 0 or 1, consult the decision tree that follows.
8. Eye Roll	Final step of full treatment procedure (page 92).

The ESM protocols are essentially recipes, worked out through muscle testing to develop the specific sequences for different problems, similar to figuring out the best microwave setting for popcorn.

Ultimately, the most important ingredient in any ESM recipe is you. You are the cook, mixing the ingredients, making sure the timing is right, measuring and monitoring as you go. But this is not rocket science. The recipes are flexible and can be adapted somewhat to your needs and temperament. An extra pinch of this or that is not going to hurt. What is needed is your intuition and attention to the procedures.

The first order of business is to choose the correct procedure. Remember, you can work with only one issue at a time. Immediate success is unlikely if you target your anxiety about losing your job, your obsession with chocolate, and your guilt over your spending habits all at one time. Each protocol narrowly addresses a specific issue; at least one tapping site is different for each protocol.

Once you have identified the problem, your task is to measure your distress level accurately on the SUD scale. It is up to you to stay focused and to reevaluate your distress during the process and, if the recipe is not working for you, to figure out what steps to take. In other words, to be a good cook. You will get positive results just by following the directions in the book, and pretty soon you won't even need the book to administer the recipes you know.

Set aside a quiet half-hour the first time you try the process. Sit comfortably, and try to minimize any distractions. You don't need a darkened room or absolute quiet, but distracting background conversations don't help, and don't try to keep an eye on the kids or check e-mail at the same time. The ESM method is very forgiving of minor imperfections in timing or tapping.

Here are some additional step-by-step notes about the process that you may find helpful.

Step 1. SUDS. Before starting the process, make sure you are clear about the emotion you are addressing. Take a minute to tune in to your thoughts and feelings about the issue. Rate the level of your distress about this problem from 0 to 10 on the SUD scale. Write down the number, so you can compare it to your distress level at the end of the process. Just tuning in to measure your distress level on the 0 to 10 scale and naming the problem will activate the thought field. You may want to review the material about SUDS in Chapter 6 before proceeding. *For more about Tuning in the Thought Field, see page 140.

Step 2. Balanced Breathing. Do the Balanced Breathing exercise for two minutes.

Step 3. Polarity Reversals. Do the Polarity Reversal exercise. As you go through the process, keep your problem in mind. You may want to substitute your own verbalization of the issue you are dealing with for the general wording "my problem." For example, you may want to say "I completely and totally accept myself, even with *my sadness."* Or ". . . even if I don't deserve to get over *my guilt."* Or ". . . even if it is not safe for others for me to get over *my anger at Bart."* This will help keep your focus on the problem.

Step 4. Tap Sequence. Here's the new part. Each tap sequence involves tapping seven times at a series of sites. (The exception is the Back-of-Hand site, where you are instructed to tap continuously.) Just follow the series of illustrations or the abbreviations and run through the entire sequence, tapping at a rate of 3–4 taps per second. Keep that thought field active by keeping in mind the problem you are working with. Here too you may want to say, aloud or to yourself, "my frustration" or "my loneliness" or "my procrastination about the annual report" as you tap each treatment point.

Some of the Tap Sequences incorporate an *Intention Statement* as you tap at certain sites. These sites are indicated by an asterisk (*). The example on page 134 indicates that there is an Intention Statement at the Little Finger site. Repeat the indicated Intention Statement three times as you *continuously* tap the designated site. If the statement does not seem to fit your situation, choose one of the alternative statements offered; or you can adjust or adapt one to be a better fit for your situation. See Custom Tailoring Intention Statements on page 142.

Step 5. Do the Bridge.

Step 6. Repeat the Tap Sequence in Step 4.

Step 7. Recheck SUDS. Recheck your distress level, and write it down. *Here is the critical point.*

- If you arrive at a 0 or 1, you can proceed to conclude the procedure with Step 8, the Eye Roll.

- If you notice a drop of 2 or more points on the SUD scale, but you are still not at 0 or 1, administer the Booster Polarity Reversals shown later in the chapter and then repeat the sequence, beginning with Step 4. If this process doesn't get you to a 0 or 1, refer to the troubleshooting tips below under **"Stuck on the Scale?"** (p. 138).

- If you *do not* see a drop of 2 or more points, see **"Stuck on the Scale?"**

Step 8. Eye Roll, as shown in Chapter 5.

The Importance of Getting to Zero

How do you know if you've gotten to zero on the SUD scale? When you tune in to the problem, there is *no distress.* You are aware of the problem and are fully cognizant of the facts of the situation, but you feel no agitation or turmoil about it. There may still be practical matters in your life that need to be dealt with, but you are able to think about them without any worry or anxiety. In fact, you may be thinking more clearly about the problem for the first time and are now able to make better decisions. Your memory suddenly improves. Perhaps you notice a drop in physical tension; your face and shoulders feel more relaxed.

There is nothing magical about achieving a zero distress level on the SUD scale. But for those who have been suffering emotional upheaval and pain, it can certainly feel like magic. On a practical level, you can finish out the process at any level you choose. For some people, dropping from a level of 8, for example, to a 2 represents great success and relief, and they are satisfied to stop. Others stop because they feel that a 1 or a 2 represents an "appropriate" level of emotional distress, especially with regard to issues such as grief or guilt, and they elect to stop there. This was the case with Phil in Chapter 7, who wanted to stop at 1 on the SUDS so he would have a reminder of the pain he'd caused his wife and family.

However, we have noticed in our clinical practice that when the distress level is reduced to zero, it is less likely to recur. When the stress level is zero, it appears that all of the disturbance in the meridians that produced the emotional distress has been dissolved or eliminated.

As discussed in Chapter 6, habit patterns and ongoing stresses often will be provoked again and need to be retreated, although the distress level probably will not be as high the next time and often subsequent treatments will last longer. We'll talk more about maintenance in Chapter 12.

But What If You Run into Difficulty?

How do you know if the process is not working? The barometer of your progress is your own SUDS rating. If, when you recheck your SUDS level after the second Tap Sequence (Step 7), it hasn't changed or has not dropped more than two points, something is not working. In most cases, when you can't reduce your distress to 0 or 1, the correction is easily made. The two-pronged "decision tree" diagrams the possible detours on the way to getting to zero. The remedies are described after the box, under *"Stuck on the Scale?"*

Troubleshooting Decision Tree

Step 7. Recheck SUDS

If SUDS has dropped 2 points or more, but not to 0 or 1:

1. *Administer Booster Polarity Reversals* (below), then repeat from Step 4. If still not at 0 or 1, go to

2. *New aspect of the same emotion:* Refocus on new aspect of distress and repeat same protocol from step 4.

3. *Layered Problem.* Repeat from Step 4, using Tap Sequence for new emotion. If still not at 0 or 1, try

4. *Comprehensive Sequence.* Repeat from Step 4, using Tap Sequence in Protocol #5.

If SUDS has not changed, or change is less than 2 points:

1. *Wrong Tap Sequence.* Tune in, identify the problem. Repeat from Step 4, using Tap Sequence for correct emotion. If still no change, go to

2. *Polarity Disorganization.* Do Five-Step Breathing exercise (in Chapter 10); repeat from Step 3. If still no change, go to

3. *Special Polarity Reversal.* Identify and administer special reversal; repeat from Step 4.

Stuck on the Scale?

If the 0 to 10 level of distress has dropped more than 2 points, but you're stuck there:

A drop of 2 or more points on the SUDS means that *something* is working, but the fact that it hasn't dropped to a 0 or 1 also indicates that something else is blocking the full effectiveness of the treatment. If the distress level has dropped by at least two points but has not fallen to the 0 or 1 level, there are four easily fixed possibilities.

1. *Booster Polarity Reversals.* This is the remedy of *first resort.* As its name implies, these add-on polarity reversals amplify, or "boost," the effec-

tiveness of the standard ones. In most cases, these booster reversals will eliminate any residual reversals, and help get you to 0, or to the level you want to be. There are two booster reversals:

Repeat three times while rubbing the Chest site: "I deeply and completely accept myself, even if I am not *completely* over this problem."

Repeat three times while tapping Under Nose: "I deeply and completely accept myself, even if I never get *completely* over this problem."

After administering the Booster Polarity Reversals, return to the protocol and repeat from Step 4.

2. *New aspect of the same emotion:* Don't give up too easily on the Tap Sequence you are using. Sometimes as we are treating an emotion, another aspect of the same problem comes up. Our grief over losing a job, for example, brings up grief over all the times we moved as a child. In such a situation, after first doing the Booster Polarity Reversal correction, focus your thoughts on the new aspect of the emotion and repeat the same Tap Sequence. Only if you still see no change in the level of distress should you move to Step 3.

3. *Layered Problems.* The third possible stumbling block is that, in clearing away your distress around one emotion, another has come to the surface. The layering of emotions was discussed in Chapter 6. One emotion can mask another the way that loud music masks a ringing telephone. At other times, our emotions don't interfere with each other or in any way overlap as we administer the treatments. Our sadness may not come up when we do the treatment for jealousy. Treating our eating habits may not bring up our fears of rejection. But when another emotion makes itself known in the midst of a treatment, we will not get complete relief from our distress until it is addressed, because in one way or another it is related to the original emotional distress.

To determine whether you have a layered problem, sit quietly and breathe calmly. Tune in to your thoughts again, and see if another feeling has surfaced. If you recognize a new aspect of your distress, turn to the protocol for the new emotion, evaluate your SUDS level for the new problem, and proceed through the new protocol, beginning with Step 3, polarity reversals. Treating for the new emotion should bring your distress level to the level you want. Of course, it is always possible that the distress level will not be erased completely, or will even *increase* because *yet another* emotion may surface and need to be treated.

4. If you get frustrated with peeling away layer after layer and still not getting to 0, or if you cannot seem to figure out what is causing your distress, try the long-winded but often effective Comprehensive Tap Sequence in Protocol #5, proceeding from Step 4. This sequence includes elements of many common and often overlapping emotions. The comprehensive sequence often does the trick when all else fails. If new emotions still arise, the sequence can be repeated.

If there is no change or if there is a drop of less than 2 points:

Any drop of less than 2 points on the 0 to 10 scale we consider "wishful thinking," probably due to your hopes and expectations rather than true relief. In such cases, the problem may be one of three things:

1. You are administering the wrong sequence. If you think this may be true, tune in to your feelings again and see if you have labeled the emotion correctly. If you suspect a different emotion is involved, use that new Tap Sequence and do the process again, beginning with Step 4. If you don't think you've mislabeled the emotion, the problem is likely to be due to the next item, polarity disorganization.

2. Polarity disorganization, in which polarity is absent or incoherent, is remedied by the Five-Step Breathing exercise in Chapter 10.

3. The least likely culprit is a special polarity reversal, an underlying negative polarity theme unique to you. The remedy for this problem is discussed under "Identifying and Treating Special Polarity Reversals," on page 142.

Tuning in the Thought Field

Don't worry about whether you are keeping your problem in mind every minute. Just tuning in to measure your distress level on the 0 to 10 scale and naming the problem during the Polarity Reversals exercise and the Tap Sequence will keep the thought field activated. On the other hand, it's best not to let your mind wander off to what you're going to be having for dinner.

Remember, it is not necessary to "relive" a painful or unpleasant experience in order to create a thought field while doing the ESM procedure. Often emotional pain has generalized in the system, and just one or two memories, or a naming of the issue, is sufficient to activate the thought field. The brain will have collected all of your experience on the same circuit.

It sometimes happens that a troubling emotion, which usually provokes a very high distress level, can be accessed only partially when the time comes to do the procedure. If you are unable to bring to mind the feelings that are troubling you or to muster up any distress as you administer the procedure, there is little for ESM to work on. Thought energy therapies operate on the emotional distress present at the time of treatment. If no distress is experienced, only intellectual awareness of the problem, there is essentially nothing to treat, no grist for the emotional management mill. It will be best to learn the protocol and wait to administer the treatment until a time when you are actively experiencing the distress. Occasionally this situation comes up with clients who have fears of driving or flying. While some phobic people are terrified by the mere sight or mention of the dreaded object, others have to be there to feel the fear.

> Henry was terrified of elevators. At home reading the newspaper or tinkering in his garage, thinking about riding in an elevator didn't distress him. Yet every day, as he entered the office building where he worked, he'd have a mini-anxiety attack just passing the elevators on the way to the stairwell and his sixteen-story walk-up. When we talked to Henry, we realized that he would need to treat his problem on-site, which would take a bit of creative problem solving. Tapping and talking his way through the protocol in the busy lobby would be embarrassing. (Of course he could treat himself for the embarrassment, but that's another matter.) What were his alternatives? He could arrange to be in the building late at night, when no one was around, to visit the elevator and bring up his fear. He might find a private place near the elevators, such as a rest room or stairwell, and administer the treatment there, or find other elevators that were more private.
>
> The option Henry chose was to administer the treatment in steps. He went to the office early, and did the Balanced Breathing exercise and the Polarity Reversals in his car before entering

the building. He walked in and saw the elevators but was calmer than usual from the procedures he'd just done: by his estimate, a 7 on the SUD scale. In the stairwell near the elevators, he administered the Tap Sequence, which he'd memorized. Henry was then calm enough to return to the lobby and ride the elevator to the sixteenth floor. Elated, he went directly to his private office, where he did the Bridge and again administered the Tap Sequence. Now his distress level was at a 2. Knowing that getting to 0 was his best guarantee that the problem would not return, Henry went through the Booster Polarity Reversals, and got his distress down to 0, before finishing with the Eye Roll. He checked out his success—and celebrated—by riding the elevator to the ground floor and back.

Custom Tailoring Intention Statements

You may find that when a Tap Sequence involves intention statements, none of the ones suggested feel right to you. The ones we have provided are the statements that we have found fit most situations. But if you feel some reservation about the wording of the statement, you can adjust it to make it more relevant to you. Ask yourself, "What would make that statement feel right for me?" or "What similar statement expresses the basic theme for me?"

For example, the standard intention statement in the love pain protocol is "I will love again" while tapping the Little Fingernail site. But Ray was still reeling from the shock of his wife's departure. In spite of their bitter and heartbreaking divorce, Ray was still in love with her. "I will love again" did not in any way resonate with Ray. He couldn't imagine falling in love with anyone else, ever. When he used the statement "I will get over this pain," he was able to move through the process in just a few minutes and erase his distress.

Identifying and Treating Special Polarity Reversals

In our practice, we have encountered a few instances where a powerful and very personal issue seems to sabotage the effectiveness of the treatment. One was a case in which a former minister could not get any relief until he acknowledged his spiritual guilt with the statement "I completely accept myself, even if God will not forgive me for getting divorced." Another man who came in because he said he wanted to stop drinking revealed, through muscle testing, that he didn't really want to quit. The statement "I deeply and completely accept myself, even if I don't have the desire to get over this problem" was able to override his unconscious resistance.

If you are stuck, ask yourself: "Are there any other aspects, themes, or perspectives on this problem that might be interfering?" Listen to your intuition for a reply. You might find "I really don't trust myself to get over this." Or "I'm going to feel deprived if I give up cigarettes."

To help you tune in to what might be blocking your progress, we present the following list of the special idiosyncratic reversals we have come across.

"I Deeply and Completely Accept Myself, Even If . . .

. . . I'll feel deprived if I get over this problem."

. . . I don't trust myself to get over this problem."

. . . I don't trust others to help me get over this problem."

. . . I'm too embarrassed to get over this problem."

. . . God will not forgive me for this problem."

. . . I cannot let this problem go."

. . . I don't have a right to get over this problem."

. . . it is not right for me to get over this problem."

. . . I'm afraid to get over this problem."

. . . I do not believe in this method of getting over this problem."

. . . I do not want this method to work."

. . . I do not have the intention of getting over this problem."

. . . this problem is too severe to get over."

. . . I'm not capable of getting over this problem."

. . . I am too angry/intolerant/guilty/unworthy (name your issue) to get over this problem."

If you identify a unique reversal, turn it into a statement. For example: "I deeply and completely accept myself, even if I don't trust myself to get over my jealousy." Repeat it three times while rubbing the NLR spot. Then return to the protocol, repeating the treatment from Step 4.

THE LAST TAP LESSON

Here are all the tap treatment points that you will use to administer the protocols. Most of these sites are bilateral, meaning that there is a tap site on either side of the body. For that matter, you can tap both sites at once, or switch from one side to the other. Locate each point on your body as you read through the descriptions. If you want to refresh your memory about tapping techniques, refer to Chapter 4, page 68.

Chest: This is the only site that employs *rubbing* instead of tapping. The Chest spot is located above the heart, about three inches off the center line of the body. It is sometimes referred to as the "sore spot," because in many people the spot is tender compared to the surrounding area. To locate the spot, probe in that vicinity until you feel a tender spot. Using two or three fingers, rub in a tight circular motion, about one revolution per second, outward toward your shoulder and down toward your heart. It is important to maintain a *firm* steady pressure as you rub, as if you were massaging oil deeply into that spot.

Eyebrow: The Eyebrow location is at the inside of the eyebrow, in a vertical line with the inner edge of the eye, close to the nose. It is best activated by tapping directly at the site with two fingers or by tapping with the flat of one finger across the bridge of the nose, covering the inner edges of both eyebrows.

Outside Eye: The Outside Eye location is on the bone of the eye socket at the outer edge of the eye, on a horizontal line with the pupil of the eye. Tap with one or two fingers.

Under Eye: The Under Eye spot is located at the bottom of the eye socket, in a direct line below the pupil of the eye. Because it is very close to the surface of the skin, it can be activated by tapping gently on the bony ridge beneath the eye with one or two fingers.

Under Nose: Tap with one or two fingers directly in the center between the nose and upper lip.

Under Lip: Tap with one or two fingers directly in the center on the chin just below the lower lip.

Collarbone: The Collarbone location is at the indentation where the collarbone joins the sternum, or breastbone. You can locate this spot by tracing along your collarbone from your shoulder inward toward the center of your body with your fingers, until you hit the hard downward angle at the juncture with the breastbone. If you press firmly at that spot, you will find a shallow spot or depression just below the junction of the collarbone and the breastbone. If you tap with all four fingers in that general vicinity, one of your fingers will always be activating the site.

Under Arm: The Under Arm location is on the side of the body about four inches below the armpit. It is best activated by tapping with all four fingers, using the opposite hand. Tapping also can be done with the hand on the same side by curving the fingers back and tapping with the backs of the fingers.

Side of Hand: Locate the Side-of-Hand spot by making a fist and noting where the palm creases on the side of your hand just below the knuckle of the little finger. It's the "karate chop" spot. The surest way to activate this spot is to do the tapping with the flat of all four fingers of the opposite hand.

Thumbnail: The Thumbnail site is located at the outside edge of your thumbnail (*not* the side that faces your index finger). Tapping with two fingers on the edge of the thumbnail seems to work best.

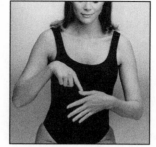

Index Fingernail: The Index Fingernail site is at the base of the fingernail of the index finger on the side nearest the thumb. Tap with the index finger or first two fingers of the opposite hand.

Middle Fingernail: The Middle Fingernail site is at the base of the fingernail of the middle finger on the side nearest the index finger. The site can be tapped with the index finger or first two fingers of the opposite hand.

Little Fingernail: The Little Fingernail location is at the base of the fingernail on the little finger on the edge closest to the ring finger. The site can be tapped with the index finger or the first two fingers of the opposite hand.

Back of Hand: To locate the Back-of-Hand spot, make a fist with one hand. On the back of your hand, locate the depression, or valley, between the knuckle of your pinky finger and the knuckle of your ring finger. Now trace back about an inch in the direction of your wrist in the valley formed between the tendons of your pinky and ring fingers on the back of your hand. This is the Back-of-Hand spot. Now that you've found it, you can release your fist.

To perform the Back-of-Hand Tap, use the flat of four fingers (that's how most people do it; you may feel more comfortable using fewer fingers) of your opposite hand and tap—or lightly slap—the Back-of-Hand spot.

Rib: There are two possible rib treatment sites. The first is directly below the nipple between the sixth and seventh ribs. On a woman, this would be about the place where the base of a bra touches the ribs. If the first site is uncomfortable to tap or difficult to access, tapping may be done on the side of the body, where the rib cage begins, at about the halfway point between the armpit and the level of the navel. This tap point is seldom used.

Prolonged Tapping: Back of Hand (50X)

In several Tap Sequences and procedures, you'll be directed to tap firmly approximately fifty times at the Back-of-Hand site. This treatment is part of the protocols for guilt, fatigue, loneliness, love pain, physical pain, regret, rejection, and sadness.

Other procedures call for you to tap *firmly* at a specified meridian site for pro-longed periods—approximately fifty times, or in some cases for as long as it takes to repeat an intention statement three times or to hold an image in mind. (See Chapter 11.) Continuous tapping seems to accelerate the development of a positive thought field associated with the goal and enhances the positive effect. About thirty seconds seems to be the optimum duration; tapping any longer doesn't seem to yield better results. In fact, there is a point of diminishing return; more tapping just slows down the process. It's a little like kneading dough. If you don't knead it enough, it won't rise well. But kneading the dough for hours doesn't make the bread rise faster or taste better. It merely takes longer to make it.

. . . .

Are you ready to tap into relief? You're finally there. Just turn the page.

NINE

The ESM Protocols

Full instructions and discussions of the procedures used in the protocols can be found on the following pages:

SUDS   page 102

Balanced Breathing Exercise   page 58

Polarity Reversal Exercise   page 70

Tap Sequence   page 144

When an asterisk ✳ appears, tap continuously at designated site while repeating the Intention Statement three times.

Bridge   page 92

Eye Roll   page 92

Protocol Reference List

1. Addictive Urges

2. Anger

3. Anticipatory Anxiety

4. Anxiety (Generalized or Free Floating)

Awkwardness: See Five-Step Breathing, page 183.

Bitterness: See Anger.

Chronic Pain: See Pain.

Clumsiness: See Five-Step Breathing, page 183.

5. Comprehensive Sequence—if all else fails

Compulsive Urges: See Addictive Urges.

Despair: See Grief.

Disappointment: See Frustration.

6. Disgust

7. Embarrassment

Envy. See Jealousy.

8. Fatigue

Fear. See Phobias.

9. Frustration

10. Grief

11. Guilt

Habits. See Addictive Urges.

Headache (Tension): See Pain.

Heartache: See Love Pain.

12. Hiccups

Hopelessness: See Grief.

Hurt Feelings: See Rejection.

Impatience: See Frustration.

Irritability: See Anxiety.

13. Jealousy

14. Jet Lag

15. Loneliness

16. Love Pain

17. Nasal Congestion

Negativity: See Balanced Breathing, page 58, and Polarity Reversals, page 61.

18. Obsessional Thinking

19. Pain

20. Phobias

21. Phobias, General

22. PMS Symptoms

23. Procrastination

24. Rage

25. Regret

26. Rejection

Remorse: See Guilt.

Resentment: See Anger

Revulsion: See Disgust.

Sadness: See Grief.

27. Shame

Sorrow: See Grief.

Stress: See Anxiety.

Tiredness: See Fatigue.

28. Trauma (Emotional)

Worry: See Anxiety.

1. Addictive Urges
(Compulsive Urges, Habits)

- Check SUDS

- Balanced Breathing

- Polarity Reversals

- Tap Sequence:

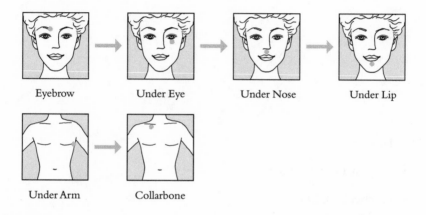

| Eyebrow | Under Eye | Under Nose | Under Lip |

| Under Arm | Collarbone |

- Bridge

- Repeat Tap Sequence

- Recheck SUDS

- Eye Roll

2. Anger

(Bitterness, Resentment)

- Check SUDS

- Balanced Breathing

- Polarity Reversals

- Tap Sequence:

Eyebrow   Little Fingernail   Collarbone

- Bridge

- Repeat Tap Sequence

- Recheck SUDS

- Eye Roll

INTENTION STATEMENT:

"I forgive them/him/her, because they didn't know how to do differently."

Alternatives:

"I forgive him/her but I do hold him/her accountable."

"I let go of this anger for my own well-being."

"There is forgiveness in my heart."

Choose a statement that fits the situation most closely or use a variation that feels appropriate to your situation.

3. Anticipatory Anxiety

- Check SUDS
- Balanced Breathing
- Polarity Reversals
- Tap Sequence:

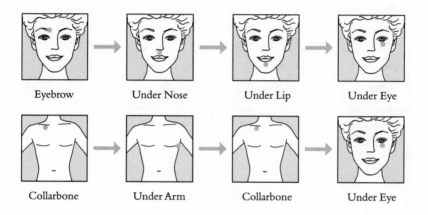

| Eyebrow | Under Nose | Under Lip | Under Eye |

| Collarbone | Under Arm | Collarbone | Under Eye |

- Bridge
- Repeat Tap Sequence
- Recheck SUDS
- Eye Roll

4. Anxiety, Generalized or Free Floating
(Irritability, Stress, Worry)

- Check SUDS

- Balanced Breathing

- Polarity Reversals

- Tap Sequence:

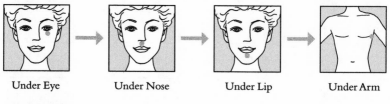

| Under Eye | Under Nose | Under Lip | Under Arm |

Collarbone

- Bridge

- Repeat Tap Sequence

- Recheck SUDS

- Eye Roll

5. Comprehensive Sequence—if all else fails

- Check SUDS
- Balanced Breathing
- Polarity Reversals
- Tap Sequence:

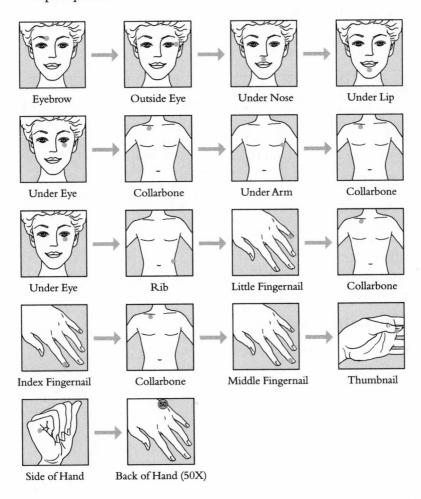

Eyebrow | Outside Eye | Under Nose | Under Lip

Under Eye | Collarbone | Under Arm | Collarbone

Under Eye | Rib | Little Fingernail | Collarbone

Index Fingernail | Collarbone | Middle Fingernail | Thumbnail

Side of Hand | Back of Hand (50X)

- Bridge
- Repeat Tap Sequence
- Recheck SUDS
- Eye Roll

6. Disgust
(Revulsion)

- Check SUDS

- Balanced Breathing

- Polarity Reversals

- Tap Sequence:

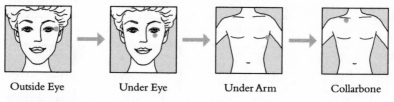

Outside Eye   Under Eye   Under Arm   Collarbone

Thumbnail

- Bridge

- Repeat Tap Sequence

- Recheck SUDS

- Eye Roll

7. Embarrassment

- Check SUDS

- Balanced Breathing

- Polarity Reversals

- Tap Sequence:

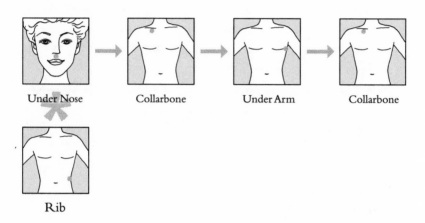

| Under Nose | Collarbone | Under Arm | Collarbone |

Rib

- Bridge

- Repeat Tap Sequence

- Recheck SUDS

- Eye Roll

*INTENTION STATEMENT:

"I release myself from this feeling."

Alternatives:

"I am relaxed and let go of the past."

"I am confident and calm."

Choose a statement that fits the situation most closely or use a variation that feels appropriate to your situation.

8. Fatigue
(Tiredness)

- Check SUDS
- Balanced Breathing
- Polarity Reversals
- Tap Sequence:

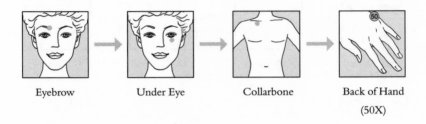

| Eyebrow | Under Eye | Collarbone | Back of Hand (50X) |

- Bridge
- Repeat Tap Sequence
- Recheck SUDS
- Eye Roll

9. Frustration
(Disappointment, Impatience)

- Check SUDS
- Balanced Breathing
- Polarity Reversals
- Tap Sequence:

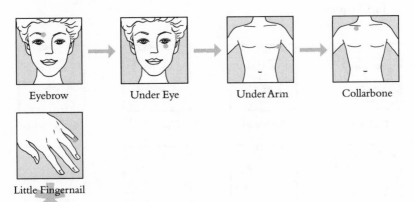

| Eyebrow | Under Eye | Under Arm | Collarbone |

Little Fingernail

- Bridge
- Repeat Tap Sequence
- Recheck SUDS
- Eye Roll

INTENTION STATEMENT:

"I let go of this frustration for my own well-being."

Alternatives:

"It really doesn't matter."

"I let go of my disappointment for my own well-being."

"I feel peace and tranquility."

"I feel balance and harmony."

"I can persevere and prevail."

Choose a statement that fits the situation most closely or use
a variation that feels appropriate to your situation.

10. Grief

(Despair, Hopelessness, Sadness, Sorrow)

- Check SUDS

- Balanced Breathing

- Polarity Reversals

- Tap Sequence:

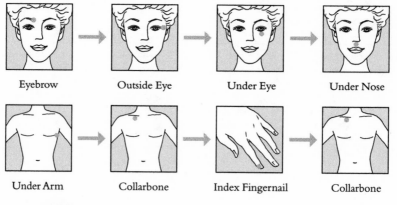

Eyebrow   Outside Eye   Under Eye   Under Nose

Under Arm   Collarbone   Index Fingernail   Collarbone

Back of Hand (50X)

- Bridge

- Repeat Tap Sequence

- Recheck SUDS

- Eye Roll

11. Guilt

(Remorse)

- Check SUDS
- Balanced Breathing
- Polarity Reversals
- Tap Sequence:

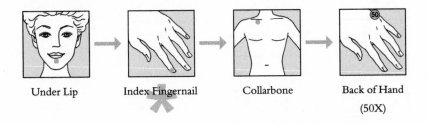

| Under Lip | Index Fingernail | Collarbone | Back of Hand (50X) |

- Bridge
- Repeat Tap Sequence
- Recheck SUDS
- Eye Roll

INTENTION STATEMENT:

"I forgive myself, I know that I could not have done differently."

Alternatives:

"I forgive myself, I did the best I could under the circumstances."

"I couldn't help it at the time."

"There is forgiveness in my heart for my own well-being."

Choose a statement that fits the situation most closely or use
a variation that feels appropriate to your situation.

12. Hiccups

- Balanced Breathing
- Polarity Reversals
- Tap Sequence:

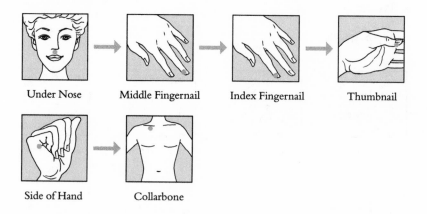

| Under Nose | Middle Fingernail | Index Fingernail | Thumbnail |

| Side of Hand | Collarbone |

- Bridge
- Repeat Tap Sequence
- Eye Roll

13. Jealousy
(Envy)

- Check SUDS

- Balanced Breathing

- Polarity Reversals

- Tap Sequence:

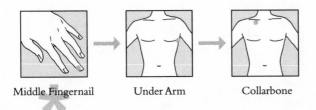

Middle Fingernail   Under Arm   Collarbone

- Bridge

- Repeat Tap Sequence

- Recheck SUDS

- Eye Roll

INTENTION STATEMENT:

"I am filled with peace and harmony."

Alternatives:

"I am generous and loving."

"I let go of the past."

Choose a statement that fits the situation most closely or use
a variation that feels appropriate to your situation.

14. Jet Lag

- Balanced Breathing
- Polarity Reversals
- Tap Sequence:

Going West:

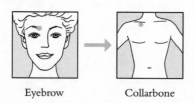

Eyebrow → Collarbone

Administer once per hour during flight.

Going East:

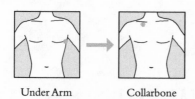

Under Arm → Collarbone

Administer once per hour during flight.

- Bridge
- Repeat Tap Sequence
- Eye Roll

15. Loneliness

- Check SUDS
- Balanced Breathing
- Polarity Reversals
- Tap Sequence:

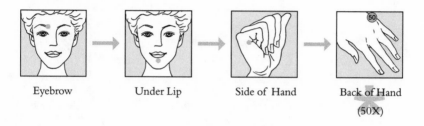

| Eyebrow | Under Lip | Side of Hand | Back of Hand (50X) |

- Bridge
- Repeat Tap Sequence
- Recheck SUDS
- Eye Roll

* INTENTION STATEMENT:

"I am comfortable with myself and others."

Alternatives:

"I am buoyant with hope."

"There is lightness in my soul."

Choose a statement that fits the situation most closely or use a variation that feels appropriate to your situation.

16. Love Pain
(Heartache)

- Check SUDS
- Balanced Breathing
- Polarity Reversals
- Tap Sequence:

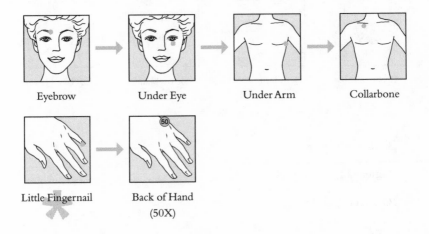

| Eyebrow | Under Eye | Under Arm | Collarbone |

| Little Fingernail | Back of Hand (50X) |

- Bridge
- Repeat Tap Sequence
- Recheck SUDS
- Eye Roll

INTENTION STATEMENT:

"I will love again."

Alternatives:

"I release the past."

"There is forgiveness in my heart."

"My heart is filled with hope."

Choose a statement that fits the situation most closely or use a variation that feels appropriate to your situation.

17. Nasal Congestion

- Balanced Breathing
- Polarity Reversals
- Tap Sequence:

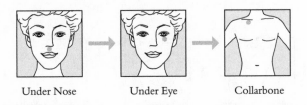

Under Nose   Under Eye   Collarbone

- Bridge
- Repeat Tap Sequence
- Eye Roll

18. Obsessional Thinking

- Check SUDS

- Balanced Breathing

- Polarity Reversals

- Tap Sequence:

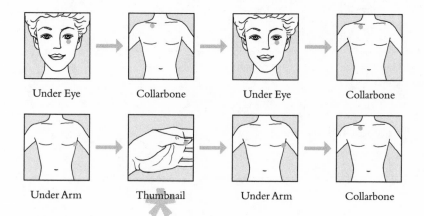

| Under Eye | Collarbone | Under Eye | Collarbone |

| Under Arm | Thumbnail | Under Arm | Collarbone |

- Bridge

- Repeat Tap Sequence

- Recheck SUDS

- Eye Roll

INTENTION STATEMENT:

"I release these thoughts for my own well-being."

Alternatives:

"My mind is calm and relaxed."

"I am at peace with myself and others."

"I renounce the past."

Choose a statement that fits the situation most closely or use
a variation that feels appropriate to your situation.

19. Pain
(Chronic Pain, Tension Headache)

- Check SUDS
- Balanced Breathing
- Polarity Reversals
- Tap Sequence:

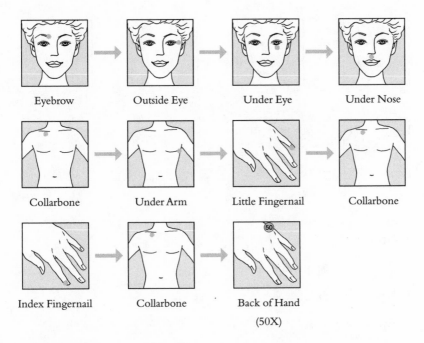

Eyebrow	Outside Eye	Under Eye	Under Nose
Collarbone	Under Arm	Little Fingernail	Collarbone
Index Fingernail	Collarbone	Back of Hand (50X)	

- Bridge
- Repeat Tap Sequence
- Recheck SUDS
- Eye Roll

20. Phobias

(Spiders, Claustrophobia, Air Turbulence)

- Check SUDS

- Balanced Breathing

- Polarity Reversals

- Tap Sequence:

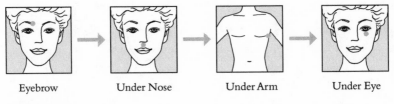

| Eyebrow | Under Nose | Under Arm | Under Eye |

Collarbone

- Bridge

- Repeat Tap Sequence

- Recheck SUDS

- Eye Roll

21. Phobias, General
(Fear)

- Check SUDS

- Balanced Breathing

- Polarity Reversals

- Tap Sequence:

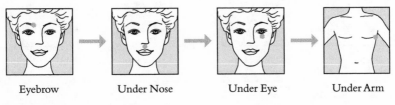

Eyebrow   Under Nose   Under Eye   Under Arm

Collarbone

- Bridge

- Repeat Tap Sequence

- Recheck SUDS

- Eye Roll

22. PMS Symptoms

- Check SUDS

- Balanced Breathing

- Polarity Reversals

- Tap Sequence:

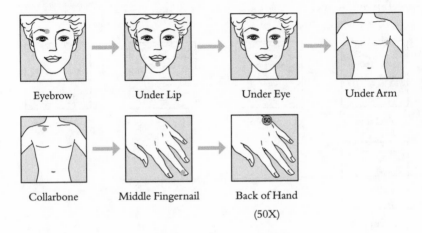

| Eyebrow | Under Lip | Under Eye | Under Arm |

| Collarbone | Middle Fingernail | Back of Hand (50X) |

- Bridge

- Repeat Tap Sequence

- Recheck SUDS

- Eye Roll

23. Procrastination

- Check SUDS

- Balanced Breathing

- Polarity Reversals

- Tap Sequence:

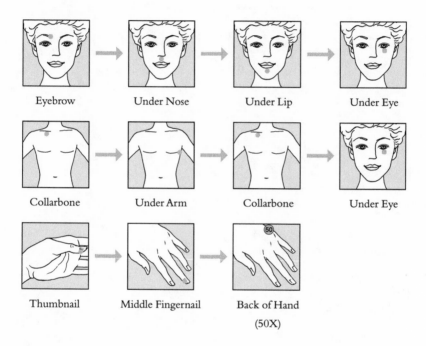

| Eyebrow | Under Nose | Under Lip | Under Eye |

| Collarbone | Under Arm | Collarbone | Under Eye |

| Thumbnail | Middle Fingernail | Back of Hand (50X) |

- Bridge

- Repeat Tap Sequence

- Recheck SUDS

- Eye Roll

24. Rage

- Check SUDS

- Balanced Breathing

- Polarity Reversals

- Tap Sequence:

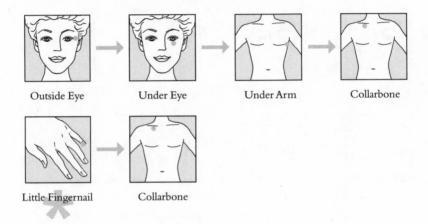

| Outside Eye | Under Eye | Under Arm | Collarbone |

Little Fingernail | Collarbone

Bridge

- Repeat Tap Sequence

- Recheck SUDS

- Eye Roll

✳INTENTION STATEMENT:

"There is forgiveness in my heart for my own self-control and peace."

Alternatives:

"I am at peace and in control."

"Reason and wisdom are within me."

Choose a statement that fits the situation most closely or use
a variation that feels appropriate to your situation.

25. Regret

- Check SUDS
- Balanced Breathing
- Polarity Reversals
- Tap Sequence:

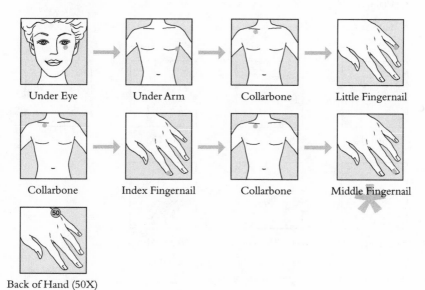

| Under Eye | Under Arm | Collarbone | Little Fingernail |

| Collarbone | Index Fingernail | Collarbone | Middle Fingernail |

Back of Hand (50X)

- Bridge
- Repeat Tap Sequence
- Recheck SUDS
- Eye Roll

INTENTION STATEMENT:

"I release the past, I did the best I could under the circumstances."

Alternatives:

"I release the past, I did not know then what I know now."

"My focus is on my life ahead."

Choose a statement that fits the situation most closely or use
a variation that feels appropriate to your situation.

26. Rejection
(Hurt Feelings)

- Check SUDS
- Balanced Breathing
- Polarity Reversals
- Tap Sequence:

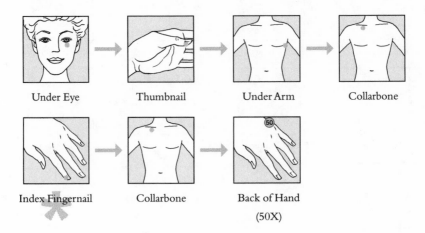

| Under Eye | Thumbnail | Under Arm | Collarbone |

| Index Fingernail | Collarbone | Back of Hand (50X) |

- Bridge
- Repeat Tap Sequence
- Recheck SUDS
- Eye Roll

INTENTION STATEMENT:

"I deeply accept myself and remain open to new possibilities."

Alternatives:

"I am worthy of love and affection."

"I am confident in my personal powers."

"I have good fortune and peace within."

Choose a statement that fits the situation most closely or use
a variation that feels appropriate to your situation.

27. Shame

- Check SUDS

- Balanced Breathing

- Polarity Reversals

- Tap Sequence:

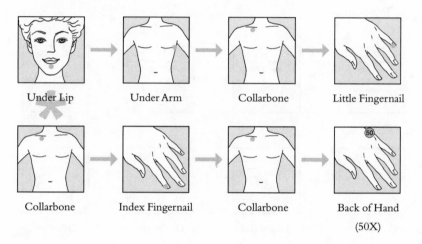

| Under Lip | Under Arm | Collarbone | Little Fingernail |

| Collarbone | Index Fingernail | Collarbone | Back of Hand (50X) |

- Bridge

- Repeat Tap Sequence

- Recheck SUDS

- Eye Roll

INTENTION STATEMENT:

"I deeply and profoundly forgive myself and others, and I accept a new beginning."

Alternatives:

"I am a unique human being."

"I hold serenity within me and I look ahead in my life."

Choose a statement that fits the situation most closely or use a variation that feels appropriate to your situation.

28. Trauma
(Emotional)

- Check SUDS

- Balanced Breathing

- Polarity Reversals

- Tap Sequence:

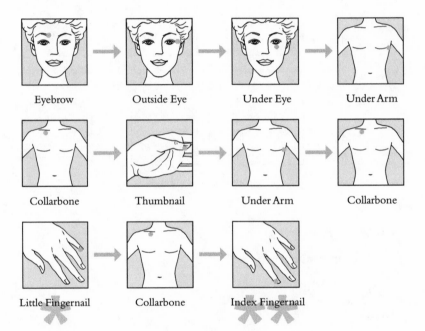

Eyebrow	Outside Eye	Under Eye	Under Arm
Collarbone	Thumbnail	Under Arm	Collarbone
Little Fingernail	Collarbone	Index Fingernail	

- Bridge

- Repeat Tap Sequence

- Recheck SUDS

- Eye Roll

* INTENTION STATEMENT — ANGER:

"I forgive them/him/her, because they could not have done differently."

Alternatives:

"I forgive him/her but I do hold him/her accountable."

"I let go of this anger for my own well-being."

"There is forgiveness in my heart."

** INTENTION STATEMENT — GUILT:

"I forgive myself, I know that I could not have done differently."

Alternatives:

"I forgive myself, I did the best I could under the circumstances."

"I couldn't help it at the time."

"There is forgiveness in my heart for my own well-being."

Choose a statement that fits the situation most closely or use a variation that feels appropriate to your situation.

Haywire

Correcting Polarity Disorganization

Success with ESM protocols assumes that the body's electrical energy and other energy systems are properly polarized. The Balanced Breathing and Polarity Reversal exercise at the beginning of each protocol ensure that both the polarity of the body and thoughts are properly aligned.

If you have tried the standard remedies outlined in Chapter 8 and have been unable to get any significant reduction in your distress level, you are probably in that small percentage of people who are dealing with a phenomenon called polarity disorganization. With polarity disorganization, *there is no detectable polarity.* So there is nothing to reverse, or to put right. Picture a supermarket parking lot with no painted lines, so the cars are parked every which way—a real mess. This is what seems to happen with some people's electromagnetic energy. When the electromagnetic energy goes haywire, treatment progress is at a standstill. Because polarity disorganization affects the polarity of the whole system, nothing we do to treat for emotional distress will work in the presence of this problem. Before we can even address any reversals, we have to get those cars lined up.

There is a hierarchy of ways in which emotional disturbances can manifest. First, an intense emotional experience by itself can persist long after the incident that provoked it has passed. Reversals in polarity of the body or of thought energy can be responsible for the looping of emotional circuits and for the interruption of the body's natural mechanisms for dissipating emotional distress. Polarity disorganization is a more complicated and serious disruption of the system and can itself spawn polarity reversals. Polarity disorganization may be traceable to energy toxins, such as electromagnetic radiation or an allergen, which block any attempt to treat the fundamental problem. While all the causes of polarity disorganization are not known, it can be corrected.

Five-Step Breathing: The Remedy for Polarity Disorganization

Before you conclude that Emotional Self-Management techniques are not working for you, we encourage you to do the Five-Step Breathing exercise outlined next. But first, drink a large glass of water. As electrical beings, we require a lot of water for our wiring to function properly. The electrochemical processes in our bodies depend on water to provide a medium for electrical conductivity. Just as your car battery needs water in order to be able to accept a charge, and will short out without it, the human body will have a similar reaction without adequate water. Water facilitates the body's electrolyte balance for optimal chemical and cellular functioning, and it also amplifies the electrical signals sent by the tapping. Whereas most people are sufficiently hydrated, for a rare few, drinking water seems to help.

Dr. Roger Callahan developed the correction for polarity disorganization that we call the Five-Step Breathing exercise. This method uses what behavioral kinesiology calls the "brain buttons." These "brain buttons" are the two Collarbone sites, which stimulate a meridian circuit and stimulate the carotid arteries to provide oxygen-rich blood to the brain.

Breathing provides a method for internal regulation and has long been recognized as a stabilizing process in the fight-or-flight response. Dr. Herbert Benson demonstrated how specific breathing exercises can reverse the "adrenaline response" and move the body in the direction of the "relaxation response," restoring calm and composure. Certain forms of slow, deep breathing have something of a cascade effect. The chain of events precipitated by sustained relaxation breathing may include most aspects of the autonomic nervous system that control automatically regulated body functions. Most of the symptoms reflective of emotion are created through various operations of the autonomic nervous system.

At the bioelectrical energy level, our breathing is one intimate connection with our "energy atmosphere," in the sense of sharing molecules and atoms and subatomic particles with our entire planet. The vital life forces, according to Eastern Ayurvedic philosophy, enter and exit our body through breathing.

The structured breathing of the Five-Step Breathing exercise, in some ways like the Balanced Breathing exercise, utilizes principles of yoga and meditation to stimulate vital life forces. As author and psychologist Dorothea Hover-Kramer, Ed.D., states, "When we work with the breath, we are working with our life force, our energy. Therefore, focusing on the breath produces a relaxed state, providing a direct experience of the unceasing flow of energy in the body." This five-step treatment involves crossing the center line of the body with alternating hands while tapping the Back-of-Hand spot and following a specific breathing sequence. It serves to reestablish the absent or disorganized electromagnetic polarity and to properly polarize the electromagnetic flows in the body, restoring a proper balance to its organization.

In our clinical practice, we have seen how polarity disorganization, whatever the source, interferes not only with ESM treatments but with hypnosis, EMDR treatments, and cognitive and other therapies. The Five-Step Breathing exercise is a potent process for organizing the body's electromagnetic energy, at least long enough for the ESM protocol to work. If polarity disorganization is preventing a treatment from working, and the emotional distress is related to the past, do the Five-Step Breathing and then treat for the problem. You will get relief, and even if your polarity becomes disorganized again, the odds are that it will not cause the old problem to resurface, and the effect will hold. But if the issue is an ongoing source of stress, or if your polarity goes haywire again, the emotional distress may return and require a readministration of the Five-Step Breathing exercise. This situation often occurs with problems such as addictive urges for cigarettes, foods, or other substances, where something in the ingested item acts as an *energy toxin,* such as the nicotine in cigarettes, some artificial sweeteners and preservatives, or high levels of refined sugar. It may take a period of abstinence before the substance is metabolized out of the body and its toxic effects have ceased. More about energy toxins at the end of the chapter.

THE FIVE-STEP BREATHING EXERCISE

The Five-Step Breathing procedure only takes a few minutes, but its effect is powerful. Although it is a bit intricate, it is not difficult to learn. It entails doing a five-step breathing technique eight times, each time holding one hand or the other in different positions on the Collarbone sites while continuously tapping the Back-of-Hand spot with the opposite hand.

If this seems confusing, it may help to think about it in terms of polarity. What's happening with this exercise is that you are generating polarity continuity, by first holding the palm side of the fingers (we'll call that the south pole) to the Collarbone spot, and then touching the back of the fingers (the north pole) to the Collarbone spot. The best way to accomplish touching the back of your fingers to the Collarbone site is to make a fist with your thumb tucked inside or alongside your index finger.

Let's look at the breathing procedure first. Here are the five steps of the breathing process:

1. Take a deep breath and hold it for five seconds.

2. Exhale *half* of the breath and hold for five seconds.

3. Exhale completely and hold for five seconds.

4. Inhale *halfway* and hold for five seconds.

5. Breathe normally for about five seconds.

Note: *Half breaths in or out are approximate; there is no precise halfway point.*

Here are the eight hand positions. Remember, in each position you will do a complete cycle of Five-Step Breathing while continuously tapping the Back-of-Hand spot with the opposite hand.

1. Palm side of the right hand touching the right Collarbone spot.

2. Palm side of the right hand touching the left Collarbone spot.

3. Backside (make a fist) of the right-hand fingers touching the right Collarbone spot.

4. Backside of the right-hand fingers touching the left Collarbone spot.

5. Palm side of the left hand touching the right Collarbone spot. *Switch hands.*

6. Palm side of the left hand touching the left Collarbone spot.

7. Backside of the left-hand fingers touching the right Collarbone spot.

8. Backside of the left-hand fingers touching the left Collarbone spot.

Practice suggestions: In order to become comfortable with the procedure:

a. Practice just the Five-Step Breathing sequence until you can do it comfortably.

b. Then practice going through the eight hand positions to become familiar with them.

c. Finally, add the continuous tapping on the Back-of-Hand spot with the opposite hand.

The first time you try it, do the whole procedure very slowly, so that you feel confident and relaxed. In subsequent applications, you can move as quickly as feels comfortable for you. Pretty soon the whole process will take three to five minutes.

. . . .

The Five-Step Breathing exercise often leaves people feeling relaxed, perhaps even sleepy. It's not just boredom; it's the effects of establishing general body polarity. Once you have completed the procedure, return to the protocol you were struggling with and repeat the process from Step 3, correcting for polarity reversals. You should now be able to reduce your distress to the desired level.

If the Five-Step Breathing exercise does not correct the problem, then it is likely that an energy toxin is at work.

Energy Toxins

Energy toxins can take many forms: electromagnetic radiation, chemicals such as pesticides and solvents, food additives and even certain foods, profoundly stressful circumstances, and the proximity of others with disorganized polarity. Not all people are affected by these factors in the same way. While most people are susceptible to the effects of electromagnetic radiation and insecticides, what acts as an energy toxin for one person may have no effect on another. These toxins can exist below the threshold of provoking a physiological allergic reaction yet can totally disrupt the body's electromagnetic energy system, and can themselves be the cause of polarity disorganization. The Five-Step Breathing exercise often offsets the effects of the toxin long enough to have time to administer the emotion-specific protocol and to have the treatment hold.

Electromagnetic radiation is a toxin that affects many people, although studies to this point have shown only weak correlations between electromagnetic radiation and disease processes such as cancers. But no study has been under way long enough to evaluate long-term effects for physical illness. It is difficult to measure the effects of electromagnetic fields because there is no reliable way to get a control sample. Almost all of us are exposed to some level of electromagnetic contamination—in the environment, and through our proximity to the gadgets of modern life: computers, cell phones, microwave ovens. The spike in the electromagnetic field at high power lines or near microwave or radio transmitters is often the focus of study.

When energy toxins are present in your environment but are not related to a substance you are discontinuing, professional treatment for the toxicity may be necessary. Qualified professionals often can identify energy toxins and treat them using thought energy therapy techniques. In our clinical practice, we identify and treat the toxin itself as a problem, just as we would treat anger or fear. In most cases, once it is treated, the substance is no longer a toxin to the system. But the diagnostic and treatment process is quite complex, involving muscle testing, holding the toxic substance against certain points in the body while tapping, and other procedures. In situations where even this treatment is not successful, Total Body Modification (TBM) can resolve these problems. A homeopathic or naturopathic practitioner in your area can locate a TBM specialist for you. Specialists in the diagnosis and treatment of energy toxins also are listed in the Resources appendix.

PART IV

Maintaining and Optimizing ESM's Benefits

ELEVEN

Performance and Productivity

The Bonus Round

Up to this point you have been using Emotional Self-Management techniques to eliminate long-standing emotional problems, or to manage ongoing stresses. But the absence or minimizing of stress is not the final destination of ESM. The goal is to be happy, to feel confident, productive, and fulfilled. In the words of author Joseph Campbell, its goal is to enable you "to follow your bliss." Now that you've had some practice with going from 10 to 0 on the distress scale, we're going to show you how to use ESM techniques to go from 0 to 10 on the plus side. ESM procedures can work wonders to boost your motivation and confidence and open pathways to more fun and enjoyment of life. If the treatment protocols for emotional distress are like fixing a short circuit in a battery, then installing positive thoughts about your goals can be compared to putting in a full charge.

Sometimes we can become so emotionally distressed that just feeling OK, not distraught or frightened, is all we imagine or hope for. Desperate for relief, we are content when ESM helps us merely to manage our unhappiness. The idea that we might actively pursue our dreams and feel good about ourselves and our accomplishments may at first seem too much to ask. But now that you have moved from negative to neutral, this chapter will show you how to shift into forward gear with the three-phase Optimizer Protocol to achieve your goals and dreams. *This is the bonus round.*

Do you recall Suzanne, from the introduction, who, among many other things, was terrified of driving on the freeway? She is a good example of the way that ESM can be applied to performance and productivity. In our session, we first worked to get her anxiety down to a zero, so that she would be able to negotiate the freeway. But then I encouraged her to take the next step— to install the positive cognition that "I enjoy driving on the freeway." She thought I had rocks in my head when I said, "Let's not just neutralize this, let's install the positive thought." I told her to call me when she got home to let me know what happened. Well, what she told me was that she was *delighted* to be driving on the freeway. She was still laughing when she called, in spite of her mystification.

What's Holding You Back?

Are you as successful and productive as you would like to be? Are you confident of your abilities at home and work, in your social life or on the playing field? Are you motivated to grow and learn and use all your skills and abilities? If not, what is holding you back? Jack Nicklaus has written that 90 percent of being a golf champion is mental. Since ESM theory says that thoughts and emotions are intertwined, our feelings regarding performance and productivity are also candidates for Emotional Self-Management.

Issues of performance and productivity come up in all areas of life. Some people want to be better partners or parents, or want to develop their effectiveness as leaders in their community, church, school, or service organization. Others desire to improve their tennis game or to make the Olympic team. The issue might be public speaking, or taking tests, or feeling more comfortable at parties. Who among us, at one time or another, has not procrastinated, or shied away from challenges that might end in failure, or berated ourselves for our shortcomings? Who among us doesn't have something holding us back from achieving our dreams? In other words, who doesn't have room for improvement in one or another area of life?

What stands in the way of achieving our goals? In the most general terms, stress. Dr. Daniel Goleman, whose work on emotional intelligence was discussed in Chapter 5, reports that in 126 studies involving 36,000 people, it was shown that as a person's worry increases, academic performance decreases, as reflected in test grades, grade-point averages, and other measures of performance. In other words, anxiety degrades performance.

Most of the impediments to our optimum performance in work, recreation, or athletics are rooted in anxiety. Mental tension and anxiety can cause loss of concentration, memory lapses, fuzzy thinking, and impaired motor skills. Stress may show up as procrastination or lack of confidence or motiva-

tion, as writer's block or test anxiety or any number of thinly disguised variations of self-sabotage. Much distress is based on fear. An athlete who has done
poorly on her last couple of outings loses confidence in her ability to do well
the next time. Or she is frustrated and angry with herself. Someone who is
terrified of failure finds it hard to muster the motivation to try again. Fear of
failure is often behind procrastination and the kind of perfectionism that keeps
us from getting our work done.

Most of us are familiar with the fear of failure. We are afraid of trying
something that carries too great a risk of our *not* reaching our goal. Not trying becomes a safe haven from the pain and shame of mistakes. Of course,
not trying also means giving up the possibility of reaching beyond our comfort zone toward the rewards that come with facing our hobgoblins. More-
over, the fears and anxiety we hope to avoid don't really go away; they just
lie in wait, continuing to fester—until the next challenge arises.

Benevolent Stress

Not all stress is bad. The term "eustress," literally "good stress," refers to the
kind of motivating energy that fuels our activities in a positive way. Nervous
excitement about an upcoming vacation or job promotion is an example of
positive stress.

There is a complex relationship between performance/learning and stress
or anxiety. The optimum level of stress depends on the nature of the task at
hand and the temperament of the individual performing it. Generally, moderate levels of stress tend to produce the best performance. At the low end of
the stress curve a person is underactivated, similar to a speaker whose presentation is flat and emotionless. At the other end of the spectrum, overactivated
stress responses can lead to paralysis, such as stage fright and the tightness a
golfer might experience in an important tournament.

Performance enhancement is not always about resurrecting oneself from
a slump or fighting the demons of fear or procrastination. It is a powerful
tool for high-level achievers who want to do even better, as Ellen's story
demonstrates.

> A capable and confident project manager for a large defense con-
> tractor, Ellen came to us for what she called "risk management."
> Having come up with an innovative solution to one of her firm's
> long-standing challenges, Ellen was now on the high-level team

presenting the new concept. She'd been given the responsibility for facilitating the meeting and introducing her idea.

There seemed to be very little on the negative side for Ellen. Whatever anxiety she had seemed to be productive in nature, keeping her motivated and enthused. Her one fear was of something unforeseen that might interrupt or spoil the presentation. Ellen knew that her fear was largely irrational and that even the worst-case scenario—a failure of the projection equipment or sound system—would not be catastrophic, merely annoying.

We targeted Ellen's fear and got it down from a 5 to a 0 on the 0 to 10 scale of distress. We came up with this positive statement in the second phase of the process: "I am confident, composed, and enthusiastic about this presentation under any circumstances." In a short time, Ellen's belief in her goal statement went from a +6 to a +10 on the Validity of Cognition (VOC) scale. In the final phase, Ellen imagined herself, in great detail, making her presentation. She pictured herself standing at the head of the meeting room, easily answering questions, moving through the slides and charts in the most confident and convincing way.

Ellen left the office feeling terrific, promising to call after her meeting the following week. But I didn't get her report until three months later. "The presentation went extremely well," she said. "I felt great, and the vice president complimented me on a wonderful job immediately afterward. I apologize for not calling sooner. But it felt to me like the real test was whether we got the contract or not. With the government you're dealing with a lot of contractual constipation, and I didn't get the results until this week. We secured a multimillion-dollar contract, and I know that the work we did together contributed to the job I did. I make it a point to recommend your risk management procedures to all my colleagues. Thanks."

The Optimizer Protocol

The purpose of the ESM performance and productivity protocol is to short-circuit negative beliefs and install positive and optimistic cognitions about our goals and dreams. It allows us to replace fears and doubts about ourselves with an optimistic and productive way of thinking about what we hope to accomplish. In this process, we internalize realistic self-concepts in a particular area of our lives.

There is power in discovering that you have the ability to take charge of your life. The Optimizer Protocol will provide the momentum for you to cross the river of avoidance, procrastination, and other defenses and reach the destination you seek.

All issues having to do with performance and productivity, whether winning a race, giving a speech, passing a test, or writing a weekly report, follow the same three-phase protocol. Our colleague, psychologist Greg Nicosia, made invaluable contributions to the performance enhancement applications used in Emotional Self-Management. We greatly appreciate his creative inspiration and assistance.

Here is a capsule description of the Optimizer process:

1. Phase 1 is very similar to what you have already been doing. The first step is to identify the negative thoughts and emotions that keep you from attaining the goal or desire you're struggling with. Then you address the underlying negative feelings and beliefs using the pertinent emotion-specific protocols (the whole procedure, including Balanced Breathing and polarity reversals) until you've reduced your stress around that issue as close as possible to zero. In most cases of underperformance and underproductivity, the underlying emotions are fear and anxiety, frustration, and disappointment.

2. The whole performance and productivity process is focused on goal-setting. In Phase 2 you clearly define your goal and state it as a positive thought. Then you rate your level of belief in that thought on the Validity of Cognition (VOC) scale. Next you do a variation of the Polarity Reversal exercise that addresses your doubts about reaching your goal. You follow with a sequence of continuous tapping at each of four sites, as you verbalize your positive statement three times. You'll continue with this process, working through any problems that come up until you get to a +10 on the VOC scale, or very close to it.

3. You begin Phase 3 by coming up with mental images of yourself in the process of accomplishing, or having reached, your goal and then rating your belief in those images on a scale similar to the VOC scale in Phase 2, which we call the Validity of Imagery (VOI) scale. The next step is another round of polarity reversals similar to those in Phase 2. These are followed by a sequence of prolonged tapping at three sites for about thirty seconds each, while you hold in mind images of

achieving your goal, again until you have gotten to a level of +10 on the VOI scale.

The Optimizer in Action

We'll use the following story about Ron to illustrate the procedures and expand on the fine points of the Optimizer Protocol.

Ron is a retired business executive with a passion for golf. But by the time he showed up in our office, his once-beloved golf outings had turned into a kind of self-torture. Every time he went out on the course lately, he'd play worse than the time before, and he'd go home feeling tense and discouraged. He was not terribly optimistic about getting help from this odd process. "What can you possibly do for me, Doc?" he asked in a tone that belied his low expectations.

1. *Phase 1:* The first step was to see what feelings and beliefs were undermining Ron's desire to play golf at the highest level possible. He described himself as distressed and discouraged, but most of all frustrated. "I just can't seem to get in a groove," he complained. "There's no consistency. One minute I slice, then I shank the next shot. I'm in the rough or the woods on every other hole. With every move I make, there's a little voice in there telling me how stupid and inept I am." Ron was in a lather of self-criticism, and claimed his distress was a 12 on the 0 to 10 point distress scale.

The Balanced Breathing exercise seemed to relax him a bit, and we began to correct for polarity reversals. Before we could even get started, his skepticism had him asking endless questions. What was the point of the exercise? Why did he have to say things about safety that made no sense to him? Finally he calmed down enough to go through the process, as he kept in mind the negative thoughts and feelings about himself. As is often the case with performance and productivity issues, just doing the Polarity Reversal exercise had a noticeable effect in clearing out the underlying negative emotions and thoughts.

At that moment, Ron's primary feeling was one of anxiety about his game and even anxiety about sitting in my office working on the problem. So we targeted his anxiety first. When his distress level wouldn't come down below a 6, I had him tune in to see if there were any other emotions interfering with getting to 0. Now he reported feeling frustrated that nothing he did seemed to get his game out of the doldrums. We next did the Tap Sequence for frustration, and his distress level went down a few more points. But something still seemed to be in the way. He was stuck at a 3 on the SUD scale. I again asked him to tune in to see if there was yet another layer of emotion. "Disappointment," he admitted. "I'm very disappointed in myself." Looking closer at his feelings of disappointment, his distress level rose to a 5. After doing a sequence for disappointment, Ron's distress level finally fell to 0. We closed the procedure with an Eye Roll. I could see that Ron was gaining confidence in the methods. We were ready to move over to the plus side and install a positive cognition about his golf game.

2. *Phase 2:* Now the task for Ron was to clarify his goal and to phrase that goal as a positive statement. Ron spent a few minutes reflecting about what he really wanted with regard to golf. Closing his eyes and recalling how he had once enjoyed the game was helpful. Ron offered that it wasn't about winning tournaments, but he did want to improve his score on his home course. Then he realized he didn't even really care too much about how he played compared to his golfing buddies. To help him clarify his objectives, I asked Ron, "How would you like to feel about playing golf? What exactly would you like to accomplish with your golf game?" Ron replied that he wanted not to feel so worried and anxious before he went out to play and not to feel so frustrated every time he made a bad shot. We worked on forming the statement to be positive rather than "not" something. "I'd like to feel like I once did about golf, having fun, playing my best, and being more confident about my game," he finally said.

After running through a number of possible statements and weeding out negative language, Ron settled on the active and positively worded goal statement "I'm relaxed, confident, and I enjoy the game." Now that Ron's goal was clearly articulated and in the present tense, Ron rated his belief in the statement on the VOC scale. He gave it a +1 on a scale of 0 to +10, indicating that he didn't believe his goal statement, but that he was willing to consider it a possibility. We did the Balanced Breathing exercise again and the exercise to correct polarity reversals. This time around Ron adapted the wording of the Intention Statements as he went through the reversals, to acknowledge the underlying doubt and disbelief he had about his stated goal. Now Ron went through the Tap Sequence for installing his positive statement: Eyebrow, Under Nose, Under Lip, Middle Fingernail. As he tapped continuously, Ron repeated his goal statement three times at each site. "I'm relaxed, confident, and I enjoy the game." Then Ron did the Bridge and repeated the Tap Sequence, after which he again evaluated the VOC level of his statement. This time it was +8. By this time Ron was enthusiastic about his progress. He felt good and wanted to continue on to see if we could get to a +10. The booster polarity reversal "I totally and completely accept my-self even if I don't want to *completely* believe this statement," while rubbing the Chest spot, did the trick for Ron. After finishing out Phase 2 with an Eye Roll, Ron was a +10 on the VOC.

3. *Phase 3:* This stage amplifies and integrates the effect of the new cognition by installing an internal picture of the desired goal, which for Ron meant imagining himself in the act of playing well and enjoying himself both on the course and afterward, regardless of his score. Again we corrected for polarity reversals (using an-other variation, with minor changes in the wording, see page 208). Then I encouraged Ron to bring to mind as vivid a picture as possible of his playing golf and enjoying himself, one that in-volved all his senses. In his case this involved envisioning the course, picturing the weather, seeing in his mind's eye what he was wearing, imagining his grip on the club. He imagined hearing the wind in the trees, joking with his playing partners, and feeling the breeze against his face as he noticed the clubhouse in the distance. He was smiling, he could smell the new-mown grass on the fair-ways and hear the click of the putter tapping the ball into the cup. I asked him to picture his feeling of success at the end of the game. What would it look like? Would he be savoring a drink and staring into the sunset? Would club members be coming up to slap him on the back and congratulate him on his great game or some ter-rific shot? I encouraged Ron to make his vision as real and three-dimensional and as active as possible.

When he had the image he wanted fully in mind, Ron rated his belief in his imagery on the VOI scale, page 208. Then he tapped for about thirty seconds on each of three treatment sites: Under Arm, the Eyebrow, and Under Lip. Tapping continuously at these locations, he imagined himself shooting his best game and even feeling good and learning something when he missed a putt or landed in a trap. When he finished, he did the Bridge and re-peated the Tap Sequence and imagery. Ron again rated his belief in the validity of his imagery on the VOI and went through the process again until he reached a +10.

Ron said that he now felt completely at ease thinking about the next time he'd play golf. That in itself seemed pretty remark-able to him. "This crazy stuff really works, doesn't it?" he said. But of course no matter how positive Ron felt when he left, what really counted was how it would affect his golf game.

What happened for Ron is what happens with most people. When their worry and anxiety abate, their underlying talents and abilities can be displayed without interference. Ron called the fol-lowing week to report "That tapping thing you did with me really worked. I still don't know what to make of it, but I just shot a 74. That's the lowest score I've ever had on the course."

Of Course There's More

You didn't think you were going to get off that easily, did you? By now you've probably figured out that we have a lot more to tell you about *exactly* how to execute these procedures to be sure you are doing them correctly and to get the best and quickest results. Success with this ESM application assumes that you've done your homework and have gotten some practice, and suc-cess, with the basic procedures. The Optimizer Protocol is shown later in the chapter. Next we provide a more detailed discussion of each of the three phases of the protocol.

More About Phase 1: Letting Go of Fear and Denial

The words may vary, but the common thread underlying most core beliefs is fear. Fears can come in many guises: fear of being found out, fear of dying, fear of being taken advantage of, fear of embarrassment, fear of rejection, fear of feeling stupid, fear of losing respect, fear of feeling inadequate, even fear of never being happy can stand in our way. Often a long list of fears and doubts are implicated in the formation or maintenance of negative core beliefs. Fear can block our most valiant efforts to achieve our goals. Taking a closer look, we find that most of our fears are about outcomes or circumstances that have never happened in the past or are very unlikely to occur in the future. This observation has led to reframing of the word "fear" to mean "false evidence appearing real." Looking closer, we are likely to discover that most of our fears are based on rather flimsy evidence. Nonetheless, these fear-based hitches in our stride toward success can have self-fulfilling side effects. They've got to go.

The first rule of improving your productivity or performance is to be scrupulously honest with yourself. Ready or not, here is the place to surrender to your fear and self-doubts and to your denial of those same fears and doubts. If you have even a shred of doubt about whether fear of failure or self-defeating beliefs are holding you back, you are better off accepting it and treating yourself for it than getting stuck in denial. In acknowledging fear and self-doubt, you gain power over it, and you move one step closer to eliminating it. Trust us. *Trust yourself.*

The goal of Phase 1 is to neutralize any snags (negative emotions and thoughts) to your positive intentions. What unacknowledged feelings lurk behind "I will pass that test," or "I will knock 'em dead with my presentation," or "I will win that tournament?" Is the critic-in-residence taunting "No, you can't," or "You'd better not," or "You'll be sorry"?

Gary Craig, the developer of Emotional Freedom Techniques™, calls these negative beliefs "tail-enders." Tail-enders have a way of sneaking up behind our positive affirmations or intentions and rear-ending them. We say, "I'm going to go to my boss tomorrow and convince him that I deserve a pay raise." That's great, but watch out for the tail-ender. That's the inner voice saying "Yeah, but . . . then more will be expected of me, and what if I can't keep it going?" Phase 1 removes the debris from our lives, and establishes a foundation for a stronger self-concept. The motto of Phase 1 is "Give it up and let it go!"

More About Phase 2: Conceiving and Believing in Your Goals

While the whole performance and productivity protocol is goal-oriented, Phase 2 concentrates on helping you to articulate your goal and to install a firm belief in that goal. Any area of life can be approached from a goal-setting perspective, as David's story demonstrates. The key is to root out the negative emotions and replace them with a clear and positive intention statement about your objective.

> Negative and unproductive emotions chip away at the healthy communication and mutual respect in relationships. David, a bright and sensitive entrepreneur, was finding this out, as one after another of his relationships fell apart. If you looked at David's history, this wasn't surprising. After the death of his parents at age six, he was raised by his grandparents. No woman he's ever been with has been able to reassure David that she won't abandon him. No amount of attention could assuage his insecurity. Each loss renewed his old aches and made him more needy. Now he was falling in love with a woman whom he was already terrified of losing.
>
> David understood full well that his difficulty in sustaining a relationship was not the fault of the women he'd been with but due to his fear and the behaviors that stemmed from it. After working with David on his underlying fears of abandonment and the frustration he felt at not finding a partner, the next step was to come up with a constructive statement that articulated a more positive self-concept about the way he wanted to behave in a relationship. How did David want to feel? What would he like to say about himself with regard to being in a relationship? There was no "right" answer. What David came up with was "I trust Eileen's love for me, and I am comfortable when I'm not with her." This intention statement connected to the way his fear had caused him to act in clinging, needy ways that eventually drove women away.

A Few Pointers About Goal-Setting

Goal-setting is the heart of the Optimizer Protocol. We cannot overemphasize the fundamental necessity of having a clearly defined goal. Just as a ship with no destination finds no favorable wind, if you do not have clearly defined goals, you will not be successful at making the changes you desire. The following guidelines will help you clarify your goal.

- *Be specific about your objective.* "I learn to play a musical instrument" doesn't cut the mustard. Even "I enjoy learning to play the piano" is too general. "I enjoy taking piano lessons twice a week at the Stapleton School" is far better. "I want to be a great coach to my soccer team" isn't specific enough. What exactly would make you a better coach? More intricate strategies? More patience and understanding? More pep talks? More games won? Meeting goals set by the team owner? Lack of clarity can lead to muddled objectives.

The more specific the statement, the better the chance of a positive outcome. Vague or unclear statements are hard to follow through on and difficult to evaluate for change. They leave a lot of wiggle room. Without a clear definition of success, it is difficult to judge our progress.

- *Break down big goals into intermediate steps.* Suppose your overall objective is to make the Olympic rowing team. Think about the ingredients of reaching that goal and set staged objectives. Your first goal might have to do with your training schedule for the next tryouts; your second, for your performance at the tryouts. Then you might focus on building endurance or strength.

- *Have a positive goal,* about something you do want to accomplish rather than what you *don't* want to happen. Think in terms of what you want to gain, not what you fear losing. Usually it is effective to connect the goal with a positive emotional memory. Linking a goal with a past success is one way to bring a positive feeling to your current quest. If your goal is to give an inspiring keynote speech at a fund-raising dinner, associate this objective with the feelings you had when you won the high school debating contest.

- *Make your goals realistic and reachable.* It is fine to have lofty aspirations, but we tend to work harder if our goals are based in reality. If you are forty-five years old, cannot read music, and your goal is to become a world-renowned jazz flautist . . . well, let's hope you have *a lot* of practice time available. Aim to play at the local club before you set your sights on Carnegie Hall. When our goals are overinflated, they leave too much room for fear and self-doubt to take up residence. Failure is built in to unrealistic goals.

Fine-Tuning the Positive Statement

Now it's time to *state your goal as a positive statement.* The phrasing of your goal is very important.

The following list of questions will help you focus on articulating just what you want to accomplish.

- How would I like to feel about the situation?

- If there were no obstacles in my way, how would I feel about
  this situation?

- What would I like to accomplish that I seem unable to do right now?

- What would I like to believe that I'm not believing now about the
  situation or challenge?

- What statement expresses how I would like to feel?

- What is the positive thought I would like to have?

At this point you can begin to *articulate what you would like to happen.*

- "I'd like to feel confident and capable of taking this test (or whatever
  the task might be)."

- "I'd like to believe I can do a good job on this task and then get on
  with my life."

- "I'd like to feel like I deserve to win."

- "I would like to think that I can overcome this threat to my health."

- "What would make me happy is to be able to get things done and to
  break this pattern of procrastination."

When you have taken some time to reflect, *phrase your goal as a positive statement.* This statement can take any number of forms. The essential ingredients are that it be totally positive and avoid the use of negative words, such as "no," "not," and "never." In other words, say "I eat only healthy food" rather than "I no longer eat junk food." Say "I pass my geometry test with flying colors," not "I don't choke and forget what I studied during my geometry test." The more active the statement, the more powerful it seems to be.

Make the statement in the present tense. An athlete might say "When under pressure, I use the pressure to perform at my best." A business executive might say "My presentation goes smoothly and is received with enthusiasm." There are times when stating the goal in the present tense sounds hollow or out of place. However, we have found that present-tense statements seem to engage a more active response.

Here are some examples of positive goal statements:

- "I present my case convincingly and speak calmly and clearly."

- "I recall everything I've read while preparing for the bar exam."

- "I come up with a creative solution to our personnel shortage."

- "I *look forward* to presenting to the book club on Sunday."

- "I am relaxed and confident as I speak to the school board about my suggestion for after-school programs."

- "Going to parties where I meet new people is fun."

When you're in a slump, it's not easy to come up with a positive goal statement, and it's even harder to believe it. Hector, a high-ranked power lifter, was depressed and desperate when he came to see me, having won only two lift events in his last competition, where much more was expected from him. "I kept thinking 'I'm not gonna make it' every time I approached a lift," he lamented. His coach was baffled about how to get Hector out of his doldrums and back on track.

Hector was fascinated by the muscle testing I used to diagnose his polarity reversals. This world-class weight lifter found his muscles turning to jelly in the presence of an unconscious negative thought! Now he was curious. We went through the process, first using the emotion-specific sequences to root out the negative thoughts and emotions that were dogging Hector.

But in Phase 2, Hector had a hard time coming up with a goal statement in positive terms. "I won't be nervous" and "Next time I won't think about giving up" were the best he could muster at first. We kept working with his negative thoughts and finally came up with two statements that dealt with different aspects of his difficulty, one to address his concentration and the other to help him gather his physical resources as he lifted the enormous weights. His final statements were "As I grip the bar, my concentration is as tight as a vise" and "As I lift, all the muscles in my body work together, and I feel and respond like the champion I am."

Now we were cooking. In Phase 3, Hector now imagined himself at a competition, hearing his coach's encouragement, approaching the bar and the weights in the competitors' circle, feeling the cold steel bar, smelling the sweat in the arena. He saw himself accepting the winner's trophy, hearing the applause and the praise, and the interview with sports reporters afterward.

Hector made all six of his lifts in the championship tournament and continued to perform at the high levels that he and his coach knew were possible for him. "My coach and I are incredibly impressed and happy," he told me after the event. "It's hard for me to understand what the heck you did, but I feel so confident now, and stronger than ever."

Once you decide on your positive statement, evaluate it on the Validity of Cognition (VOC) scale and proceed with the protocol. Sometimes the way the goal is stated leads to complications that keep people from getting to a +10 on the VOC scale. One of our clients, for instance, got stuck on the goal statement "I am an effective leader and conduct my meetings with enthusiasm and fairness." That statement brought up fear and wondering about whether in fact he was always fair. We went back and did the anxiety Tap Sequence around his negative thoughts of unfairness, to neutralize his distress. Then he was able to continue through Phase 2.

You may encounter an unexpected negative emotion as you install the positive intention statement or as you install the imagery in Phase 3. If so, go back and apply the appropriate Tap Sequence until it is no longer a block; in other words, until you reduce the intensity of the negative emotion to a 1 or 0 on the distress scale.

The VOC Scale: Taking the Measure of the True Believer

The VOC (Validity of Cognition) scale used in Phase 2 of the Optimizer Protocol measures the strength of belief that a person has in a positive statement. It begins at zero, meaning that, without reservations, you believe the statement is untrue, and goes up to a +10, meaning that you feel that the statement is totally and completely true and valid. In her EMDR work, Dr. Francine Shapiro rates the VOC on a scale that goes from 1 to 7. We've reworked this to be the 10-point scale most people are familiar with.

Validity of Cognition (VOC) Scale

0   No belief in the statement at all.

1   Able to consider the possibility of the statement.

2   Able to feel some hope that the statement could be true.

3   Able to relate to some prior experience that supports the possibility of believing the statement.

4   The statement has a grain of truth to it.

5   The positive statement begins to be believable.

6   Able to see that the positive statement already has been partly true.

7   The statement feels true but there are some reservations or disclaimers.

8   The statement feels mostly true but there is still some doubt.

9   The statement feels almost completely true.

10   The statement feels completely true—I believe it without a doubt.

Phase 2 Polarity Reversals

Polarity reversals are corrected in each phase of the Optimizer Protocol. But in Phase 2 the portion of the Intention Statement that normally refers to "the problem" now focuses on the negative thought or self-doubt that interferes with your total belief in yourself. This variation eliminates the negative themes that prevent you from totally accepting and believing the positive statement. *The target of these polarity reversals is simply the disbelief in general.* It is not necessary to articulate the specifics of the belief or difficulty. As you can see, the structure remains the same, although the words vary.

In preparation for doing the polarity reversals, think about whatever might be interfering with your total belief in your positive statement. As you do the following Polarity Reversal exercise, repeating each one three times, think about the disbelief that stands in your way.

POLARITY REVERSAL EXERCISE: PHASE 2 VARIATION

The Global Polarity Reversal correction remains exactly the same.

While rubbing the Chest spot:
Intention Statement: "I deeply and completely accept myself, even with all my problems and limitations."

Keeping PR. While rubbing the Chest spot:
Intention Statement: "I deeply and completely accept myself, even if I want to keep this difficulty in believing my goal statement."

Future PR. While tapping under the nose:
Intention Statement: "I deeply and completely accept myself, even if I will continue to have this difficulty in believing my goal statement."

Deserving PR. While tapping under the lower lip:
Intention Statement: "I deeply and completely accept myself, even if I don't deserve to get over this disbelief."

Safety PR. While rubbing the Chest spot:
Intention Statement: "I deeply and completely accept myself, even if it isn't safe for me to get over this disbelief."

Safety of others. While rubbing the Chest spot:
Intention Statement: "I deeply and completely accept myself, even if it isn't safe for others for me to get over my disbelief."

Permission PR. While rubbing the Chest spot:
Intention Statement: "I deeply and completely accept myself, even if it isn't possible for me to get over my difficulty in believing in my statement."

Allowing PR. While rubbing the Chest spot:
Intention Statement: "I deeply and completely accept myself, even if I will not allow myself to get over this difficulty in believing my positive statement."

Necessary PR. While rubbing the Chest spot:
Intention Statement: "I deeply and completely accept myself, even if I will not do what is necessary to get over this disbelief."

Benefit of Self PR. While rubbing the Chest spot:
Intention Statement: "I deeply and completely accept myself, even if getting over this disbelief will not be good for me."

Benefit of Others PR. While rubbing the Chest spot:
Intention Statement: "I deeply and completely accept myself, even if getting over this disbelief will not be good for others."

Unique PR. While rubbing the Chest spot:
Intention Statement: "I deeply and completely accept myself, even if I have a unique block to getting over this disbelief."

. . . .

More About Phase 3: Imagining the Future Now

The central element of Phase 3 is the use of imagery to heighten the positive thought. It is widely understood that imagery is the language of the unconscious mind. This method of tapping on meridian sites while vividly and actively imagining our goal is powerful. By holding an image in our minds of the process or end result of our goals, we believe you are programming the brain to acquire the information and materials needed to make our goals materialize.

The best imagery encompasses more than just visual cues. We have found from our work with hypnosis that guided imagery is most effective when it utilizes as many of the five senses as possible. The best imagery is also active and includes an evocation of both the process through which the accomplishment will occur and the end result, in the most positive possible way.

Performance imagery falls into two distinct categories. *Process imagery* is just what the term implies, actively imagining yourself going through the task or activity involved with your goal. Ron, for example, imagined the entire process of making a putt, feeling himself holding the putter, lining up the putt. Ron mentally imagined these process steps:

1. Looking at the break and the grain of the green

2. Determining the amount of incline or decline

3. Gently gripping the putter as if there were a baby bird in his hands

4. Visualizing a line that the ball will travel to roll into the hole

5. Imagining hearing the ball dropping into the hole

The process image for making a successful speech or presentation might involve imagining yourself rehearsing comfortably, feeling confident about your material, delivering the presentation smoothly and with enthusiasm, seeing the audience respond positively, and even applauding or complimenting the presentation. This is what Ellen did earlier in this chapter.

The effectiveness of process imagery has been demonstrated in a number of areas. In one of the earliest of these experiments, Barbara Kolaney of Hunter College asked two groups of people either to practice making basketball free throws on a court with real basketballs or to spend an equal amount of time practicing mentally, just imagining shooting the free throws. She discovered that the group imagining shooting free throws did as well as those who practiced on the court. There is no doubt that mental rehearsal enhances certain fine motor skills and performance results. Recent reviews of over a hundred studies of mental imagery have shown significant positive results in over three-fourths of the studies. It is not uncommon to see Olympic skiers waiting their turn to compete, their eyes closed and their bodies shifting and swaying as they run through every turn of the slalom course in their minds. Mental processes are excellent adjuncts to the development of physical capabilities. Of course, for imaging techniques to work, first you must have learned the fundamentals of activities such as golf, tennis, billiards, skiing, snowboarding, or hitting a baseball. The combination of physical training and imagery is powerful.

The flip side of process imagery is *end result imagery,* which focuses intention past the event and on to the outcome. End result imagery might include the audience's applause after your speech, or imagining the tournament trophy that you win on a shelf in your living room. Imagining the end result of our efforts as if it has already occurred appears to program the goal-directing mechanisms in the brain responsible for filtering information that is relevant to us. These mechanisms communicate with our body to enhance the learning process and in other ways to create the imagined experience.

Validity of Imagery (VOI) Scale

0   No belief in the imagery at all.

1   Able to consider the possibility of the imagery being real.

2   Able to feel some hope that the imagery could be real.

3   Able to relate to some prior experience that supports the possibility of believing the imagery is real.

4   The statement has a grain of reality to the imagery.

5   The positive imagery begins to feel real.

6   Able to see that the positive imagery already has become partly true.

7   The imagery feels true but there are some reservations or disclaimers.

8   The imagery feels mostly real but there is still some doubt.

9   The imagery feels almost completely real.

10   The imagery feels completely real—I believe it without a doubt.

During Phase 3, the wording of the polarity reversals is adjusted to reflect potential negative themes about our imagery. The VOI, or Validity of Imagery, scale tracks our level of belief in our mental picture as we move toward a +10.

POLARITY REVERSAL EXERCISE: PHASE 3 VARIATION

Remember to repeat each statement three times.

The Global Polarity Reversal correction remains exactly the same:

While rubbing the Chest spot:

Intention Statement: "I deeply and completely accept myself, even with all my problems and limitations."

Keeping PR. While tapping the side of hand spot:
Intention Statement: "I deeply and completely accept myself, even if I want to keep this difficulty in believing my imagery."

Future PR. While tapping under the nose:
Intention Statement: "I deeply and completely accept myself, even if I will continue to have this difficulty in believing my imagery."

Deserving PR. While tapping under the lip:
Intention Statement: "I deeply and completely accept myself, even if I don't deserve to get over this disbelief."

Safety of Self PR. While rubbing the Chest spot:
Intention Statement: "I deeply and completely accept myself, even if it is not safe for me to get over this disbelief."

Safety of Others PR. While rubbing the Chest spot:
Intention Statement: "I deeply and completely accept myself, even if it isn't safe for others for me to get over my disbelief."

Permission PR. While rubbing the Chest spot:
Intention Statement: "I deeply and completely accept myself, even if it isn't possible for me to get over my difficulty in believing in my imagery."

Allowing PR. While rubbing the Chest spot.
Intention Statement: "I deeply and completely accept myself, even if I will not allow myself to get over this difficulty in believing a positive image."

Necessary PR. While rubbing the Chest spot:
Intention Statement: "I deeply and completely accept myself, even if I will not do what is necessary to get over this disbelief."

Benefit of Self PR. While rubbing the Chest spot:
Intention Statement: "I deeply and completely accept myself, even if getting over this disbelief will not be good for me."

Benefit of Others PR. While rubbing the Chest spot:
Intention Statement: "I deeply and completely accept myself, even if getting over this disbelief will not be good for others."

Unique PR. While tapping the side of hand:

Intention Statement: "I deeply and completely accept myself, even if I have a unique block to getting over this disbelief."

. . . .

That, at long last, is the whole story. Before we get to the protocol, here's one more anecdote about using ESM, to show you how Kristi came to believe the impossible.

Seventeen-year-old Kristi was referred by her father, who was concerned about her mounting test anxiety. An attractive and athletic 4.0 student, she was so worried about getting good SAT scores that she was scoring poorly on the practice tests. Trying to explain her current difficulty, Kristi said that she'd always gotten anxious before tests, and sometimes got sick to her stomach before athletic events. But this time it was much worse. For the first time in her life, Kristi found herself avoiding studying, and looking for excuses not to put in the hours she knew were necessary to succeed. During the tests, she would revise her answers so much in an attempt to make them perfect that she would run out of time. Perhaps because the SAT test was such a crucial factor in getting into the college she hoped to attend, Kristi felt pushed beyond her coping abilities. "I'm just not up to it," she said. "I don't think I'm as smart as everyone thinks I am."

I asked Kristi if she believed that, before she left my office, she would look forward to taking tests. She gave me one of those exasperated looks that teenagers have perfected for the adults in their lives. "You've got to be kidding," she replied. "It's not possible."

As we began Phase 1 Kristi reported that her distress about taking the SAT was a 9 on the distress scale. After having her bring to mind her negative thoughts about herself as we corrected for polarity reversals, while going through the sequence for anticipatory anxiety, relief showed on her face, and her clenched jaw relaxed. This got her attention. Kristi may have been placating her father when she arrived, but now something had changed. She knew there had already been an improvement. We finished Phase 1 with one more Tap Sequence, to address the procrastination that was creeping into her study habits.

In the next phase, we spent some time helping Kristi come up with the right statement to express her goal. I asked her what she would like to believe about herself with regard to taking tests. "Well, it would be pretty amazing if I could feel that taking tests was fun," she said. Apparently my earlier comment, and her growing confidence, invited her to challenge how strong a positive statement she could make. She acknowledged that at the moment she was not distressed or anxious about taking tests. Why not move on to feel good about it?

The goal statement that Kristi arrived at was "I do well on tests and enjoy taking them." At first she rated her belief in the statement as a +1 on the VOC scale. When we concluded Phase 2, with the Polarity Reversal exercise and the Tap Sequence for performance, she was at a +10.

In Phase 3 Kristi imagined taking tests in the future under many different circumstances, feeling comfortable and confident, enjoying the experience, seeing her test scores. When her dad came to pick her up she announced, "You know, Dad, I'm actually looking forward to taking the test on Thursday." He was shocked. Now *he* gave me a funny look. I just shrugged my shoulders. Several weeks later he called to tell me that Kristi had increased her practice SAT scores by 172 points.

The ability to use thoughts to improve performance is not new. What's new is involving the body's electrical energy to install and enhance those thoughts, bringing about a powerful integration of mind and body. In many situations you will notice positive results immediately. As you apply the Optimizer Protocol to long-range situations or goals, work with the method daily for several weeks before you assess its success.

THE OPTIMIZER PROTOCOL

Phase 1

- SUDS, while thinking about the blocks to achieving your goal

- Balanced Breathing exercise

- Polarity Reversal exercise, while holding in mind negative themes about yourself

- Apply Tap Sequences for the specific emotions interfering with your goal. If you run into trouble, you might first try the Booster Polarity Reversals (page 258) or Comprehensive Tap Sequence in Protocol #5. If you still cannot reduce the SUDS, refer to the information about working with layered emotions in Chapter 6 and the troubleshooting section of Chapter 8. Follow each Tap Sequence with:

- Bridge

- Repeat Tap Sequence

- Recheck SUDS

- Eye Roll

Phase 2

- Decide on a positive statement that clearly expresses your goal.

- Rate your level of belief in that statement using the VOC scale. (Page 208.)

- Balanced Breathing. (This is optional if you are doing all three phases in one sitting.)

- Polarity Reversals. (Use the alternative version shown on page 209.)

- Tap Sequence:

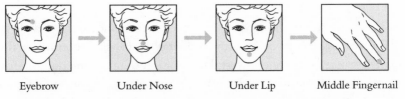

| Eyebrow | Under Nose | Under Lip | Middle Fingernail |

Tap continuously while stating your goal three times at each location.

- Bridge

- Repeat Tap Sequence, as above.

- Recheck VOC; if it's a +10, or if you are satisfied with a +8 or +9 at this stage, move to:

- Eye Roll.

Note: If you become stuck and are not able to get to the level you want, first apply the Booster Polarity Reversals on page 258. Go through the Tap Sequence again with your positive goal statements, then the Bridge and the Tap Sequence with positive goal statement.

Phase 3

- Bring to mind images of the process and result of achieving your goal.

- Rate your belief in your imagery on the VOI scale. (Page 212.)

- Balanced Breathing (This is optional if you are doing all three phases in one sitting.)

- Polarity Reversals (Use the version on page 212.)

- Tap Sequence:

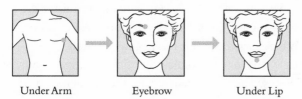

| Under Arm | Eyebrow | Under Lip |

Tap continuously for thirty seconds each while fully imagining the process and result of achieving your goal.

- Bridge

- Repeat Tap Sequence and imagery, as above.

- Check VOI; if it's a +10, or if you are satisfied with a +8 or +9 at this stage, move to:

- Eye Roll.

Note: If you become stuck and are not able to get to the level you want, apply the Booster Polarity Reversals on page 258. Go through the Tap Sequence again with your imagery in mind, then the Bridge and the Tap Sequence with positive goal statement. You can prolong this third phase or repeat it as desired to reinforce your goal statement.

. . . .

Wish fulfillment

Will the improvements that we make with our goal-setting last? In part it comes down to whether we are working with a single and specific incident or a large, ongoing issue. If our goal has to do with one test, one big date, one track meet, or one speech, one treatment will likely take care of it. For ongoing issues—school in general, career growth, regular competition—where the circumstances are likely to be complicated and varied, you may need to reapply the Optimizer Protocol. Sometimes the effect will last until there is a change in the usual situation: We move up to a higher competition level, or move to a job with a new company.

Even if the improvement does not last, you now have the tools to reapply the procedures as needed. With goal-setting issues, polarity reversals will crop up frequently and need to be corrected. For example, as part of a regular "tune-up," Ron (remember his golf improvement?) corrected for polarity reversals every time he went out to play. Replaying the imagery of achieving your goal is another good reinforcement. Each time you administer the protocol, you are building a stronger foundation of self-confidence and motivation under that issue. You are crowding out the negative beliefs.

The knowledge that we have tools to create positive change in our lives is very empowering. When we have internalized a positive cognition consistent with our goals and self-concept, we become better workers, better friends, and better parents. We are filled with positive intentions. Our personal sense of self-worth is good for everyone.

The Optimizer Protocol just scratches the surface of the applications that we are discovering and developing for ESM. We hope to expand on this new direction for Emotional Self-Management in a future book. Enjoy your successes and remember that each experience can be appreciated and utilized as part of the learning process. And have fun sharing these methods with your friends and family.

Maintaining Emotional Fitness

We are confident that by now you have had some success with the methods presented in this book. If you have learned the procedures well, you should be feeling less stressed and more confident in your ability to think clearly about the issues that come up in your life. You will have eliminated or managed the emotional distress that prompted you to invest in this book. Perhaps for the first time in years you even entertain a new vision for your future.

But if you're like most people, once you're no longer in emotional pain, you move on to other pressing obligations or issues in your life. The unhappy memory fades, and life goes on. It's just human nature. Although people generally seek pleasure and want to avoid pain, they tend to be crisis-oriented. After careful and strenuous adherence to a program of healthful eating and exercise to reach their ideal weight, people frequently stop doing whatever worked to achieve their goal, and pretty soon they've gained it all back. Couples spend months in therapy to learn how to work out problems with their partners. With new understanding, and using their new skills, life is again calm and happy at home. But then they may forget what they learned about kind words and attentive listening, leaving the door open for conflict and criticism to creep back in.

We've certainly learned a lot about human nature in our years of clinical practice. We've seen that people will go to extraordinary lengths to alleviate their devastating emotional pain. They are thrilled with the relief they experience through ESM, hypnosis, EMDR, cognitive, or other therapy approaches and with the positive changes in their lives. They leave treatment with renewed hope, with a new sense of direction and new skills to help them cope with life's challenges. But without some level of distress to motivate them, people tend to neglect, and then to forget, the tools that helped them overcome their problems. It happens all the time. They slowly slide into a state of stress or unhappiness, perhaps about some new issue. But they're out of shape emotionally and have only a vague idea about how to get back on track.

Becoming Fluent in ESM

Maintenance is a crucial component of Emotional Self-Management. Like brushing our teeth, it's not terribly entertaining or exciting, but it saves us a lot of unnecessary pain and inconvenience in the long run. Just as regular dental visits stave off cavities, root canals, and even dentures, keeping up a regular schedule of ESM practice will maintain your emotional well-being. Think of it as "emotional hygiene."

We urge you not to put this book on the shelf, to be consulted only in the event of future crisis. It takes but a few minutes a day to incorporate elements of ESM into your daily life. Daily maintenance is the best way to prevent the buildup of emotional distress and to provide you with the clarity to make decisions and solve problems. When you feel calm and balanced, you can make optimum use of all your personal resources.

The more you practice ESM techniques, the easier and more comfortable they will seem, and the more confidence you will have in your ability to use them to maximum benefit. It won't be long before you will be able to administer some of the techniques without even referring to the book. You'll always have the ESM tools on hand. Perhaps that's already happening. When you become fluent in ESM, we are confident that your success, and its noticeable benefits, will motivate you to continue to utilize these skills in all areas of your life, with whatever issues come up.

> Gregory originally used ESM to ease the pain of his grief over his father's death, when it had not diminished after nearly three years. "I had my life on hold, as if I expected him to call me. I guess I never really accepted that he was dead," he said. "It's hard to explain. What's strange is that now that I've let him go, I think about him in new ways, sort of like he's still with me in a silent, internal way." Being able finally to say good-bye to his father allowed Gregory once again to concentrate on his work, to be more attentive to his wife and two daughters, and to play and have fun.

Gregory recognizes the value of ESM techniques for many aspects of his life. He does the Balanced Breathing exercise each morning, along with the Global Polarity Reversal, and administers the Rapid Relaxer before making his weekly presentations at work. An avid tennis player, he finds that correcting for all polarity reversals before a match makes a big difference. In short, Gregory feels he has the tools he needs to better manage his life.

Make It a Habit

The most reliable way to make a productive and beneficial behavior part of your life is to make it a part of a regular ritual. This is what we do with regard to bathing, taking our vitamins each morning, or exercising. We maintain our friendships with weekly phone calls or periodic lunch dates. Sunday dinners are family rituals; children come to count on nightly bedtime stories.

A regular program of ESM keeps your emotional life in tune. When you balance your energy on a regular basis, it does not mean you never get angry, anxious, or sad. It means you *move through* those emotions, gathering what you need to learn and then letting go. You learn to check in with yourself on a regular basis, to see what you're feeling. You learn to evaluate whether you need to address your stress or quell the buildup of anger or fear. The check-in is like a smoke detector, alerting you to early signals of trouble brewing.

The following box provides a suggested schedule of regular ESM practice. It consists of a simple daily tune-up and a weekly check-in. It assumes that you have administered the appropriate protocols for any emotional distress and that you are free of emotional turmoil. The purpose of the regular ESM maintenance program is to help you maintain a sense of balance and clarity.

Some types of emotional distress are likely to require more aggressive follow-up. Habits and compulsive urges, for example, have a built-in recurrence factor. Systemic stresses like chronic pain and the hormonal cycles associated with PMS need regular treatment. Ongoing stresses like grief or loneliness, or frustration with a critical boss, often call for more aggressive management. Following this general maintenance schedule is the Six-Week Stabilizer program for more complex situations.

Daily Tune-Up

Once each day, do the two-minute Balanced Breathing exercise, to center your thoughts, balance your judgment, and activate your creative mind. Follow

Maintaining Balance and Clarity with ESM

Daily Tune-Up:	Balanced Breathing (2 minutes)
	Global Polarity Reversal (15 seconds)
Weekly Check-in:	Correct for all Polarity Reversals (3 minutes)
	Tune in; check SUDS (1 minute); if needed, address any troubling issues or feelings with full protocol
Always on Hand:	The Rapid Relaxer
Make Use of:	The Optimizer

up by aligning your body's polarity. Administer the Global Polarity Reversal, rubbing the Chest spot while thinking about self-acceptance and repeating three times: "I deeply and completely accept myself even with all my problems, limitations, and frustrations." The Global Polarity Reversal helps to maintain focus and clarity about one's life and promotes an overall sense of self-acceptance. You may notice that you are apt to take yourself less seriously and feel lighter about the world in some small or big ways after the Global Polarity Reversal correction. Do it as often as you like, for a well-being build-up. The Global Polarity Reversal can be done anywhere; to most observers it would appear that you were massaging an achy muscle. You can say the statement silently to yourself, or imagine the words being written out.

You can perform this daily tune-up in bed before arising, in your office, in an easy chair, or while sitting in your car. Try to do it at regular times each day, in a quiet spot.

Weekly Check-in

To make sure that there are no hidden saboteurs of your emotional stability, take a few minutes once a week to do the full Polarity Reversals exercise (page 255). Focus on any challenge or current struggle as "the problem" in the intention statements. Even if you're not aware of any distress, it is still good practice to take a quiet minute to tune in to your feelings, to catch any emotional problems before they become troubling or distracting. Check the distress level of any emotions that come up, and, if needed, administer the full protocol for the problem.

The Rapid Relaxer Is Always on Hand

Don't forget the secret weapon of ESM. You can use the Rapid Relaxer (page 257), anywhere and anytime, to cut your distress level in half in just thirty seconds. This quick fix comes in handy for the day-to-day stresses that come up or when you don't have the time or opportunity to administer a full treatment. Remember that the Rapid Relaxer's effects are temporary—they last about half an hour to an hour—and it provides symptomatic relief, not a longer-lasting therapeutic solution. For even greater relief however, you can repeat it. Are you getting nervous as you get ready to go out to a company function? Are you still winding down when you arrive home from work to face the demands of your three young kids? Did you just rear-end the car in front of you? While you're waiting for the highway patrolman to write up his report, it's Rapid Relaxer time.

Doing the Rapid Relaxer can make a big difference in a pinch. It's like fixing a rip in the seat of your pants with a quick row of stitching. It probably won't last, and you'll have to repair it properly when you get home. But meanwhile, it saves the day. We recommend that you learn it by heart, so you can administer this emotional first aid at any time. A good way to remember it is to think of it as a Bridge sandwiched between two Eye Rolls. To refresh your memory, refer to page 257. Repeat this procedure as often as you like, as many times as you need.

Make Use of the Optimizer

You can further enhance your emotional well-being by making regular use of the Optimizer procedures. With a solid foundation of emotional stability, you'll be able to devote more time and energy to thinking in terms of your personal goals, dreams, and objectives. Just what is it that you would like to do? Can you envision a promotion? Would you like to improve your investment strategies? Run for PTA president? Do you feel ready to take up the tuba? Learn to tell stories or be a better conversationalist? Be creative in using the Optimizer Protocol. There are many areas where the Optimizer can improve the quality and satisfaction in our lives.

As a regular practice, spend five minutes a day doing this streamlined version of the Optimizer.

DURING YOUR WEEKLY CHECK-IN:

1. Identify a goal that you want to work on, and come up with a positive statement that expresses that goal. You may want to refer to "Fine-Tuning the Positive Statement" on page 204 for guidance.

DAILY:

2. Do the Global Polarity Reversal.

3. Follow it with the Tap Sequence Eyebrow, Under Nose, Under Lip, Middle Fingernail as you make your positive goal statement three times at each site, while tapping continuously.

4. Vividly imagine yourself going through the process of achieving your goal, using the Tap Sequence Under Arm, Eyebrow, Under Lip, continuously tapping at each site for about thirty seconds.

5. Finish with the Eye Roll.

Stay with this process until you have achieved whatever you envisioned. Then devise another goal statement, perhaps related to another aspect of the original situation, and continue as before.

Note: If you do not notice an increase in your feeling of belief in the positive statement (VOC) or in the imagery (VOI), return to Chapter 11 and administer the complete version of the Optimizer. This abridged version is intended as a reinforcement and may not be effective if you're working on a totally new area or topic.

The Six-Week Stabilizer Program for Managing Chronic and Ongoing Stress

If your original problem returns or if the source of your distress is an ongoing stress that won't just go away with one ESM treatment, what can't be banished must be managed. The Six-Week Stabilizer is a maintenance program for tenacious recurrent or ongoing stresses.

DAILY:

1. Balanced Breathing.

2. Administer the Global Polarity Reversal ten times a day for six weeks. This means taking fifteen seconds every hour to rub the Chest spot while repeating three times: "I deeply and completely accept myself, even with my problems and limitations."

3. The full polarity reversal exercise. Name the issue as you do the reversals: "I deeply and completely accept myself even if I never get over the compulsion to shop," or ". . . even if I don't deserve to get over this pain," ". . . even if I will continue to be lonely," or ". . . even if it's not possible to lose this weight."

WEEKLY:

Once a week, as part of your weekly check-in, administer the full protocol for your problem. Write down the SUDS level as a way of tracking your progress from week to week.

In most cases, the Six-Week Stabilizer will lead to a complete resolution of the problem. By using this program to stay ahead of the stress curve, the correction will hold and become permanent after about six weeks. Thereafter, you may be fine with just the standard maintenance schedule, as long as you check in periodically to see how you're doing. This six-week maintenance program was an important ingredient of the program Donna from Chapter 7 used to knock out her pastry habit. Of course, if at any point you feel that the habitual behavior is getting out of hand, do whatever it takes—twice-daily administration of the complete Polarity Reversals exercise, daily application of the full protocol—to bring your distress back under control.

Who Needs the Six-Week Stabilizer?

Most of the ongoing stresses addressed by the Six-Week Stabilizer fall into four categories: habits and compulsive or addictive urges; pain and chronic physiological symptoms; ongoing stress and problems related to the future; and ongoing aggravations.

Habits and Compulsive or Addictive Urges

The Six-Week Stabilizer program is always indicated when the target problem is an addictive or compulsive urge for such things as cigarettes, food, nail-biting, shopping, or gambling. The effect of administering the full protocol for the first time may last anywhere from a few hours to a few days. Because the trigger for the behavior is still present, or because the addictive substance itself is toxic to the body, the urge is likely to come back sooner or later. Substances such as nicotine, caffeine, or refined sugar are powerful triggers for polarity reversals, and regular retreatment with the full protocol is often necessary.

Pain and Chronic Physiological Symptoms

Emotional distress associated with physical discomfort or pain may return even after a successful ESM treatment. It is possible that the physical source of discomfort generates polarity reversals that undermine the effect of the Tap Sequence. Other factors specific to the physical nature of the pain also may necessitate periodic retreatment.

Many times the Six-Week Stabilizer is successful in lowering the frequency and intensity of chronic pain sensations. While it is unlikely that the level of *misery* experienced before ESM treatment will return in full force, it helps to catch the distress at its earliest stage. As soon as you notice your distress level beginning to increase as a result of some chronic pain or ongoing physical discomfort, readminister the full protocol for pain. Reapplying the Tap Sequence will bring a measure of relief, and the sequence can be repeated as often as needed. Remember that ESM may not eliminate all physical discomfort with pain. The treatment objective is to minimize or neutralize the emotional misery and suffering that accompany pain.

Ongoing Stress and Problems Related to the Future

Loneliness, guilt, grief, and jealousy may be woven into the fabric of our days. Fears and anxieties about the future can keep us in their clutches until the dreaded event or situation is past. You probably have experienced some relief from these issues with the administration of the specific ESM protocol, which can be reapplied at any time if needed. If the emotion resurfaces, it is unlikely to be as strong as it was at first, and its intensity will diminish with each treatment. But with a problem that is ever present, the best way to get lasting relief is to commit to the Six-Week Stabilizer program.

You may recall Kathy, who was anxious about a business venture as she was grieving the recent death of her son. For her, emotional management included the Six-Week Stabilizer program. The loss of her relationship with her boyfriend left a void in her social life, which meant getting back into the swing of dating again. Kathy used the ESM protocol for anxiety to help her feel more calm and composed on first dates (and especially, she reported, on third dates). She also found that doing the Balanced Breathing again just before going to sleep helped her enjoy a restful night.

But what really made the difference for Kathy was when she committed to doing the Global Polarity Reversal at least ten times daily for six weeks. "I fought it at first," Kathy says. "Doing something every hour seemed like a lot to ask. But then I realized that most times I did it I felt more calm and focused. Now the change seems permanent, although I still do it several times a day, because it feels good."

Ongoing Aggravations

Sometimes emotional upheaval persists because of an ongoing provocation. Continued aggravations such as a dictatorial boss, a constantly complaining coworker, recurring frustrations with the kids, or noisy neighbors may need a special program.

The best approach for this type of ongoing problem, in addition to the Six-Week Stabilizer, is to use the Optimizer process to focus on a goal related to solving the problem. The performance enhancement sequences of Phase 2 and Phase 3 particularly can help you move to a higher level of effectiveness in dealing with an ongoing challenge. You may want to refer back to Chapter 11 to refresh your memory about how to apply the full Optimizer treatment, or you can use the streamlined version shown earlier in this chapter.

The idea is to look at how you might apply goal-setting techniques to the management of your situation. Jonathan, who, you may recall, was horribly disfigured in a mugging, uses Optimizer skills to manage several aspects of his situation.

Jonathan faced many ongoing challenges, after having experienced tremendous relief from his emotional distress with the initial ESM procedure. Not surprisingly, he was frequently embroiled in struggles with his insurance company, as it repeatedly questioned his claims in its desire to minimize its expenditures in his behalf. He could always anticipate delays in providing authorizations and reimbursements.

Jonathan found that he was able to manage these situations more effectively when he applied the Optimizer methods. His goal statement was "I am patient, calm, and I persevere against institutional frustration."

In addition to installing that positive cognition, Jonathan also used the Phase 3 imagery to instill active images of himself remaining calm and making reasoned arguments on his own behalf. He envisioned his success at getting fully reimbursed, finding checks in his mailbox, and hearing the insurance claims adjuster agree to his claims. He found that by reinforcing this process with a four- or five-minute session each day, he was able to maintain a very high level of patience and equilibrium in the face of recurring frustrations.

Tracking Your Progress

You may find it helpful, as part of your daily or weekly practice, to keep some kind of log of your experiences with ESM. Keep a record of the feelings that come up and the circumstances that provoked them. Make a note of which Tap Sequence you used. Write down what the distress level was at the beginning and how you felt at the conclusion. Even simple notations will help you keep track of your progress, so that you can see what processes were especially helpful and how you handled certain issues. Make note of your successes and good feelings to remind yourself that your hard work is paying off.

Anna's PMS mood swings had become so debilitating that she had recently resorted to antidepressant medication. Even so, she pretty much isolated herself for nearly two weeks each month, in order to stave off confrontations with friends, family, and coworkers. No boyfriend could withstand her moodiness for more than a few months. Before coming to see us, Anna had tried cognitive therapy, hypnosis, and group therapy in addition to prescription medication. She was resigned to feeling alone and miserable a good deal of the time.

For Anna, the Polarity Reversal exercise was a major breakthrough. Just correcting for reversals improved her mood and her outlook. Her negativity and irritability abated almost immediately, and she was able to acknowledge some of the positive aspects of her life for the first time in years. She had a good job and was valued by her supervisor. She had friends who understood and accepted her, and knew when to leave her alone.

Anna essentially followed the Six-Week Stabilizer program, but made it a practice to correct for *all* polarity reversals *three times* daily, with the focus or problem targeted in the statements as "my PMS symptoms." The ability to make these corrections enabled Anna to manage her extreme moods and gave her a feeling of control over her life after years of feeling at the mercy of her monthly cycles.

Keeping a log of her moods, her symptoms, and the procedures she used to treat herself was a major factor in Anna's progress. She tracked the pattern of her monthly mood swings, noting each time she did the polarity reversals, when she used Balanced Breathing, and when the Rapid Relaxer came in handy. She found out when it made sense to administer a full treatment for the intense emotions that sometimes came up. Over a period of several months, Anna learned just what worked for her and when to use each ESM technique. And it was the record of her feelings and treatments that enabled Anna to see the progress she was making. This clear picture of the gains she was making gave her the impetus to continue. At times when she was most discouraged and irritable, Anna made it a point to review her log and remind herself out loud, "This is working for me."

The Buddy System: Sharing ESM with Friends and Family

If you exercise regularly, you already may recognize the value of having an exercise buddy. Having someone with whom you regularly work out provides motivation and structure, to ensure that you stay on your program. An exercise buddy shares our struggles and triumphs. Buddies encourage us—or motivate us with guilt—into staying the course when we are feeling tired or lazy. An ideal way to make the most of what Emotional Self-Management offers is to have a friend or family member who uses it also.

The first step is to introduce potential buddies—your friends or family members—to ESM. Letting others know what helped you is a good place to begin. The process of positive attraction is the best enticement. Allow your own positive outcomes and newfound sense of well-being to attract others. Begin by demonstrating basic procedures, like Balanced Breathing and the Rapid Relaxer. As others experience positive results, they naturally will be inclined to ask you to share more with them.

Choosing an appropriate time to introduce ESM is especially important when it comes to suggesting to a spouse or partner that ESM might work for them. If you've just had an argument with your partner, and he or she is obviously angry, it's generally not a good time to say you have the solution to his or her distress. People are likely to be defensive at such times, and they are not going to respond positively to your suggestion. It's best to wait for a time when there is no reason for them to reject your suggestion, which means a time when you don't have anything to gain or win in the transaction. The right occasion may present itself when you see that they are upset with someone else or with a situation at work. Introducing the Balanced Breathing exercise at such a moment may help with their distress and to convince them of how well ESM works.

The most effective way to teach ESM to others is simply to model the exercises as you do them together. Now that you have done the work of learning ESM procedures by following the instructions in this book, you can easily demonstrate the position for the Balanced Breathing exercise, or the tapping techniques. As you do the exercises, say the intention statements along with your friend, partner, or teenager. The first time you show an exercise to others, pay careful attention to be sure that they are doing it correctly. Are they tapping firmly enough, and not too slowly? Are they repeating each statement three times? You can help aspiring ESM buddies to trace the eye movements by having them follow the movements of your hand as you show them the Bridge and Eye Roll. By talking with them, you may be able to help them determine what is troubling them and choose the appropriate treatment protocol.

ESM buddies can work together to support and encourage each other in many ways, as Jay and Danielle's story shows:

> "When we came to your ESM workshop, we were having all kinds of problems," Jay told us on the phone several months later. "Danielle was dealing with her sister's breast cancer, which was bringing up long-standing animosities among the four sisters. I was just swamped with work. We were expanding our hardware store to nearly triple its original size. Our separate problems were spilling over into our marriage, and we were making things worse for each other, instead of being supportive."
>
> During the workshop, in addition to learning all the ESM procedures, Jay and Danielle used ESM treatment protocols to

treat their specific emotional dilemmas. By the time they left, they were already feeling much calmer and felt that they had tools to help them maintain their equilibrium. In addition to the standard maintenance, Danielle did the Six-Week Stabilizer to address her ongoing anger and frustration with her sisters. Jay followed the standard maintenance program and worked daily with the goal statements and imagery components of the Optimizer Protocol to help him move forward through the challenges of his business expansion. Both reported that what helped them most was the encouragement each provided for the other. They got into the habit of doing the Balanced Breathing exercise and the Global Polarity Reversal together when they got into bed at night. They did their weekly check-ins together, which they felt kept them tuned in to what was going on in each other's emotional life. If one of them needed to go through a treatment protocol, the other coached them through it.

"If Jay noticed that I was forgetting to do the GPR correction, he'd make a circular motion on his own Chest spot to remind me," Danielle reported. "I felt he was really looking out for me. I do the same thing when I notice that he doesn't seem to be keeping up with his goal-setting exercise."

"Our problems have not disappeared," Jay says. "Jan's sister is still recovering from surgery and chemotherapy, and I'm still working far too much, though I'm developing new strategies and can see that things will change very soon. But we are so much calmer now, and we feel more supported by each other. There's no more blame or criticism. Jan has taught all her sisters to use ESM, and it's been a major help in their relationships with each other. I haven't convinced my coworkers to try it yet, but they can see the difference in my attitude and energy. I figure it's only a matter of time."

As you follow one of these suggested maintenance programs and become more familiar with the ESM practices, we hope you will gain enough confidence in your ESM skills to customize your own program. You can tailor your personal emotional hygiene program to reflect your own emotional challenges and your own schedule and lifestyle, and to take advantage of the ESM practices that have worked best for you.

Teach the Children Well

Using ESM with Kids

The joy of parenting is inevitably leavened with a measure of worry and sorrow. It is heartbreaking when we cannot console a crying infant. Seeing our children in emotional turmoil, as they try to cope with the predictable stresses of growth and development, can be as painful and confusing for us as for them. It can be taxing to try to make sense of adolescents' struggles, especially when they seem determined to blame us for their anger and pain. Challenge and heartache are part and parcel of parenthood.

The good news is that ESM techniques can work wonders with children of all ages, from a week-old infant to a world-weary teenager. It is wonderful to be able to soothe a hysterical infant, to help a second-grader get over her fear of walking to school, or to teach a teenager how to use ESM to stay calm for a final exam. ESM tools are a boon not only for parents but for teachers and childcare providers.

The individual's level of cognitive and emotional development determines the way in which ESM treatments are applied. The younger the child, the more elementary the emotional disturbance, and thus the simpler the technique that will restore calm. With infants and babies, the usual treatment is for the parent to administer a variant of the Global Polarity Reversal, tapping on the side of the baby's hand while holding her in their arms.

With grade-schoolers, a polarity disturbance is still at the root of most distresses. Of course, while young children tend to be less complex than adults in terms of the level of their emotional disturbance, they also have fewer social skills to contain their distress or to self-soothe. It is up to the parent to diagnose and treat the problem. In some cases, where specific fears or maladaptive patterns have developed, the parent can administer a full protocol, doing the tapping and saying the intention statements for the child.

Adolescents are at the mercy of a full complement of hormone-fueled emotions and a vast array of social pressures and decisions. Despite their struggles with authority, teenagers can be taught how to use ESM techniques for themselves. Kids who've been exposed to ESM, with their parents tapping for them, usually are eager to move on to doing it on their own.

Understanding Your Child's Feelings

Part of the process of socialization is to teach our children how to manage their feelings and impulses in a way that fosters cooperation and good relationships with others in the family and beyond. In your role as parent, you teach your child how to cope with his feelings. You become attuned to what your child is feeling and what will help to relieve his distress. Will talking about what's wrong help him to feel better? Does she need to be cuddled first? Is distracting her by making cupcakes together the best way to soothe her feelings? Should she be scolded or reprimanded? Should you withhold her allowance? Or impose a curfew?

Emotional Self-Management as applied to children is not meant to be a substitute for talking with your child about ways to deal with angry feelings, or how to overcome fear of losing a toy, or frustration about having to share it with other kids. Children need direct guidance from caring adults to understand what they are feeling and to develop healthy habits and productive ways to respond to powerful emotions.

It is beyond the scope of this book to discuss how to handle specific emotional problems with children. Every child is unique. Every family is different. We do want to point out that where there are problems in the family, it is unlikely that the child can be helped unless the parents first deal with their own emotional distress. The best way for parents to teach their children to manage their emotions is to model constructive behaviors for them. In families with dysfunctional patterns, the parents are struggling themselves and can't look beyond their own concerns to see what is necessary to correct the system. They need professional help to resolve their own problems so they can help their children. *Also, when a child's problem is severe, either emotionally or behaviorally, consultation should be sought with a qualified medical or mental health professional.*

In the majority of situations, ESM techniques can relieve a youngster's stress. The most frequent use for ESM with children is to treat polarity reversals, which if not corrected have the effect of destabilizing a child's composure. But these techniques also are helpful for breaking up behavior patterns before they cause trouble. These patterns make themselves known when you see that natural corrective mechanisms are not kicking in, and your child is not able to work his way through disturbing emotional states. He doesn't calm down from the tantrum. She never figures out a way to make friends or to get along with her older sister. He cannot find a solution to his distress and keeps having the same problem over and over.

Having these tools keeps stresses from building up to the point where the child becomes trapped in an emotional loop that she can't quickly break out of. The procedures can nip habits in the bud that, unchecked, might carry into larger and more complex problems in adulthood. Often simply correcting the reversals will cut a child's stress considerably, so that she can calm down enough to think through the situation, to talk about it more calmly, and to correct it. Because the complexity of the issues and the treatment differ by age, we have broken the discussion of using ESM into three stages: using ESM with infants and toddlers, grade school–age children, and adolescents.

Infants and Toddlers

It happens to every parent. Their darling baby is cooing and happy one minute, and the next he is fussing and agitated. He isn't wet or hungry or tired. Talking or cuddling or playing his music box or twirling the mobile above the crib doesn't work to distract or soothe him. Sometimes there seems no way to pull the child out of his state, and the cries are heartbreaking.

It can be very distressing for parents to see their child shift from a loving bundle of joy to an ornery and obstinate bundle of agitation. The most common explanation, when there is no apparent provocation, is that the child has experienced a sudden polarity reversal. These reversals seem to appear "out of thin air." Sometimes the squall passes over as quickly as it arrived; other times it goes on for hours, while the parents fret and go a little mad themselves. Remember that we can be affected by the polarity reversals or disorganization of others—our children included—with whom we are in close or frequent contact.

It is also true that children eventually get past their upsetting moods naturally. Like adults, they have their own self-correcting polarity kit built in.

It's unusual for a child's bad mood or tantrum to last more than a few hours, let alone for days. But it does seem that as children get older, and move from being infants to toddlers to preschoolers, they may sustain longer periods of down moods. When negative response patterns get established, they may develop into more serious mood swings later in life. ESM can be used to treat these moods before they go on too long.

> Miguel and Lily came to the office because eighteen-month-old Javier recently had begun having uncontrollable tantrums. One minute he was sweet and pleasant, and the next he was a scream-ing terror, crying and inconsolable. There seemed to be no expla-nation—he wasn't hungry or in pain; he wasn't even tired. Noth-ing they could think of seemed to stop the tantrums. When he was in this agitated state, he kicked the sides of his crib and threw his toys and struggled when they picked him up or hugged him. As soon as one demand was fulfilled, he'd make a new one. Lily was at the point of throwing up her hands at Javier's tantrums. They made Miguel angry.
>
> Miguel and Lily left the office after some tutoring and with instructions on how to use ESM with Javier, who, predictably, had been calm and composed during our visit. That same evening, when Javier went ballistic, they tried the treatment, which basi-cally involved tapping, gently but firmly, on the side of his hand while saying "I love you, Javier, even when you are angry and up-set." It worked immediately. Javier calmed down right away; his tears stopped and he became "reasonable" once again, and they were able to distract him with one of his pull toys—all in the space of about two minutes. Miguel and Lily reported that the treat-ment didn't always work, but most of the time it was successful in shortcircuiting Javier's tantrums, and the frequency and dura-tion of new episodes diminished.

ADMINISTERING THE REVERSAL REMEDY

To correct an infant or young child's polarity reversal, hold the child in your arms. Gently but firmly tap the treatment point on the side of the hand while saying three times, "I to-tally love you, honey [or child's name], even when you're feeling this way." With infants less than six months old, you do not even need to make the statement. Simply tapping the side-of-hand spot (see page 146 for a refresher on the location) may be sufficient.

Often it helps to stroke the back of the child's hand as you tap the side of the hand. If the child tries to pull away, do not hold the hand by force. If the child is resistant, it will be better to wait for a minute and then try again.

As you know from earlier discussions, there is nothing absolute or fixed about the statements you use. It is the theme or intention that matters, not the specific words used to convey it. Any message of loving intention directed at the child tunes the thought energy field related to love and self-acceptance. We believe that when a loving parent or caring adult creates a thought field related to the child, the adult's thought field encompasses and affects the child. Making the statements aloud also focuses the child's thoughts.

. . . .

Growing Pains

The trajectory of emotional development in the early years of life is nothing short of breathtaking. Infants from day one are able to express their pain and discomfort, their frustration or contentment, their hunger or thirst, with a variety of coos and cries and facial expressions. By the time they are six months old, babies can register anger or fright or glee or excitement. By the time they are two, young children exhibit guilt or jealousy, impatience or stubbornness.

As the child's emotional range broadens, it helps to identify exactly what emotion the child is feeling, even if he cannot name it exactly. Infants and toddlers are always in the present moment. You can be sure that whatever is causing their distress is foremost in their minds. You never need to prompt toddlers to "tune in" to what is bothering them, because they are constantly "in the now." But it is helpful if you can label your child's emotion accurately, so that your intention statement truly mirrors what the child is feeling.

If you know the child is feeling frustrated, say "I completely and totally love you, darling, even when you are frustrated." If it is anger, then the statement is ". . . even when you are angry." If the child seems to be throwing a generic tantrum and there is no specific emotion to pin it on, say "I love you always, even when you are upset," or "I deeply love you, even when you are feeling this way." Also, singing the intention statements, or saying them in a singsong voice, is especially soothing with infants and toddlers.

It is always best if you can embrace or hold the child at the time you administer the treatment. Sometimes it is more convenient for one person to hold the child while another person, even an older sibling, does the tapping. The child may be distracted momentarily by your words and tapping. But most of the time he'll be so absorbed in his emotional state that he will barely notice what you are doing. After you administer the Reversal Remedy, let the child alone for a moment or two and watch for him to become calmer. Then you can proceed with distraction or play or whatever else you think might be helpful.

Often the results are surprising. More than half the time, the child's mood will change from distress to calm in less than a minute. But don't become discouraged if it doesn't work the first time. Recognize that it doesn't need to be effective 100 percent of the time for it to be useful. It's nice to know that you have another tool to help you and your children.

Marci and Vincent's daughter Kimmy was just as sweet as can be—until she turned three, when she began having fits of whining almost every other day, talking back to her parents, refusing to eat food they knew she loved, taunting her nine-year-old brother. When after ten minutes, and sometimes as long as half an hour, she wouldn't calm down, Vincent would send her to her room for a "time-out." It seldom worked. Kimmy would become even more hysterical, and she'd add foot-stomping and piercing screams to her repertoire.

We taught Marci how to apply the Reversal Remedy. She began by holding Kimmy's small hand gently in her own and stroking her daughter's forehead with the other hand. Tapping gently on the side of Kimmy's hand, Marci softly repeated, "I love you, Kimmy, even when you're upset." She repeated the phrase a few times and continued holding Kimmy until she pulled her hand away or struggled to be set loose. When they used the Reversal Remedy, Kimmy usually calms down quickly and returns to being their darling and lovable little girl.

Vincent was reluctant to use the technique at first, convinced that stern threats or a raised voice was the best solution. In the beginning, Vincent would point to the times when the polarity correction *didn't* work as evidence that the whole idea was "ridiculous." It took a while for Vincent to recognize that the Reversal Remedy was working. Kimmy was having fewer tantrums, and they were not so dire. Although Vincent has not stopped using time-outs when he gets frustrated, he now frequently does the Reversal Remedy with Kimmy, and he sees how it's helped her "spells."

Grade-Schoolers

Kids in kindergarten through about sixth grade move through profound leaps in their emotional range and their ability to understand and manage their feelings. Of course, they still may get into a state when they simply, and for no explainable reason, have a tantrum or are out of control. They're so upset that they cannot be consoled or reasoned with.

Grade school children usually are dealing with more complicated emotions: selfishness, shyness, pouting, hurt feelings, embarrassment. As children grow up, so do the complexity of their polarity reversals. At this stage, there are situations in which a complete ESM treatment is called for.

Of course, young children usually are not sophisticated enough to clearly identify just what is troubling them. A small child may not say "I don't feel confident at school" or "I feel embarrassed at school." The child may not even understand what is triggering their fear or resistance. "I don't *want* to go to school" is the way the child may express it. This is where the parent's understanding comes in. Is the child scared? Of what? Or angry, or embarrassed, or lonely? At this stage of development there is still no need to ask your child to reflect on the problem. Activating the proper thought field is automatic.

In most cases, it is also too early to have the child do the tapping him- or herself. Try getting an angry six-year-old to say "I'm totally OK, even if I'm feeling lousy." However, by the age of eight or nine, often children can do the tapping sequences and make the statements for themselves, with an adult's guidance. Even so, when young children are struggling to make sense of feelings or when they are having a "hissy fit," they are not in a position to focus on the ESM process and will need their parents' help.

ESM can have a powerful effect on children when there is an ongoing pattern or problem. For example, you may notice that your child is developing resistance to doing homework, or refusing to go to school, or acting shy around classmates, or having difficulty with sharing toys. In this kind of situation, it is important to treat the behavior before it becomes more serious or before the child becomes even more distressed. The danger of letting these feelings go on indefinitely is that they can become an ingrained pattern that gets carried into adolescence and adulthood. Once unproductive coping mechanisms become established, it takes a great deal of parental support and focused attention to break the pattern.

Before you approach your child to work on what seems to be a cumulative pattern of behavior, be sure that *you* are calm and centered. A parent's stress can inadvertently provoke the child's stress, which can make the situation more difficult to deal with. The challenge as a parent is to be calm in the face of the child's distress, which may involve first treating yourself using ESM techniques. The usual power and authority conflicts that arise between parents and children also may complicate administering the treatments, especially to a child in turmoil.

The best time to use ESM techniques with children is when the distressing emotion or behavior first presents itself. If, for example, the problem is shaping up as a nightly struggle about doing homework, you might begin each homework session with a treatment. The trick here is not to get into difficulty with "teaching" ESM to a child who is already struggling with emotional difficulty and inciting a new level of frustration. The parent can do the tapping on the child, up until the child is able to or shows interest in doing it for himself.

Ten-year-old Bobby's struggle in school and with his homework was making life difficult for everyone in their household. He'd told the school counselor, who had screened him for learning disorders and other serious problems, that he didn't understand why reading and composition were so hard for him. Often he didn't understand the assignments, and then he felt stupid and frustrated. Bobby worked with a tutor for a while, but the tutor became frustrated with the way that Bobby tended to give up easily on difficult tasks. His parents had tried hard to teach Bobby patience and good study skills—and they'd worked hard to learn patience themselves—but it seemed that each evening turned into a battle at homework time.

When they first came to our office, Bobby's parents related how painful it was for them to see their son so unhappy and struggling so hard with his homework. Lately, when he became frustrated, he would grit his teeth and sometimes pound the palm of his hand against his forehead, saying things like "I'm stupid, I just don't get this." They wondered if hypnosis might help Bobby. I suggested to them that if low frustration tolerance was part of

Bobby's difficulty, we might try using ESM to see if it would improve his ability to be patient with himself. I explained that they would need to be able to administer the procedure with Bobby, and he would need to be willing to try it. So the stage was set.

Bobby appeared bright-eyed, inquisitive, and curious, but a bit cautious as well. When I asked him what he thought of all this, he said, "I don't know yet. Sometimes I feel stupid, because I just don't understand what we're reading in school. And with my homework, most of the time I'm lost."

I explained to Bobby and his parents that they would be learning a skill to help him reduce his frustrations and improve his concentration and focus. We all agreed those were good goals. With his parents doing the exercises along with Bobby, we went through the Balanced Breathing, polarity reversal corrections, and the Tap Sequence for frustration. Certainly Bobby's parents benefited from that as well.

Sitting in my office, Bobby was not feeling the intense frustration that he typically experiences while doing his homework. In order that they would have this tool whenever it was needed, it was important for Bobby and his parents to learn to run through the whole process easily and confidently. We all practiced it together a few times, like a chorus line, and I made an audiotape of the instructions. Bobby enjoyed learning it together as a family.

Within two weeks, his parents reported, Bobby's frustration had dropped considerably. It was now time to move into the Optimizer protocol. Meeting again with Bobby and his parents, I showed them how to develop a positive goal statement. Bobby came up with "I get this; I understand this stuff." Bobby's statement had all the necessary elements. It was a positive statement in the present tense, and specific to the problem. While not the way an adult would have phrased it, Bobby understood exactly what was meant—that he would be able to understand and make sense of his assignments.

Bobby's grades improved within six weeks. What is more important, he had stopped hitting himself in the head in frustration, which he had explained was an effort to "pound this stuff into my head." He now took his time reading the assignments and asked good questions in class. His parents also helped him use other ESM processes to reduce his anxiety on test days and before oral presentations. As a result of his active participation in solving his problems, Bobby also felt more self-confident. He was calmer and even a little more patient with his younger brother, an unanticipated bonus for his parents.

The whole family had gained something from using ESM. They would tease each other, saying "I think you need to tap," whenever one or another was getting upset or frustrated. They were all making use of these valuable new tools.

ADMINISTERING ESM TO GRADE-SCHOOL CHILDREN

The following series of drawings is meant to help young children measure their distress. Although there are only half as many levels here as on the 0 to 10 scale, you will get a pretty good reading of the intensity of your child's feelings. Ask your child to point to the face that looks most like the way he or she feels. You might also ask "Are you feeling sad? Or are you worried? Are you frustrated with your homework?"

Your attention and your knowledge of your child will help you to formulate the right intention statement. You can say "I love you very much, honey, even if you won't share your toys." Or, "I completely love you, even if your feelings are hurt." Make the statement three or more times as you tap the Side-of-Hand spot or rub the Chest spot, whichever feels most comfortable for the child. It's always good if you can hold the child, though a distressed child may at first resist being comforted.

After administering the treatment, ask your child to again point to the face that looks like what they're feeling now, as a way of monitoring the effect of the treatment.

Administering a Full Treatment:

When your child is dealing with a more complex problem, such as a fear or a phobia, it may be necessary to administer a full treatment sequence. For example, parents who detect that a child is being repeatedly embarrassed at school can help by administering the protocol for embarrassment. Heading off feelings of humiliation early in life can insulate a child from developing inappropriate feelings of shame. An inability to handle frustration that is causing a child to struggle with friendships, or with studying, and that seems to be leading to problems with self-esteem can be addressed with a complete protocol. Kayla's story illustrates how a full treatment can be administered to a young child:

. . . .

Waiting her turn for a swimming lesson at her friend's home, six-year-old Kayla suddenly let out a scream. When her mother ran to her, she saw that Kayla's legs were covered with ants. The ants were quickly washed off, but Kayla was traumatized. She refused to stay for her lesson and had to be carried to the car. An ice cream cone and a good night's sleep helped, but her fear of ants remained. She'd come screaming into the house at the first sight of an ant in the backyard. Of course, there were *always* ants in the backyard. She insisted on being carried every time she went outdoors, which soon became tiresome and inconvenient. When Kayla's mom learned to administer the protocol for phobias, she explained to Kayla that she could do something to help her. Kayla had a hard time even talking about her fear of ants, so her mom had her point to one of the faces in the chart to show how she felt. Not surprisingly, Kayla picked out the very unhappy face #5.

Taking Kayla on her lap, her mother corrected for all polarity reversals. First she administered the global reversal, saying "I completely love and accept you, Kayla, even with your problems and frustrations." She continued through the list of reversals: ". . . even if you want to keep your fear of ants," ". . . even if you will continue to have your fear of ants," ". . . even if you don't deserve to get over your fear of ants," through to ". . . even if getting over your fear of ants will not be good for others." Then they went through the Tap Sequence for phobias, with Kayla's mother doing the tapping, while Kayla said "fear of ants" at each site. Then her mother tapped on the Back-of-Hand spot for Kayla and led her through the steps of the Bridge, with Kayla following her mother's finger as she went through the eye movements. They repeated the Tap Sequence again. Kayla now picked out the smiling face when her mother asked her to show how she felt on the chart. Finally Kayla did the Eye Roll, with her mother demonstrating how to do it. Kayla was fascinated by the simple tapping procedure that took just a few minutes. The next thing her mother knew, Kayla was out playing in the yard. "I'm not afraid of ants anymore," she now tells her friends.

Adolescents

Adolescents can be very responsive to ESM. Teenagers find that having some way of controlling their feelings is empowering. They like the idea that they can self-administer these procedures at any time to get relief from their worries and frustrations.

There is no substitute for knowing what your child is experiencing in his or her social, academic, and family life. Before using ESM techniques, focus first on what the distress is about and what it is teaching the child. Especially with adolescents, taking away their distress before they have a grasp of how the feeling may serve a purpose, and before they have a chance to experience the emotional consequences of their actions, can ultimately be unproductive. Let the teenager complain about having the "blahs" or upset about not making the soccer team. The discussion itself may relieve some of the distress and may offer the opportunity to introduce him or her to ESM.

Most teenagers respond positively to learning ESM when they feel like they've suffered enough, but teaching an adolescent may prove tricky, if she is angry or defensive or in an emotional state where she resents any show of authority. Waiting for the right moment, or sharing with your teenager the way that the process has worked for you, are good strategies. Refer to Chapter 12 for more tips on teaching ESM to others.

When it comes to fears and phobias, a rational explanation is like a bucket against a raging tide. Fourteen-year-old Grace was terrified of high winds and thunderstorms, which are common at certain times of year in the high desert town in which she lives. The howling winds made her feel like the house might collapse or a tree might fall on it, even though there were no large trees outside and even though the storms rarely caused any significant damage.

During the storms, Grace would shiver and tremble under the covers or insist on sleeping the night in her parents' bed. She became embarrassed about her fear, because sleepovers at her friends' were out of the question. One night, as they were talking about her fear, Grace asked her mother for help. That was all her mother needed to hear. Searching out a variety of treatments, eventually she was referred to me. I talked by phone with Grace's mother and sent her some literature and a tape, so she could learn the procedure and teach it to Grace.

Grace was initially skeptical about "this weird tapping thing," but she also saw little reason not to try it. At the time of the treatment, Grace was only able to feel a stress level of 2 on the distress scale as she recalled the storm that had scared her so much the month before. With no actual thunder and lightning to create a fully active thought field, it was unlikely that this one treatment would hold. But just so that she would learn the techniques, Grace corrected for polarity reversals and went through a complete cycle of the phobia sequence, with her mother modeling the tapping for her. When she had repeated the Tap Sequence for the second time, her mother asked her to again think about the thunderstorms. "I was remembering the big storm we had just after school started last fall," Grace said. "I remembered how scared I was then and how I'd be scared if there was another storm like that. But right now, I feel kind of silly for having been so scared." Now her distress level was zero.

Of course, the true test for Grace was her reaction to the next storm. As it happened, a windstorm with forty-five-mile-per-hour gusts blew through the town the following week. This was just the sort of storm that would find Grace under the covers, except that this time she "forgot" there was a windstorm and continued to watch television all that Saturday. Her mother was hopeful that now Grace would be able to weather the thunderstorms.

Nature kept the suspense short. A thunderstorm brewed up a few days later. Not as big as the last one, but wild enough to have sent Grace running for cover. This time Grace was acutely aware of the thunder and the lightning-streaked sky, and although she stayed up, her anxiety level rose to a 6. As the thunder cracked and rolled overhead, her mother again led Grace through the complete sequence for fears and phobias. Grace's anxiety level dropped to a 2 and remained there for the duration of the storm.

This was a tremendous success for Grace. She felt pleased with herself, because she had done the tapping herself and it had worked. She was relieved that she was no longer "acting like such a weirdo."

This time Grace's treatment seemed to be permanent. When the next thunderstorm came up, her stress level never went above a 2, a reasonable level of concern with lightning and thunder clapping overhead.

Dating is one of the most anxiety-producing situations for teens. By mid-adolescence boys and girls are beginning to do things together socially, have crushes, and become involved in their first relationships outside of their family. Young men and women feel socially awkward, sensitive about their appearance, and unsure of themselves. Emotional Self-Management methods can help your teenagers cope with these and other uncomfortable situations more effectively.

Fifteen-year-old Angela was slightly overweight and very self-conscious about her appearance, with little confidence in her popularity at school. Now a classmate had asked her to go to the movies, and what should have been a very pleasant and positive experience was causing Angela only dread and anxiety. Would he like her? What would they talk about? What would her classmates think? She was considering canceling the date when her parents became concerned about how anxious and upset she seemed. She was setting up a self-fulfilling scenario that could easily turn into what she feared most: rejection.

Angela's parents were experienced with ESM and only too happy to show her how it might help her. Angela was willing to learn, as long as no one found out about it. With her parents to guide her, she was able to overcome her anxieties and self-doubt by administering the protocol for anticipatory anxiety.

Then she used the Optimizer protocol to install positive thoughts about herself and the upcoming date. She was able to enjoy the evening and, although the boy did not ask her out again, she didn't take it personally. Again using the Optimizer procedure to reach her personal goals, Angela installed positive thoughts and images of herself talking and being at ease with boys. Her parents reported that over the following months Angela appeared to gain self-confidence at school and with her friends. Her dating life picked up considerably. In following up with her parents about six months later, I learned that Angela was dating a boy she liked and who liked her. She was even beginning to give dating advice to her girlfriends.

In dealing with teenagers, parents need to be aware of how open teens are to parental suggestion or authority. If your son or daughter is like Angela, you may be able to coach him or her directly in using the ESM methods. But adolescents who are withdrawn or rebellious will simply tune their parents out. In such situations it may be better to make the book available and merely comment on how ESM has helped you. Another way of piquing a teen's interest in ESM is to point out that these are techniques used by athletes, performers, or others whom the adolescent might admire.

Helping one's own children cope more effectively with the stresses of life and learn new skills is a rewarding part of being a parent. Learning Emotional Self-Management can be a wonderful way to ease the stresses of parenthood and model the skills for impressionable youngsters.

Energy Futures

The Sky Is Not *the Limit*

For all the innovative and powerful advances in energy psychology in recent years, the field is still in its infancy. Considering the steep curve at which this field is evolving, there will certainly be new breakthroughs in understanding the mechanisms of human thought and emotion. There may be as-yet undiscovered dimensions of energy that illuminate the human condition. New instrumentation, such as magneto-encephalography (MEG), and new applications of existing technologies like functional magnetic resonance imaging (fMRI) and positron emission tomography (PET) scans, directed toward the physiological phenomena associated with thought energy therapies, will provide new information about the composition of thought. Exploration of acupunc-ture processes and the body's meridian system are under way. Soon we may be able to decipher the vibrational band of discrete emotions, just as we measure levels of physical stimulus and response with an electroencephalograph. Once such effects are measurable and repeatable, acceptance and utilization of energy therapy modalities will follow at a rapid pace. Just as biofeedback teaches people to control physiological states, future technology may help people recognize and cultivate specific emotions. The July 1999 issue of *Nature Neuroscience* reported a study by John Chapin, Ph.D., in which electrical activity in rats' brains associated with their intention to get water activated a robotic arm that provided water to them. To us, it provides evidence that specific thought activity can be identified and utilized constructively.

The coming years will see a sweeping change in treatment approaches related to human health and development. Energy therapies are pointing the way to harness what may be the most powerful force of all: *human intention.* Quantum physics shows that the focusing of thought energy can have an effect on matter. In other words, our ability to focus our thoughts with intention can have an effect on energy in the body, which manifests in physical form. We are on the threshold of discovering highly effective ways to use thought energy to maintain physical as well as mental health and balance. Fueled by new understanding of the energy systems of body and mind, we will fully activate the "power of positive thinking."

A Vision of the Future

Eventually nearly everyone, in one way or another, will use energy therapy tools for managing emotions, because they are portable, easy to learn, and without harmful side effects. Energy psychotherapies will be part of the treatment for a variety of medical disorders. The ability to eliminate self-sabotaging polarity reversals will facilitate more effective response to existing treatments, neutralizing distress and unblocking pathways to healing. The reduction of stress alone, with its ability to reduce the incidence and severity of disease processes, is fertile ground for comprehensive energy psychotherapeutics. The day is not so far off when all members of the healing professions will be familiar with these procedures and use them within their own approach to helping people.

Already, in our own practices, physicians refer clients with difficult-to-treat illnesses, for help with the emotional components of their distress. We also train physicians and other clinicians in the use of ESM as an adjunct treatment. As of this writing, we are running a pilot study on the effectiveness of ESM for people who suffer from claustrophobia. The study examines changes in brain wave patterns, muscle tension, heart rate, skin temperature, respiration, and electrical properties of the meridian system, using the AMI (Apparatus for Meridian Identification) device in addition to a number of psychological measures. Though as yet incomplete, the study reveals evidence of physiological changes in muscle tension, automatic nerve activity, and other readings after an ESM treatment. Significant behavioral changes are also being observed, with subjects able to tolerate confinement in a small elevator-size room with greater comfort. We will be updating the findings of this study on our website: www.gem-systems.com.

Thought Field Therapy (TFT) has proven highly effective in crisis situations. In 1998 a team of visiting therapists that had been conducting a local training in TFT were able to respond immediately to the bombing of the U.S. Embassy in Nairobi. Working with translators, they went from bed to bed administering treatment to people severely injured and traumatized in the blast. They were also able to help family members grief-stricken by the loss of loved ones or devastated by seeing family members with missing limbs. One of our students, a missionary and nurse practitioner, traveled to Albania in 1999 as part of a medical team, administering ESM to distraught refugees fleeing Kosovo. She reported many successes in treating severe emotional trauma and in helping to lift the psychic burden of these men, women, and children, in addition to treating their medical needs.

ESM and the Evolution of Consciousness

ESM and energy psychotherapies are emblematic of the evolution of human consciousness. When we first began our practices, our objective was to alleviate psychological distress—to neutralize negative effects. Then, along the same continuum, we began applying these same principles to performance enhancement in business and sports. The training we have conducted in corporate and organizational settings has shown us that ESM methods are powerful tools for building teams, resolving conflicts, reducing stress, and increasing overall performance. We are just beginning to explore the vast potential for the Optimizer capabilities of ESM.

Now we see ourselves moving further along that continuum to apply these methods to global consciousness and the healing of the human spirit. The wider applications for ESM move beyond the personal arena to adding positive energy to larger systems: the family, the school, the local and global community. When people have tools to resolve personal issues and to manage their practical problems and difficulties, they have more energy to focus on others. No longer self-consumed, they are less defended and can look beyond their narrow interests to the larger world. The ability to make a contribution to society and to have a positive effect on one's world is key to spiritual growth and self-actualization.

In the wake of recent school and community violence, it is vital to find new ways to teach young people to manage their emotions and to foster self-esteem. Poorly channeled rage, anger, and the pain of rejection can lead all too easily to senseless violence. Increasing the emotional intelligence of young people before problems arise may be the most direct solution to some of the problems in our society. Children deserve to have skills to enable them to cope with the complexities of life more effectively. Emotional Self-Management techniques, life skills that promote a sense of competence, confidence, and social awareness, directly address the impulse control problems so often associated with violent behavior. We are now developing a program for coaching teachers and counselors in methods of introducing ESM at the middle school level.

At this time in human evolution, as the acceleration of new technologies and information threatens to overwhelm us, we are being given life-saving and life-enhancing psychological tools with which to face the new millennium. ESM tools are the foundation for focusing intention beyond oneself, ultimately connecting people on a level that bridges language differences and diversities. With these tools, we can all become agents of change, not only at home but in our communities. We can each contribute to making the global village a safe and happy place to live.

PROCEDURES AT A GLANCE

Tap Site Reference Key

Subjective Units of Distress Scale

Balanced Breathing Exercise

Polarity Reversal (PR) Exercise

The Rapid Relaxer

The Eye Roll

The Bridge

Booster Polarity Reversals

The Optimizer Protocol

Stress Self-Assessment for Children

The Five-Step Breathing Exercise

Tap Site Reference Key

Eyebrow

Outside Eye

Under Eye

Under Nose

Under Lip

Little Fingernail

Index Fingernail

Middle Fingernail

Back of Hand

Back of Hand
(50X)

Collarbone

Under Arm

Rib

Chest

Side of Hand

Thumbnail

Subjective Units of Distress Scale

0   The absence of any distress. Feeling calm and totally relaxed.

1   Neutral feeling or just OK, not as relaxed as could be.

2   A mild irritation. First awareness of tension or vague stress.

3   Increased discomfort, unpleasant, but in control.

4   Noticeable discomfort or distress, perhaps agitation, but tolerable.

5   Discomfort is very uncomfortable, but I can stand it.

6   Discomfort worsens and affects my life.

7   Discomfort is severe and emotional pain interferes with life.

8   Discomfort increases and it is in my thoughts constantly.

9   Discomfort is nearly intolerable.

10   Discomfort is extreme and the worst imaginable. I feel panicky and overwhelmed.

Balanced Breathing Exercise

Balanced Breathing takes about two minutes. Sitting in a straight-back chair is best, but Balanced Breathing can be done while lying down or in a standing position.

1. Cross your left ankle over your right ankle.

2. Extend both arms straight out in front of you.

3. Cross your right arm over your left arm at the wrist.

4. Rotate the palms of your hands so that they are facing and interlock your fingers.

5. Rotate your hands down toward your stomach.

6. Continue rotating inward so that you bring your hands up close to your chest. At this point you have crossed the center line of your body with your hands, arms, and legs.

Note: If it is more comfortable for you, you can reverse the order—right ankle over left, left wrist over right. It doesn't make a difference, as long as they are opposite.

Once in the proper position, inhale through your nose while touching the tip of your tongue to the roof of your mouth. Exhale through your mouth, resting your tongue on the floor of your mouth.

Focus your thoughts on the concept of *balance*. It might be the idea of the balance of mind and body or just the word "balance." At the same time picture in your mind, if you can, an image that represents balance. This could be the image of a scale, or a seesaw, or standing on one foot. Throughout the two-minute process, breathe comfortably. Don't worry if you are not always able to hold the thought or image; come back to it if you drift away.

Polarity Reversal (PR) Exercise

Begin by doing the Balanced Breathing exercise to align the body's polarity. Then, sitting comfortably, tap or rub the designated point while saying each intention statement three times. It does not matter how quickly or slowly you speak each statement, do whatever feels right to you. With the exception of the Global PR, you can substitute a verbalization of the issue you are dealing with for the phrase "my problems and limitations." For example, "my anxiety" or "my anger about my divorce."

Global PR. While rubbing the Chest sore spot:
Intention Statement: "I deeply and completely accept myself, even with all my problems and limitations."

Keeping PR. While rubbing the Chest spot:
Intention Statement: "I deeply and completely accept myself, even if I want to keep this problem."

Future PR. While tapping under the nose:
Intention Statement: "I deeply and completely accept myself, even if I will continue to have this problem."

Deserving PR. While tapping under the lower lip:
Intention Statement: "I deeply and completely accept myself, even if I don't deserve to get over this problem."

Safety of Self PR. While rubbing the Chest spot:
Intention Statement: "I deeply and completely accept myself, even if it isn't safe for me to get over this problem."

Safety of Others PR. While rubbing the Chest spot:
Intention Statement: "I deeply and completely accept myself, even if it isn't safe for others for me to get over this problem."

Permission PR. While rubbing the Chest spot:
Intention Statement: "I deeply and completely accept myself, even if it isn't possible for me to get over this problem."

Allowing PR. While rubbing the Chest spot:
Intention Statement: "I deeply and completely accept myself, even if I will not allow myself to get over this problem."

Necessary PR. While rubbing the Chest spot:
Intention Statement: "I deeply and completely accept myself, even if I will not do what is necessary to get over this problem."

Benefit of Self PR. While rubbing the Chest spot:
Intention Statement: "I deeply and completely accept myself, even if getting over this problem will not be good for me."

Benefit of Others PR. While rubbing the Chest spot:
Intention Statement: "I deeply and completely accept myself, even if getting over this problem will not be good for others."

Unique PR. While rubbing the Chest spot:
Intention Statement: "I deeply and completely accept myself, even if I have a unique block to getting over my problems."

The list of polarity reversal themes below can be memorized so that you can do the exercise without referring to the written instructions. The tap site for each reversal appears in parentheses.

Global PR (Chest)

Keeping PR (Chest)

Future PR (Under Nose)

Deserving PR (Under Lip)

Safety of Self PR (Chest)

Safety of Others PR (Chest)

Permission PR (Chest)

Allowing PR (Chest)

Necessary PR (Chest)

Benefit of Self PR (Chest)

Benefit of Others PR (Chest)

Unique PR (Chest)

The Rapid Relaxer

The Rapid Relaxer consists of an Eye Roll, then a Bridge, followed by another Eye Roll. Because the Eye Roll and Bridge are used independently in the ESM protocols, the two procedures are presented separately below.

The Eye Roll

The Eye Roll is a continuous eye roll, which is done while continuously tapping the Back-of-Hand spot. Throughout the exercise, keep your head level, facing straight ahead. *Move only your eyes, not your head.*

Begin with your eyes closed. Open your eyes, look down (at the floor if you're standing, or into your lap if you're sitting), and with your eyes, slowly trace an imaginary line straight forward across the floor to the wall in front of you. Continue slowly rolling your gaze up the wall to where it meets the ceiling and then back toward you across the ceiling, until you are looking above you. The whole sequence should take about eight seconds.

The Bridge

The Bridge consists of a series of eye movements, humming, and counting, all the while keeping up the Back-of-Hand Tap. The whole sequence takes about fifteen seconds.

 1. Start with your eyes open.

 2. Close your eyes.

 3. Open your eyes and glance down toward the floor to your right.

 4. Glance down to your left.

 5. Rotate your eyes in a full circle in one direction. *Make sure you are not skipping any part of the circle. It may take a little practice to be sure you are making a complete circle.*

 6. Now rotate your eyes around in a complete circle in the opposite direction.

 7. Hum about five notes. *This might be a familiar tune, such as "Happy Birthday," or just make up a few notes of your own.*

1 · 2 · 3 · 4 · 5   8. Count from one to five.

 9. Hum a few notes again.

Booster Polarity Reversals

 Repeat three times while rubbing the Chest site: **"I deeply and completely accept myself, even if I am not** *completely* **over this problem."**

 Repeat three times while tapping Under Nose: **"I deeply and completely accept myself, even if I** *never* **get completely over this problem."**

The Optimizer Protocol

Phase 1

- SUDS, while thinking about the blocks to achieving your goal

- Balanced Breathing exercise

- Polarity Reversal exercise, while holding in mind negative themes about yourself

- Apply Tap Sequences for the specific emotions interfering with your goal. If you run into trouble, you might first try the Booster Polarity Reversals or Comprehensive Tap Sequence in Protocol #5. If you still cannot reduce the distress level, refer to the information about working with layered emotions in Chapter 6 and the troubleshooting section of Chapter 8. Follow each Tap Sequence with:

- Bridge

- Repeat Tap Sequence

- Recheck SUDS

- Eye Roll

Phase 2

- Decide on a positive statement that clearly expresses your goal.

- Rate your level of belief in that statement using the VOC scale (page 208).

- Balanced Breathing. (This one is optional if you are doing all three phases in one sitting).

- Polarity Reversals, the alternative version shown on page 209.

- Tap Sequence:

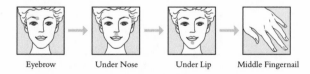

| Eyebrow | Under Nose | Under Lip | Middle Fingernail |

tapping continuously while stating your goal three times at each location.

- Bridge

- Repeat Tap Sequence, as above.

- Recheck VOC; if it's a +10, or if you are satisfied with a +8 or +9 at this stage, move to:

- Eye Roll.

Note: If you become stuck and are not able to get to the level you want, first apply the Booster Polarity Reversals on page 258. Go through the Tap Sequence again with your positive goal statements, then the Bridge and the Tap Sequence with positive goal statement.

Phase 3

- Bring to mind images of the process and result of achieving your goal.

- Rate your belief in your imagery on the VOI scale on page 212.

- Balanced Breathing. (This is optional if you are doing all three phases in one sitting.)

- Polarity Reversals. (Use the version on page 217.)

- Tap Sequence:

| Under Arm | Eyebrow | Under Lip |

or thirty seconds each while fully imagining the process and result of achieving your goal.

- Bridge

- Repeat Tap Sequence and imagery, as above.

- Check VOI; if it's a +10, or if you are satisfied with a +8 or +9 at this stage, move to:

- Eye Roll.

Stress Self-Assessment for Children

Have your child point to the face that best reflects how s/he feels.

The Five-Step Breathing Exercise

Five-Step Breathing entails doing a five-step breathing technique eight times, each time holding one hand or the other in different positions on the collarbone sites while continuously tapping the Back-of-Hand spot with the opposite hand.

Here are the five steps of the breathing process:

1. Take a deep breath and hold it for five seconds.

2. Exhale *half* of the breath and hold for five seconds.

3. Exhale completely and hold for five seconds.

4. Inhale *halfway* and hold for five seconds.

5. Breathe normally for about five seconds.

Note: Half breaths in or out are approximate; there is no precise halfway point.

Here are the eight hand positions. In each position do a complete cycle of Five-Step Breathing while continuously tapping the Back-of-Hand spot with the opposite hand.

1. Palm side of the right hand touching the right Collarbone spot.

2. Palm side of the right hand touching the left Collarbone spot.

3. Backside (make a fist) of the right-hand fingers touching the right Collarbone spot.

4. Backside of the right-hand fingers touching the left Collarbone spot.

Switch hands.

5. Palm side of the left hand touching the right Collarbone spot.

6. Palm side of the left hand touching the left Collarbone spot.

7. Backside of the left-hand fingers touching the right Collarbone spot.

8. Backside of the left-hand fingers touching the left Collarbone spot.

Practice suggestions: In order to become comfortable with the procedure:

a. Practice just the Five-Step Breathing sequence until you can do it comfortably.

b. Then practice going through the eight hand positions to become familiar with them.

c. Finally add the continuous tapping on the Back-of-Hand spot with the opposite hand.

G L O S S A R Y

Acupuncture. A traditional Chinese therapeutic technique wherein specific points on the body's *meridian* system are stimulated with very fine needles to produce healing effects. Stimulation also can be achieved with heat, pressure, electrical current, tapping, and other means of activating the meridians.

Applied Kinesiology. A therapeutic methodology that utilizes manual *muscle testing* to diagnose and treat various imbalances in the body's systems.

Aspect. A new facet of the emotion being treated by an ESM protocol that arises during the treatment process.

Back-of-Hand Tap. A frequently used ESM procedure that involves actively tapping on a spot located on the back of the hand between the knuckles of the ring and pinky fingers, about an inch back toward the wrist.

Balanced Breathing. An exercise derived from yoga and from the innovations of engineer Wayne Cook. This breathing exercise acts to organize and balance the body's electrical energy.

Bioelectrical Energy. Energy generated through biological processes such as nerve impulses, the electrical energy generated by muscle contractions, and the electrical charges that exist within cell membranes and other parts of the body.

Booster Polarity Reversal. A specific correction for *Polarity Reversals* that sometimes occur during the administration of the *Tap Sequence.* It represents an aspect of a *polarity theme* that has not been completely corrected.

Bridge. An *ESM procedure* that integrates thoughts related to a specified problem or objective into different regions of the brain, through the use of activities such as eye movements, counting, and humming. It is part of the emotion-specific *protocols* and the *Rapid Relaxer.*

Chi. (also recognized as Qi) The word for vital life energy in Traditional Chinese Medicine.

Electromagnetic Fields. The field of force associated with electric charge in motion, with both electric and magnetic components. The surrounding sphere of magnetic energy, such as is generated by the conduction of electricity through wires.

Emotional Target. The specific feeling or issue that is the focus of an ESM *protocol.*

Emotional Self-Management (ESM). A system of self-administered procedures for correcting mental and emotional balance and relieving emotional distress based on Thought Field Therapy and other techniques in the fields of energy psychology and cognitive therapy.

Energy Psychology. An emerging branch of psychology that incorporates electromagnetic and other energy processes in the treatment of mental, emotional, and physical problems.

ESM Procedures. A variety of techniques that function to organize the body's energy, relieve distress, and install positive thoughts and images for success.

Eye Movement Desensitization and Reprocessing (EMDR). A methodology for treating emotional distress through the use of eye movements and other methods of lateralization developed by Dr. Francine Shapiro.

Eye Roll. An ESM procedure that involves slow, sweeping eye movements. It is part of the *Rapid Relaxer* and also concludes a successful *protocol,* as a way of closing the effect of the treatment.

Five-Step Breathing. A breathing exercise that restores the body's *polarity* when it has become incoherent or undetectable. See *polarity disorganization.*

Intention. Thought that is focused with some goal orientation.

Intention Statement. Declaration of a specific objective, spoken softly or silently to oneself as part of an ESM procedure.

Labeling Emotions. Identifying or naming specific feelings so that the correct *Tap Sequence* treatment can be applied.

Layered Emotions. Levels of emotional distress perceived at varying levels of consciousness. Much as an onion only reveals its top layer at any one time, emotions may stack up one on top of the other, so that only the most intense or recent is noticeable.

Major Points. The *meridian* locations that make up the *Tap Sequence* of an ESM *protocol.*

Meridians. The system of pathways that include the target sites of *acu-puncture* and ESM treatments, which are organized primarily around specific organs or systems of the body.

Morphic Fields. Theoretical fields of energy that contain information useful to forming or maintaining an organism. The theory of morphic fields is supplementary to the genetic theory of formation.

Muscle Testing. A methodology that uses the detection of muscle weakness to diagnose the presence of unconcious distress, polarity reversals, and external influences, such as toxic foods or medications.

Neurolymphatic Reflex Spot. An acupuncture site and a nerve bundle associated with the lymph system. In ESM, this treatment site frequently is used to correct for *polarity reversals.*

Nonlocal Effect. The phenomenon in quantum physics in which action in one place causes like reaction in another. For example, a photon mirrors the change of direction when the rotation of another photon with which it is paired is altered.

Optimizer Protocol. An ESM treatment sequence for addressing issues of performance and productivity that incorporates goal-setting and imagery strategies.

Neuropeptides. Chemical structures that serve as messengers to communicate information from one location in the body to another.

Paradigm. A pattern for knowing, or model of understanding, a given domain. Generally a set of rules and parameters for addressing a specific area or topic.

Piezoelectric Effect. Mechanical phenomenon wherein certain crystals, when bent and released, produce an electrical discharge. Frequently used to ignite gas burners.

Polarity. A characteristic of electromagnetism that organizes energy into opposing attributes or tendencies, such as plus/minus or north/south.

Polarity Disorganization. A state of electrical polarity incoherence that has the effect of interfering with the effectiveness of therapies and may produce negative emotional and sometimes cognitive symptoms.

Polarity Reversals. An electromagnetic state in which the plus/minus pole has become inverted. This effect can interfere with thought processes and emotional stability. Also, the name of an exercise to correct the effect.

Polarity Themes. Topics of thought about universal human issues. Categories of life themes, such as deserving, possibility, or safety, as well as uniquely individual themes, are the target of the *Polarity Reversals* exercise.

Protocol. A complete ESM treatment sequence for a specific emotion or issue.

Quantum Mechanics. In physics, a theory of the structure and behavior of atoms and molecules.

Quantum Theory. A mathematical theory in which subatomic particles can display behavior significantly different from the behavior of large objects in the macro world.

Rapid Relaxer. An ESM procedure consisting of a *Bridge* between two *Eye Rolls*, used to provide rapid, though temporary, emotional relief.

Reversal Remedy. The procedure for administering *Polarity Reversals* to young children, which involves an adult tapping on the side of the child's hand while repeating an *intention statement* for the child.

Subtle Energy. A reference to energy systems that are barely, or not directly, detectable.

Subjective Units of Distress Scale. A scale whereby individuals can self-assess the level of their emotional or physical distress. Developed by psychologist Joseph Wolpe, Ph.D., the scale rates distress in levels from zero to ten or zero to one hundred.

Tap (Treatment) Points. The specific *meridian* locations that are used as the tapping sites in *thought field therapies.*

Tap Sequence. The grouping and order of *tap points* used to address a particular emotion or issue in an ESM *protocol.*

Target Emotion. The specific feeling or emotional state that is the target of a *Tap Sequence.*

Thought Field. A hypothesized electromagnetic field of energy believed to correspond to individual categories of thought associated with specific emotions.

Thought Field Therapy. A range of therapies, which use characteristics of thought, combined with certain electromagnetic characteristics of the body, to effect the release of emotional, and sometimes physiological, distress.

Traditional Chinese Medicine. An umbrella term for a broad range of Eastern medical practices, including acupuncture and herbal remedies.

VOC. Validity of Cognition. A self-assessed rating scale for an individual's belief in a particular thought or cognition, developed by psychologist Francine Shapiro, Ph.D., as part of *EMDR* treatment. In ESM, it is part of the *Optimizer* protocol.

VOI. Validity of Imagery. A self-assessed rating scale for measuring an individual's belief in a particular mental image or set of images. In ESM, it is part of the *Optimizer* protocol.

R E S O U R C E S

Contact us with your comments and questions, or for further information at:

Global Emotional Self-Management Systems™
Peter Lambrou, Ph.D. and George Pratt, Ph.D.
Scripps Memorial Hospital Campus
9834 Genesee Avenue, Suite 321
La Jolla, CA 92037
(858) 457–3900
http://www.gem-systems.com
Our website features updates and more information about Instant Emotional Healing and energy therapies. You'll find more tips and instruction, along with tapes, courses, and other products and services related to Emotional Self-Management. E-mail the authors and explore links to relevant websites.

The following organizations and information sources are leads to exploring and learning more about energy psychotherapy and related topics discussed in *Instant Emotional Healing*.

Energy Psychotherapy

ACT (Acupressure, Chakra Technique)
http://www.meridiantherapies.co.uk/phil.html
This website contains information about several variations of meridian-based therapeutic methods.

Association for Comprehensive Energy Psychology
http://www.energypsych.org
Organization that promotes the practice of energy psychology.

Attractor Field Therapy (AFT)

http://www.the-tree-of-life.com

An outgrowth of the seminal work of David R. Hawkins, M.D., Ph.D., author of *Power vs. Force: The Hidden Determinants of Human Behavior.* This site provides information about the application of energy principles to a variety of emotional and physical problems.

Be Set Free Fast™

Larry Phillip Nims, Ph.D.

1400 East Chapman Avenue

Orange, CA 92866

(714) 771-1186

http://members.aol.com/dnnn/whatisbsff.html

A highly focused energy therapy method for eliminating the negative emotional roots and self-limiting belief systems that are embedded in the subconscious mind and are "locked" together by specific energy circuits.

Callahan Techniques®, Ltd.

78-816 Via Carmel

La Quinta, CA 92253

(760) 564-1008

http://www.tftrx.com

Callahan Techniques™ of Thought Field Therapy offers information on professional training, research, products, and other information.

EMDR

P.O. Box 51010

Pacific Grove, CA 93950-6010

(831) 372-3900

http://www.emdr.com

Information source about Eye Movement Desensitization and Reprocessing, a therapeutic method that uses some processes similar to energy psychotherapy.

Emotional Freedom Techniques™

Gary H. Craig

P.O. Box 398

The Sea Ranch, CA 95497

(707) 785-2848

http://www.net-energy.com/index.html

http://www.emofree.com

This variation of Thought Field Therapy provides a simplified version of the basic TFT procedures. Craig's website provides in-depth information on incorporating TFT/EFT into one's life. Features the "Palace of Possibilities," an extended set of essays on living well and using energy psychotherapy methods as a part of eliminating unconscious obstacles to success.

Energy Diagnostic & Treatment Methods (EDxTM)
Fred P. Gallo, Ph.D.
40 Snyder Road
Hermitage, PA 16148
http://www.energypsych.com
Comprehensive energy psychotherapy services and professional-level training as well as public presentations on Thought Energy Therapy.

Tapas Acupressure Technique™
P.O. Box 7000–379
Redondo Beach, CA 90277
http://www.tat-intl.com
TAT (Tapas Acupressure Technique) is an accelerated information processing technique, useful in the treatment of traumatic stress, allergic reactions, and fixed negative emotional states. Based on Traditional Chinese Medicine.

Thought Energy Synchronization Therapies™ TEST®
Greg Nicosia, Ph.D.
4927 Centre Avenue
Pittsburgh, PA 15213
(412) 683-8378
Comprehensive energy psychotherapy services and professional-level training as well as public presentations on Thought Energy Therapy.

Acupuncture/Acupressure

Acupressure Institute
1533 Shattuck Avenue
Berkeley, CA 94709
(510) 845-1059
http://www.healthy.net/acupressure
Offers comprehensive acupressure trainings in traditional Asian bodywork and massage to students from around the world.

American Academy of Medical Acupuncture
5820 Wilshire Boulevard, Suite 500
Los Angeles, CA 90036
(323) 937-5514
http://www.medicalacupuncture.org

American Association of Oriental Medicine
433 Front Street
Catasauqua, PA 18032
(610) 433-2448
http://www.aaom.org

National Acupuncture & Oriental Medicine Alliance
14637 Starr Road SE
Olalla, WA 98359
(206) 851-6896
http://www.healthy.net/naoma

Kinesiology

Edu-Kinesthetics, Inc.
P.O. Box 3395
Ventura, CA 93006-3395
Toll Free: (888) 388-9898
http://www.braingym.com
Information about educational kinesiology as applied by Paul E. Dennison, Ph.D., including descriptions of his use of specific exercises to assist in improving dyslexia and other problems that affect learning.

Touch for Health® Kinesiology Association
11262 Washington Boulevard
Culver City, CA 90230
(800) 466-8342
http://www.tfh.org
The Touch for Health® Kinesiology Association was formed to serve the needs of TFH instructors and practitioners in the United States and to promote TFH as a system of complementary health care. A valuable resource for information about kinesiology and manual muscle testing.

Homeopathy/Naturopathy

American Association of Naturopathic Physicians
601 Valley Street, Suite 105
Seattle, WA 98109
(206) 298-0126
http://aanp.net
http://www.naturopathic.org
A resource for homeopathic physicians and Total Body Modification.

Homeopathic Academy of Naturopathic Physicians
12132 SE Foster Place
Portland, OR 97266
(503) 761-3298
http://www.healthy.net/hanp/hanp1.htm
A resource for homeopathic physicians and Total Body Modification.

Journal of Naturopathic Medicine
http://www.healthy.net/naturopathicjournal

Nambudraipad Allergy Elimination Techniques
http://www.naet.com or http://www.allergy2000.com
Another method of eliminating allergies and toxins.

National Center for Homeopathy
801 N. Fairfax Street, Suite 306
Alexandria, VA 22314
(703) 548-7790
http://www.homeopathic.org

Total Body Modification
This is a method of treating allergies and chemical sensitivities developed by chiropractor Victor Frank.
Referrals may be obtained from (800) 243-4826 or further information on the web at:
http://www.healthpyramid.com/bio-energetic/tbmbrochure.html

Hypnosis

American Psychotherapy and Medical Hypnosis Association
210 S. Sierra Street, Suite B-100
Reno, NV 89501
http://members.xoom.com/Hypnosis
This professional association to further the ethical application and research in hypnosis offers a referral service to qualified clinicians who use hypnosis.

American Society of Clinical Hypnosis
33 W. Grand Avenue, Suite 402
Chicago IL 60610
(312) 645-9810
This professional association to further the ethical application and research in hypnosis offers a referral service to qualified clinicians who use hypnosis.

Biofeedback

Association of Applied Psychophysiology and Biofeedback
10200 West 44th Avenue, Suite 304
Wheat Ridge, CO 80033
(800) 477-8892

The Biofeedback Foundation of Europe (BFE)
P.O. Box 21
3440 AA Woerden
The Netherlands.
(41) 31 348 482 757
http://www.bfe.org
BFE's purpose is to promote a greater awareness of biofeedback through training workshops and educating clinicians in the use of biofeedback techniques and technology.

Subtle Energy

Biomagnetic Technologies, Inc.
9727 Pacific Heights Boulevard
San Diego, CA 92121
(858) 453-6300
http://www.biomagtech.com
Manufacturer of magneto-encephalographs (MEGs), which are able to identify unique qualities of brain activity.

California Institute for Human Science
701 Garden View Court
Encinitas, CA 92024
(760) 634-1771, Fax: (760) 634-1772
http://www.cihs.edu
A center for higher learning, research, and professional skill building within the disciplines of general psychology, human science, and clinical-counseling psychology. Founded by engineer Hiroshi Motoyama, Ph.D., the inventor of the AMI device for measuring meridian energy.

Institute of Noetic Sciences
475 Gate Five Road, Suite 300
Sausalito, CA 94965
General inquiries (415) 331-5650
Fax (415) 331-5673
http://www.noetic.org
A research foundation, educational institution, and organization dedicated to study of the mind and the diverse ways of understanding knowledge and consciousness including research into the workings and powers of the mind, perceptions, beliefs, attention, intention, and intuition.

International Society for the Study of
Subtle Energy and Energy Medicine
11005 Ralston Road, #100
Arvada, CO 80004
(303) 425-4625
http://www.issseem.org

Alternative Health

Ener-G-Polari-T Products, Inc.
P.O. Box 2449
Prescott, AZ 86302–2449
(800) 593-6374
http://www.energpolarit.com/Newsletter1.htm
This website provides information and products based on the work of Wayne Cook. Cook spent thirty-three years studying the body's energy fields and their relationship to health. In 1964 he developed a method of enhancing the body's natural electrical field, thereby neutralizing the negative effects produced by random electromagnetic radiation. Cook's exercises form the basis of some of the corrective procedures of ESM, TFT, and other energy therapies.

EM Radiation Protection
Advanced Living Technology
2442 Meade
Denver, CO 80211
(800) 317-9969
http://www.advancedliving.com
Distributor of devices made by Clarus Systems Group, designed to neutralize the effects of electromagnetic radiation on the body. These devices have been found to re-

duce or eliminate the disruptive influence of ambient EMF radiation that can cause polarity disorganization and polarity reversals related to the body's energy systems. The authors have used the Q-Link and the Clear Wave Professional office units with noticeably positive results.

HealthWorld Online
A comprehensive resource for alternative health information.
http://www.healthy.net

HeartMath LLC
14700 West Park Avenue
Boulder Creek, CA 95006
(831) 338-8700
http://www.heartmath.com/welcome.html
This research foundation and its training programs provide human performance tools and technology specifically designed to increase productivity through enhanced job satisfaction, goal clarity, and improved health by reducing tension, burnout, physical symptoms of stress, and negative moods.

The International Academy of Bioenergetic Practitioners
2160 West Drake Avenue, Suite A-1
Fort Collins, CO 80526
(970) 224-2850
http://www.iabp.net
Bioenergetics offers a bridge between conventional and complementary medicine, because it interrelates many of the current health fields (and sciences) and incorporates training in Chinese medicine, biofeedback, holistic and natural health, herbs, homeopathy, homeotoxicology, and a nutritional approach toward wellness.

Gary Null's Natural Living Home Page
http://www.garynull.com
Exploring the nature and politics of medicine, health, nutrition, and the environment.

Andrew Weil, M.D.
http://cgi.pathfinder.com/drweil
Alternative health information and products.

Alman, Brian, and Lambrou, Peter. *Self-Hypnosis: The Complete Manual for Health and Self-Change.* New York: Brunner/Mazel, 1992.

Barinaga, Marcia. "Giving Personal Magnetism a Whole New Meaning." *Science,* May 15, 1992, p. 967.

Bassett, A. "Therapeutic Uses of Electric and Magnetic Fields in Orthopedics." In D. O. Carpenter and S. Ayrapetyan, eds., *Biological effects of electric and magnetic fields, Vol. 2, Beneficial and harmful effects.* San Diego: Academic Press, 1994, pp. 13–48.

Beck, Judith. *Cognitive Therapy: Basics and Beyond.* New York: Guilford Press, 1995.

Becker, Robert O. *The Body Electric.* New York: William Morrow, 1985.

———. *Cross Currents: The Promise of Electromedicine, the Perils of Electropollution.* New York: Jeremy P. Tarcher/Putnam, 1990.

———. Interview published in *Newsletter of the International Society for the Study of Subtle Energies and Energy Medicine* 1, no. 3 (1990): 4–10.

Beinfield, Harriet, and Korngold, Efrem. *Between Heaven and Earth.* New York: Ballantine Books, 1991.

Benson, Herbert. *Beyond the Relaxation Response.* New York: Berkley Publishing Group, 1984.

———. *The Relaxation Response.* New York: William Morrow, 1975.

Bergman, Ronald L. *Emotional Fitness Conditioning.* New York: Berkley Publishing Group, 1998.

Birkner, Kathrine M. "Magnets, Nature's Healing Energy." *MMRC Health Educator Reports,* January 31, 1997, p. 13.

Blanchard, Kenneth H., and Bowles, Sheldon. *Gung Ho.* New York: William Morrow, 1997.

Bloxham, Jeremy, and Gubbins, David. "The Secular Variation of the Earth's Magnetic Field." *Nature,* October 31, 1985, pp. 777–781.

Borysenko, Joan. *Fire in the Soul.* New York: Warner Books, 1993.

Bowsher, David. "Physiology and Patho-Physiology of Pain." *Acupuncture in Medicine: Journal of the British Medical Acupuncture Society* 7, no. 1 (1990): 17–20.

———. "The Physiology of Stimulation-Produced Analgesia." *Acupuncture in Medi-*

cine: *Journal of the British Medical Acupuncture Society* 9, no. 2 (1991): 58–62.

Braden, Gregg. *Awakening to Zero Point.* Bellevue, Wash.: Radio Bookstore Press, 1997.

Brennan, Barbara A. *Hands of Light: A Guide to Healing Through the Human Energy Field.* New York: Bantam Books, 1987.

Brewitt, Barbara. "Quantitative Analysis of Electrical Skin Conductance in Diagnosis: Historical and Current Views of Bioelectric Medicine." *Journal of Naturopathic Medicine* 6, no. 1 (1996): 66–75.

Burr, Harold S. *Blueprint for Immortality: The Electric Patterns of Life.* Essex, England: Neville Spearman Publishers, 1972.

Byrd, Randolph C. "Positive Therapeutic Effects of Intercessory Prayer in a Coronary Care Unit Population." *Southern Medical Journal,* no. 7 (1988): 826–829.

Callahan, Roger J. *Five Minute Phobia Cure.* Wilmington, Del.: Enterprise Publishing, 1985.

———. "More Scientific Support-Psychotherapy and Deep Biological Change-Rouleaux and Callahan Techniques C. T.-T. F. T." *The Thought Field* 4, no. 2 (1998): 5–6.

Callahan, Roger, and Callahan, Joanne. *Thought Field Therapy and Trauma: Treatment and Theory.* Indian Wells, Calif.: Thought Field Therapy Training Center, 1996.

Campbell, John W., Jr. "The Scientific Method." *Bridges: Magazine of the International Society for the Study of Subtle Energy & Energy Medicine,* 8, no. 3 (1997): 12–16.

Childre, Doc Lew. *Freeze Frame: Fast Action Stress Relief.* Boulder Creek, Calif.: Planetary Publications, 1994.

Cho, Z. H. "New Findings of the Correlation Between Acupoints and Corresponding Brain Cortices Using Functional MRI." *Proceedings of National Academy of Sciences* 95 (1998): 2670–2673.

Chopra, Deepak. *Ageless Body, Timeless Mind: The Quantum Alternative to Growing Old.* New York: Harmony Books, 1993.

Cofer, C. N., and Appley, M. H. *Motivation: Theory and Research.* New York: John Wiley & Sons, 1964.

Collinge, William. *Subtle Energy: Awakening to the Unseen Forces in Our Lives.* New York: Warner Books, 1998.

Crain, William C. *Theories of Development: Concepts and applications,* 2nd ed. Englewood Cliffs, N.J.: Prentice-Hall, 1985.

Cousins, Norman. *The Healing Heart.* New York: W. W. Norton, 1983.

Damasio, Antonió R. *Descartes' Error: Emotion, Reason, and the Human Brain.* New York: Avon Books, 1994.

Darras, Jean Claude, Albarede, P., and de Vernejoul, Pierre. "Nuclear Medicine Investigation of Transmission of Acupuncture Information." *Acupuncture in Medicine, Journal of the British Medical Acupuncture Society,* March 31, 1993, pp. 22–28.

Darwin, Charles. *The Expression of the Emotions in Man and Animals,* 3rd ed. New York: Oxford University Press, 1998.

Dennison, Gail, Dennison, Paul, and Teplitz, Jerry. *Brain Gym for Business.* Ventura, Calif.: Edu-Kinesthetics, 1994.

Dennison, Paul E. *Switching On: A Guide to Edu-Kinesthetics.* Ventura, Calif.: Edu-Kinesthetics, 1981.

Dennison, Paul E., and Dennison, Gail E. *Personalized Whole Brain Integration.* Ventura, Calif.: Edu-Kinesthetics, 1985.

Diamond, John. *Life Energy: Using the Meridians to Unlock the Hidden Power of Your Emotions.* St. Paul, Minn.: Paragon House, 1985.

———. *Your Body Doesn't Lie.* New York: Warner Books, 1979.

Dossey, Larry. *Beyond Illness: Discovering the Experience of Health.* Boulder, Colo.: Shambhala Publications, 1984.

———. *Healing Words: The Power of Prayer and the Practice of Medicine.* New York: HarperCollins, 1997.

———. *Meaning and Medicine: A Doctor's Tales of Breakthrough and Healing.* New York: Bantam Books, 1991.

Durlacher, James. V. *Freedom from Fears Forever.* Tempe, Ariz.: Van Ness Publishing Co., 1994.

Eden, Donna, and Feinstein, David. *Energy Medicine: Balance Your Body's Energies for Optimum Health, Joy, and Vitality.* New York: Jeremy Tarcher/Putnam, 1999.

Ekman, Paul. "Facial Expressions of Emotion: New Findings, New Questions." *Psychological Science* 3 (1992): 34–38.

Faust, Sylvain. "Acupuncture for Psychological Problems." *Acupuncture in Medicine: Journal of the British Medical Acupuncture Society,* November 30, 1991, pp. 80–82.

Figley, Charles R. Open letter to colleagues, June 27, 1995, Psychosocial Stress Research Program and Clinical Laboratory, Florida State University.

Flower, Robert G. "Real Work on the Hard Problem." *Frontier Perspectives* 5, no. 2 (1996): 38–41.

Fluhart, Karuna. "The Three Nervous Systems and Polarity Principles of Sattva, Rajas, and Tamas." *Ayurveda Today,* March 31, 1996, p. 11.

Friedman, Howard, Becker, Robert, and Bachman, Charles H. "Geophysical Variables and Behavior: X X V. Alterations in Memory for a Narrative Following Application of Theta Frequency Electromagnetic Fields." *Perceptual and Motor Skills* 60 (1985): 416–418.

———. "Psychiatric Ward Behavior and Geophysical Parameters." *Nature,* March 13, 1965, pp. 1050–1052.

Friedman, Howard S., Hall, J. A., and Harris, M. J. "Type A Behavior, Nonverbal Expressive Style, and Health." *Journal of Personality and Social Psychology* 48 (1985).

Friedman, Meyer, and Rosenman, Raymond H. *Type A Behavior and Your Heart.* New York: Fawcett Books, 1974.

Gallo, Fred. *Energy Psychology: Explorations at the Interface of Energy, Cognition, Behavior, and Health.* Boca Raton, Fl.: CRC Press, 1999.

Gerber, Richard. *Vibrational Medicine.* Santa Fe, N.M.: Bear & Co, 1996.

Gerbode, Frank A. *Beyond Psychology: An Introduction to Metapsychology.* 3rd ed. Menlo Park, Calif.: IRM Press, 1995.

Goleman, Daniel. *Emotional Intelligence: Why It Can Matter More Than IQ.* New York: Bantam Books, 1995.

Goswami, Amit. *The Self-Aware Universe: How Consciousness Creates the Material World.* New York: Jeremy P. Tarcher/Putnam, 1993.

Green, Elmer. "Cartography of Consciousness: A Functional Reexamination of Theta, Alpha, and Beta." *Subtle Energies* 5, no. 1 (1993): 135–150.

Greenspan, Stanley I. *The Growth of the Mind.* Reading, Mass.: Perseus Book Group, 1997.

Gribbin, John. *The Search for Superstrings, Symmetry, and the Theory of Everything.* New York: Little, Brown and Company, 1998.

Grof, Stanislav. *The Holotropic Mind.* New York: HarperCollins, 1990.

Groves, Philip M., and Rebec, George V. *Introduction to Biological Psychology.* New York: William Brown & Co., 1988.

Hammerslough, Jane, "The Healing Touch," *San Diego Union-Tribune,* January 5, 1998.

Hawkins, David. *Power vs. Force: An Anatomy of Consciousness.* Phoenix, Ariz.: Veritas Press, 1995.

Hou, T. Z., and Li, M. D. "Experimental Evidence of a Plant Meridian System: V. Acupuncture Effect on Circumnutation Movements of Shoots of Haselus Vulgaris L. Pole Bean." *American Journal of Chinese Medicine* 25, nos. 3–4 (1997): 253–261.

Hover-Kramer, Dorothea, and Shames, Karilee H. *Energetic Approaches to Emotional Healing.* New York: Delmar Publishers, 1997.

Hsieh, C.Y., and Phillips, R. B. "Reliability of Manual Muscle Testing with a Computerized Dynamometer." *Journal of Manipulating and Physiological Therapeutics* 13, no. 2 (1990): 72–82.

Hugdahl, Kenneth. *Psychophysiology: The Mind-Body Perspective.* Cambridge, Mass.: Harvard University Press, 1995.

Hunt, Valerie. *Infinite Mind: Science of the Human Vibrations of Consciousness.* Malibu, Calif.: Malibu Publishing Co., 1996.

Ironson, G., Barr, T., Boltwood, M., Bartzokis, T., Dennis, C., Chesney, M., Spitzer, S., and Segall, G. M. "Effects of Anger on the Left Ventricular Ejection Fraction in Coronary Artery Disease." *American Journal Cardiology,* August 1, 1992, pp. 281–285.

Jacka, Judy. *Healing Through Earth Energies,* Melbourne, Victoria, AU: Thomas C. Lothian Press, 1996.

Jacobson, Neil S. "The Role of the Allegiance Effect in Psychotherapy Research: Controlling and Accounting for It." *Journal of Clinical Psychology: Science and Practice* 6, no. 1 (1999): 116–119.

Kaplan, Harold I., and Sadock, Benjamin J. eds. *Comprehensive Textbook of Psychiatry/IV.* Baltimore, Md.: Williams & Wilkins, 1985.

Kenney, J., Clemens, R., and Forsyth, K. D. "Applied Kinesiology Unreliable for Assessing Nutrient Status." *Journal of the American Dietetic Association* 88, no. 6 (1998): 698–704.

Knave, B. "Electric and Magnetic Fields and Health Outcomes—An Overview. Electric and Magnetic Fields (EMF): What Do We Know About the Health Effects?" *International Archives of Occupational and Environmental Health* 68, no. 6 (1996): 448–454.

Korn, Errol, and Johnson, Karen. *Visualization: The Uses of Imagery in the Health Professions.* Homewood, Ill.: Dow Jones-Erwin, 1983.

Korn, Errol, Pratt, George, and Lambrou, Peter. *Hyper-Performance: The A.I.M. Strategy for Releasing Your Business Potential.* New York: John Wiley & Sons, 1987.

La Tourelle, Maggie. "Kinesiology: An Integrated Approach for Complementary Therapies." *Positive Health,* November 30, 1996, pp. 41–45.

Lawson, Arden, and Calderon, Lawrence. "Interexaminer Agreement for Applied Kinesiology Manual Muscle Testing." *Perceptual and Motor Skills* 84 (1997): 539–546.

LeDoux, Joseph. *The Emotional Brain: The Mysterious Underpinnings of Emotional Life.* New York: Touchstone/Simon & Schuster, 1996.

Leisman, Gerald, Shambaugh, Philip, and Ferentz, Avery H. "Somatosensory Evoked Potential Changes During Muscle Testing." *International Journal of Neuroscience* 45 (1989): 143–151.

Leisman, G., Zenhausern, Robert, Ferentz, A., Tefera, T., and Zemcov, A. "Electromyographic Effects of Fatigue and Task Repetition on the Validity of Estimates of Strong and Weak Muscles in Applied Kinesiological Muscle Testing Procedures." *Perceptual and Motor Skills* 80 (1995): 963–977.

Lemonick, Michael D., and Thompson, Dick. "Racing to Map Our DNA." *Time* magazine, January 11, 1999.

Levy, Susan L., and Lehn, Carol R. *Your Body Can Talk: The Art and Application of Clinical Kinesiology.* Prescott, Ariz.: HOHM Press, 1996.

Liangyue, Deng. *Chinese Acupuncture and Moxibustion.* Beijing: Foreign Languages Press, 1987.

Lipton, Bruce H. *Fractal Biology: The Science of Innate Intelligence.* Santa Cruz, Calif.: N.P., 1998.

———. "Nature, Nurture, and the Power of Love." *Journal of Prenatal and Perinatal Psychology and Health* 13, no. 1 (1998): 3–10.

Macdonald, Alexander. "Acupuncture Analgesia and Therapy—Part 1." *Acupuncture in Medicine. Journal of the British Medical Acupuncture Society,* May 31, 1990, pp. 8–12.

Manyande, Anne. "Preoperative Rehearsal of Active Coping Imagery Influences Subjective and Hormonal Responses to Abdominal Surgery." *Psychosomatic Medicine* 57 (1995): 177–182.

Marcus, Paul. "Acupuncture in Modern Medicine." *Acupuncture in Medicine: Journal of the British Medical Acupuncture Society,* December 31, 1992, pp. 101–108.

Markovitz, J. H., Matthews, K. A., Kannel, W. B., Cobb, J. L., and D'Agostino, R. B. "Psychological Predictors of Hypertension in the Framingham Study." *Journal of the American Medical Association* 270, no. 20 (1993): 2439–2443.

McClelland, David C., and Krishnit, Carol. "The Effect of Motivational Arousal Through Films on Salivary Immunoglobulin A." *Psychology and Health* 2, no. 1 (1988): 31–52.

McCraty, Rollin, Atkinson, Mike, and Tiller, William. "New Electrophysiological Correlates Associated with Intentional Heart Focus." *Subtle Energies* 43, no. 3 (1995): 251–262.

Michaud, Louise Y., and Persinger, Michael A. "Geophysical Variables and Behavior: Alterations in Memory for a Narrative Following Application of Theta Frequency Electromagnetic Fields." *Perceptual and Motor Skills* 60 (1985): 416–418.

Miller, R. N. "Study on the Effectiveness of Remote Mental Healing. The Holmes Center for Research and Holistic Healing." *Medical Hypotheses* 8 (1982): 481–490.

Milton, Richard. *Alternative Science: Challenging the Myths of the Scientific Establishment.* Rochester, Vt.: Park Street Press, 1994.

Mitchell, E. D. *The Way of the Explorer.* New York: G. P. Putnam's Sons, 1996.

Monti, D. A., Sinnott, D. C., Marchese, M., Kunkel, E. J. S., and Greeson, J. M. "Muscle Test Comparisons of Congruent and Incongruent Self-Referential Statements." *Perceptual and Motor Skills* 88 (1999): 1019–1028.

Motoyama, Hiroshi. *Measurements of Ki Energy: Diagnosis and Treatments.* Tokyo: Human Science Press, 1997.

Myss, Caroline. *Anatomy of the Spirit.* New York: Harmony Books, 1996.

Neergaard, Lauran, and Duerksen, Susan. "Offbeat Medicine Put to Serious Test." *San Diego Union/Tribune,* November 11, 1998.

Nordenstrom, Bjorn. "Electromagnetic Fields: Activation, Guidance, and Interferences of BCEC (Biologically Closed Electric Circuits)." *Acupuncture and Electro-Therapeutics Research* 23, no. 1 (1998): 84.

Omura, Yoshiaki. "Connections Found Between Each Meridian (heart, stomach, triple burner, etc.) and Organ Representation Area of Corresponding Internal Organs in Each Side of the Cerebral Cortex; Release of Common Neurotransmitters and Hormones Unique to Each Meridian and a Corresponding Acupuncture Point and Internal Organ after Acupuncture, Electrical Stimulation, Mechanical Stimulation (Including Shiatsu), Soft Laser Stimulation or Qi Gong." *Acupuncture and Electro-Therapeutics Research International Journal* 14 (1989): 155–186.

———. "Meridian-like Networks of Internal Organs, Corresponding to Traditional Chinese 12 Main Meridians and Their Acupuncture Points as Detected by the 'Bi-Digital O-Ring Test Imaging Method': Search for the Corresponding Internal Organs of Western Medicine for Each Meridian—Part 1." *Acupuncture and Electro-Therapeutics Research International Journal* 12 (1987): 53–70.

Padus, Emrika. *Positive Living and Health: The Complete Guide to Brain/Body Healing and Mental Empowerment.* Emmaus, Pa.: Rodale Press, 1990.

Patten, Leslie, and Patten, Terry. *Biocircuits,* Tiburon, Calif.: H. J. Kramer, Inc., 1988.

Penrose, Roger. *The Emperor's New Mind: Concerning Computers, Minds, and the Laws of Physics.* New York: Penguin Books, 1991.

Pert, Candace B. *Molecules of Emotion.* New York: Scribner's, 1997.

Physicians' Desk Reference. 52nd ed. Montvale, N.J.: Medical Economics Data, 1999.

Pratt, George, Wood, Dennis, and Alman, Brian. *A Clinical Hypnosis Primer.* New York: John Wiley & Sons, 1988.

"Precision Engineered Sound Waves Powerfully Focus Your Mind." *Brain Wave Technology,* November 29, 1998. www.brainsync.com.

Rabasca, L. "Anger Caused by Violence May Hinder TV Viewer's Memory of Commercials." *Monitor: American Psychological Association,* February 1999. Report on Brad J. Bushman of Iowa State University in Journal of Experimental Psychology: Applied 4, no. 4, pp. 291–307.

Radin, Dean I. "Possible Proximity Effective on Human Grip Strength." *Perceptual and Motor Skills* 58 (1984): 887–888.

Radin, Dean I., and Rebman, Jannine M. "Lunar Correlates of Normal, Abnormal, and Anomalous Human Behavior." *Subtle Energies* 5, no. 3 (1994): 209–238.

Redford, B. Williams, Lane, James D., Kuhn, Cynthia M., Melosh, William, White, Alice D., and Schangerg, Saul M. "Type A Behavior and Elevated Physiological and Neuroendocrine Responses to Cognitive Tasks." *Science,* October 29, 1982, pp. 483–486.

Restak, Richard. *Brainscapes: An Introduction to What Neuroscience Has Learned About the Structure, Function, and Abilities of the Brain.* New York: Hyperion, 1996.

Ritter, Malcolm. "Scientists Achieve a Quantum Leap that Einstein Believed Impossible." *San Diego Union/Tribune,* December 11, 1997.

Rosenfeld, Isadore. "Acupuncture Goes Mainstream (Almost)." *Parade Magazine,* August 16, 1998.

Rossi, Ernest L. *The Psychobiology of Mind-Body Healing.* New York: W. W. Norton & Company, 1986.

Rubik, Beverly. "Energy Medicine and the Unifying Concept of Information." *Alternative Therapies in Health and Medicine,* March 31, 1995, pp. 34–39.

———. *Life at the Edge of Science.* Philadelphia: Institute for Frontier Science, 1996.

Savitz, D. A. "Exposure Assessment Strategies in Epidemiological Studies of Health Effects of Electric and Magnetic Fields." *Science of the Total Environment* 168 (1995): 143–153.

Selye, Hans. *The Stress of Life.* New York: McGraw-Hill, 1956.

———. *Stress Without Distress.* New York: Lippincott and Crowell, 1974.

Shang, C. "Singular Point, Organizing Center and Acupuncture Point." *American Journal of Chinese Medicine* 17, nos. 3–4 (1989): 119–127.

Shapiro, Francine, and Forrest, Margot S. *EMDR: The Breakthrough "Eye Movement" Therapy for Overcoming Anxiety, Stress, and Trauma.* New York: Basic Books, 1997.

Shealy, Norman C., and Myss, Caroline M. "The Ring of Fire and DHEA: A

Theory for Energetic Restoration of Adrenal Reserves." *Subtle Energies* 6, no. 2 (1995): 167–174.

Sheikh, Anees A., and Korn, Errol R., eds. *Imagery in Sports and Physical Performance.* Amityville, N.Y.: Baywood Publishing Company, 1994.

Sheldrake, Rupert. *A New Science of Life: The Hypothesis of Morphic Resonance.* Rochester, Vt.: Park Street Press, 1995.

———. *Seven Experiments That Could Change the World: A Do-It-Yourself Guide to Revolutionary Science.* New York: Riverhead Books, 1995.

Siegel, B. *Love, Medicine, Miracles.* New York: Harper & Row, 1986.

Sloan, R. P., et al. "Effects of Mental Stress Throughout the Day on Cardiac Autonomic Control." *Biological Psychology* 34 (1994): 89–99.

Snellgrove, Brian. *The Unseen Self: Kirlian Photography Explained.* Essex, England: C. W. Daniel Company, 1979.

Srinivasan, T. M. "Machines with Promise: Electromedicine." *Bridges, Magazine of the International Society for the Study of Subtle Energies and Energy Medicine* 8, no. 4 (Winter 1997).

Stebbins, John. "Fundamentals of Electro-Acupuncture." *Oriental Medicine Journal,* June 30, 1996, pp. 51–61.

Tart, Charles T. "Subtle Energies, Healing Energies." *Interfaces: Linguistics, Psychology and Health Therapeutics* 12, no. 1 (March 1985): 3–10.

Taylor, Kylea. *The Breathwork Experience.* Santa Cruz, Calif.: Hanford Mead Publishers, 1994.

Thaler, David S. "The Evolution of Genetic Intelligence." *Science* 264: 224–225.

Thompson, Dick. "Acupuncture Works." *Time Magazine,* November 17, 1997.

Tiller, William. *Science and Human Transformation: Subtle Energies, Intentionality and Consciousness.* Walnut Creek, Calif.: Pavior Publications, 1997.

Tiller, William A., McCraty, R., and Atkinson, M. "Cardiac Coherence: A New, Non-invasive Measure of Autonomic Nervous System Order." *Alternative Therapies in Health and Medicine* 2, no. 1 (January 1996): 52–56.

Valberg, P. A. "Electric and Magnetic Fields (EMF): What Do We Know About the Health Effects?" *International Archives of Occupational and Environmental Health* 68, no. 6 (1996): 448–454.

Valjus, J. "Health Risks of Electric and Magnetic Fields Caused by High Voltage Systems in Finland." *Journal of Scandinavian Work, Environment, and Health* 22, no. 2 (April 1996): 85–93.

Vallbona, Carlos, Hazlewood, Carlton F., and Jurida, Gabor. "Response of Pain to Static Magnetic Fields in Post Polio Patients: A Double Blind Pilot Study." *Archives of Physical Medicine and Rehabilitation* 78 (November 1997): 1200–1203.

Veith, I. *The Yellow Emperor's Classic Internal Medicine.* Berkeley: University of California Press, 1966.

Veterans Administration Hospital, Syracuse, New York, and State University of New

York Upstate Medical Center. "Psychiatric Ward Behavior and Geophysical Parameters." *Nature,* March 13, 1965, pp. 1050–1052.

Walker, Michael M., Kirschvink, Joseph L., Chang, Shih-Bin R., and Dizon, Andrew E. "A Candidate Magnetic Sense Organ in the Yellow-Fin Tuna, Thunnus Albacares." *Science,* May 18, 1984, pp. 751–753.

Wallis, Claudia. "Healing: A Growing and Surprising Body of Scientific Evidence." *Time* magazine, June 24, 1996, pp. 59–62.

Weil, Andrew. *Spontaneous Healing.* New York: Ballantine, 1995.

Weiss, D. S., Kirsner, R., and Eaglstein, W. H. "Electrical Stimulation and Wound Healing." *Archives of Dermatology* 126 (February 1990): 222–225.

White, George L., Egerton, Charles P., and Henthorne, Beth H. "Health Effects of Electromagnetic Fields: Review of the Literature." *Health Values: The Journal of Health Behavior, Education, and Promotion* 19, no. 3 (1995): 15–21.

Wilber, Ken. *Eye to Eye: The Quest for the New Paradigm.* Boston: Shambhala Publications, 1983.

————. *The Spectrum of Consciousness.* Wheaton, Ill.: Quest Books, 1993.

Wilcher, C. C. "Chronic Subluxation Complex." *The Prover: The Journal of the Chiropractic Academy of Homeopathy,* March 30, 1995, pp. 27–38.

Wilford, John Noble. "New Data Supports Inflationary Big Bang Theory." *San Diego Union/Tribune,* February 17, 1999.

Wolf, Fred A. *Taking the Quantum Leap: The New Physics for Non-Scientists.* New York: Harper & Row, 1989.

Wolpe, Joseph. *Psychotherapy by Reciprocal Inhibition.* Stanford, Calif.: Stanford University Press, 1958.

Wood, Clive. "Acupuncture, Chi and a Credible Model for Treatment." *Acupuncture in Medicine: Journal of the British Medical Acupuncture Society,* November 30, 1993, pp. 90–94.

Wright, Susan M. "A Validity of the Human Energy Field Assessment Form." *Western Journal of Nursing Research* 13, no. 5 (1991): 635–647.

Wylie, Mary S. "Going for the Cure." *The Family Networker* (July/August 1996): 20–37.

Yerkes, R. M., and Dodson, J. D. "The Relationship of Strength of Stimulus to Rapidity of Habit Formation." *Journal of Comparative Neurology* 18 (1908): 459–482.

Zanakis, M. F. "Regeneration in the Mammalian Nervous System Using Applied Electric Fields: A Literature Review." *Acupuncture and Electro-Therapeutics Research* 13, no. 1 (1988): 47–57.

INDEX